HIGHER EDUCATION
FOR DEMOCRACY

HIGHER EDUCATION FOR DEMOCRACY

The Role of the University in Civil Society

WILLIAM G. TIERNEY

SUNY PRESS

Cover image: *Zola aux outrages* by Henry de Groux, 1898.

Published by State University of New York Press, Albany

© 2021 State University of New York

For information, contact State University of New York Press, Albany, NY
www.sunypress.edu

Library of Congress Cataloging-in-Publication Data

Name: Tierney, William G., author.
Title: Higher education for democracy : the role of the university in civil
  society / William G. Tierney.
Description: Albany : State University of New York Press, 2021. | Includes
  bibliographical references and index.
Identifiers: LCCN 2020041500 | ISBN 9781438484495 (hardcover : alk. paper) |
  ISBN 9781438484501 (pbk. : alk. paper) | ISBN 9781438484518 (ebook)
Subjects: LCSH: Education, Higher—Political aspects. | Education, Higher—Aims
  and objectives. | Universities and colleges—Political aspects. | Democracy and
  education. | Civil society.
Classification: LCC LC171 .T54 2021 | DDC 378.1—dc23
LC record available at https://lccn.loc.gov/2020041500

10 9 8 7 6 5 4 3 2 1

Contents

Acknowledgments   vii

Preface   ix

1   Globalization, Neoliberalism, and Their Discontents   1

2   The Democratic Imperative of Higher Education   25

3   Identity Matters   71

4   Understanding Academic Freedom and Free Speech
    on Campus   97

5   Understanding What Modern Universities Do:
    Goods and Services   147

6   Academic Competencies for the Twenty-First Century   183

7   Academic Responsibility: Toward a Cultural Politics
    of Integrity   217

Notes   267

References   269

Index   291

Acknowledgments

I am grateful to the support I have received from the Pullias Center for Higher Education at the University of Southern California. My students, research assistants, postdoctoral students, and colleagues helped me think through what I present here. Monica Raad and Diane Flores, who staff the Center for us, are the absolute best at what they do. Although many individuals read a part of this book, Michael Lanford provided extraordinary help in his editing and feedback. He's a gem. Rebecca Colesworthy at SUNY Press has been thoughtful, positive, fun, and reflective about how to improve the text; I've been very lucky to work with her. I had the good fortune to put the finishing touches on this manuscript first at the Rockefeller Foundation's Bellagio Center in Lake Como, Italy, and then at the European University Institute in Florence, Italy, before the pandemic closed down the world. I could not have had better environments to complete this book. Through it all, Barry Weiss has been my sounding board and best friend.

Preface

When I speak to my students about the relatively leisurely times I had when I went to college it seems like I am referring to a foreign land about which they have no knowledge. Today seems entirely different from yesterday. One point I make in this text, however, is that the past and present help determine the future; there is no linear inevitability. I started the book before COVID-19 arrived on the scene and closed down the world. Moreover, although I have long supported Black Lives Matter, the murder of George Floyd created a new urgency for me to think through what I am writing here.

We are always in a time of change, and the contexts in which we exist matter a great deal. What I resist, however, is those who say, "Everything must change" as if there is an abrupt rupture from today to tomorrow. Such an assumption is historically naïve, and frequently enables antidemocratic forces to constrict the public good. Given the fiscal challenges the pandemic has created, we hear, for example, that the end of academe as we know it is near. However, for over a generation, when higher education has faced a crisis, such a response has been inevitable.

Tech boosters now say that an online revolution is about to happen, which will disrupt all of academe. Online learning certainly has grown over the last decade, and some students seem to learn just fine that way. However, I do not find the argument that all our colleges and universities are going to fold like a house of cards very convincing. Clayton Christenson, and before him, Peter Drucker, have been academic Jeremiahs saying, "The end is near," Drucker suggested the end of higher education in 1997, and since 2011 Christenson has predicted that half of higher education will go out of business. It has not happened, however. Even today, when academe faces the worst economic crisis in a century because of the pandemic, sober predictions are that about 5% of the 4,000 postsecondary institutions face closure. Two hundred institutional closures are certainly significant, but it does not represent total disruption and devastation for the postsecondary system.

Similarly, the protests that erupted after the murder of George Floyd in Minneapolis rightfully called for dramatic reforms, not only in policing, but in all organizations, and academe is certainly included. Change, however, is not a singular event, and instead requires ways to think through bringing about systemic reforms, rather than rely on singular acts. I am pleased, for example, that racist monuments finally have fallen on our campuses and elsewhere, but the removal of a statue of a confederate general hardly suggests that we have resolved the systemic problem of racism.

I make the case here that we need to think about what we want higher education to look like after this pandemic is eliminated. Racism is not going away simply because many of us want it to be eliminated. Online higher education is not going to overwhelm all of higher education simply because business gurus say it will. And threats to democracy will not be overcome without a significant concerted effort by those of us in higher education.

Academe in the twenty-first century has four key goals. We need to educate students so that they are employable. We need to do research and conduct service in our communities that advances the public good. We need to continue to act as a gateway out of poverty and into the middle and upper class. We need to engage as an academic institution and imbue in our students the skills necessary to advance democracy in a multicultural society.

The pandemic, along with the ongoing crisis of structural racism, frame the context in which higher education functions today. The world is different from when I began the book—and it will be different still by the time the reader has the text in hand. Change is inevitable, but it does not alter what I am arguing here about the essential role of higher education in creating a more equitable and democratic future. How we define and enact that role is up to us.

CHAPTER ONE

Globalization, Neoliberalism, and Their Discontents

Why are you so afraid of the word "Fascism"? Just a word—just a word! And might not be so bad, with all the lazy bums we got pan-handling relief nowadays, and living on my income tax and yours—not so worse to have a real Strong Man, like Hitler or Mussolini—like Napoleon or Bismarck in the good old days—and have 'em really run the country and make it efficient and prosperous again. . . .

Country's too big for a revolution. No, no! Couldn't happen here!

—Sinclair Lewis, *It Couldn't Happen Here*

I entered academic life as a college freshman in 1971. I retired as a professor in 2020. What changed in almost a half-century? Don't worry. This is not yet another elegiac academic memoir. I have no interest in recalling the "good old days," as if when I was a college student everything was great and today everything is terrible. Times change. Contexts change. People change. What I will explore is how those times and contexts and people have changed. Because of these changes, I intend to put forward a new way to position higher education in what I have come to think of as a globalized economy.

When I graduated from Tufts University in 1975, I did not worry very much about finding work; jobs were plentiful for someone with a college degree. I joined the Peace Corps, learned Arabic, and spent two years in Morocco. A large part of my decision to join the Peace Corps was not only my Irish Catholic family background, in which volunteer

1

work was encouraged, but also because I got a college degree during the Vietnam War. I had a great many discussions in and out of class about what our obligations were as citizens. I worked at a homeless shelter during college to earn some money. I picked up a lot at the Pine Street Inn in Boston's red-light district. I learned not only from the guys who were homeless, but also from the hard-scrabble men who worked there, most of whom were veterans, and the police who worked to make extra cash in their off-hours in the cavernous lobby trying to maintain a semblance of peace among 300 homeless men. All the police disagreed with me—they hated my long hair, my left-leaning views, my protest against the Vietnam War. We also all got along. One cop drove me home after our shift; we argued the whole way, and we shook hands as I got out of the police car every week.

I came back from the Peace Corps, picked up a master's degree at Harvard, worked for two years at a Native American community college in North Dakota, went west to earn a PhD at Stanford, and then held a postdoctoral position in Boulder, Colorado. The rest of my adult life has been as a professor, first at Penn State and then at the University of Southern California, punctuated by time spent abroad.

It is commonplace to say that universities are among the oldest organizations in the world. India, Morocco, Italy, and the United Kingdom, to name but a few countries, have had storied institutions of higher education for several hundred years. American higher education came of age in the late nineteenth century, and only became the envy of the world after World War II. Many observers might suggest that I entered academe at the beginning of the end of its golden era. Finances are now in disarray. The workforce is undergoing a sea change in terms of desired skills and workplace benefits. Technology and social media have disrupted how one teaches and does research. What one says and does on a college campus today are under greater scrutiny than at any time in the last half-century.

The trends that are apparent in the United States are also clear in other countries and regions. I intend to discuss those developments with a special focus on Los Angeles, Hong Kong, and New Delhi. Since the pandemic hit, many in higher education have claimed that a revolution is about to occur on our campuses—that all of our 4,000 institutions will close and online behemoths will take over. My goal is not to be an academic doomsayer claiming that the end is near. Rather, I have been wondering, as I have traveled the world trying to figure out what's going on, what we might do to help higher education get its groove back.

As I will discuss, I don't think making our postsecondary institutions more productive is simply a concern to those of us who work in higher education. I link higher education to what I shall call the democratic project. The democratic project pertains to enabling individuals to have a voice about the future of their country and to reject those fascist tendencies currently at work. As I shall elaborate, that future pertains not only to material goods and services, but also to cultural and social ones. Here's the conundrum: academe reflects the tenor and events in the larger society, but our colleges and universities also have the opportunity to change those events and the discourse that surrounds them. Democracy and higher education are inextricably linked. Even in fascist countries, where universities have been a tool, not to promote democracy, but rather to distort and mute it, education plays an important role. In a democratic environment, however, universities have the ability, not only to be key arbiters of how one advances democracy, but also to reflect democratic values in their practices, objectives, and goals.

Societal changes of the twenty-first century necessitate changes to higher education—not simply to adapt to the marketplace, but also to help the larger society adhere to the democratic project. Before I flesh out what I mean by the democratic project, however, let me consider the changes that are occurring and what those changes have portended for academe.

Considering Globalization and Neoliberalism

Globalization is transforming virtually all of modern life. Goods, services, jobs, technology, and information have changed in developed and developing countries. Many scholars have argued that current economic strategies have enabled transnational corporations to gain an enormous competitive advantage in the global marketplace. The by-products of globalization are the homogenization of culture, the reduction of full-time employment, the insertion of business practices into not-for-profit and public organizations, and most important for my purposes here, the rise of a populist movement that has enabled nationalistic politicians to gain power by employing privatization as the scaffolding to construct policies (Cantwell & Maldonado-Maldonado, 2009; Diamond, 2019; Fuchs & Klingemann, 2019; Gutek, 2006).

These forces and their impacts, however, are neither well understood nor well examined, particularly in terms of how they have impacted tertiary education. Although globalization certainly has its intellectual roots in various international transformations that have occurred over the last two centuries (e.g., the rise and fall of colonialism), what many scholars mean by globalization in the twenty-first century is a relatively new phenomenon that has been shaped by advances in technology and the decline of the public sphere (Kaul et al., 1999). Indeed, change occurs so quickly now that what one meant by "globalization" at the turn of the century differs from the meanings that are evoked by the term today. For example, whereas "globalization" was, at one point, frequently employed as little more than a synonym for American imperialism, today scholars have a more sophisticated understanding of the manifold ways in which culture, technology, politics, and the market interact to create new relationships that have both positive and negative impacts on a society and its people. Nevertheless, because these changes are taking place so quickly, and because their manifestations vary so significantly across regions and by country, "globalization" remains a nebulous term (Tierney & Lanford, 2021). One result is that policies that deal with these forces quickly become irrelevant or of little use, or even worse yet, dysfunctional.

While globalization has afforded great opportunity, it also has brought about great inequality. Americans, for example, will trumpet that more individuals participate in higher education than a generation ago; college students also graduate with greater debt, encounter greater uncertainty in the job market, and face greater inequality in wealth accumulation (Baum, 2015; Berliner, 2013; Fry, 2014; Piketty, 2014; Saez, 2018). The entrepreneurial ambition and grit of some people mask the stratification and shortchanging of opportunity for many others. One can no longer ignore the diminished opportunities for the least privileged among us when contrasted with the expanding economic, human, and social capital of the most privileged (Hartmann, 2008; Thurow, 2000). As I shall elaborate, such a point can be made whether we are talking about Los Angeles (LA), Hong Kong, or New Delhi.

We also can acknowledge that poverty, hunger, and child mortality have decreased worldwide. Half a billion people escaped extreme poverty between 1990 and 2011. The child mortality rate has gone down by over 50 percent (Ebner, 2017, p. 15). However, coupled with positive news are worrying trends about the erosion of civil rights, a greater sense of economic insecurity among the middle classes, and a rise on the attacks of civic organizations such as the judiciary and the press.

Hand in hand with globalization has been the idea of neoliberalism. Although there are certainly many ways in which one might interpret globalization, the dominant interpretative framework has been neoliberalism. Neoliberalism has been around for over a century and currently is the primary mode of thought in the United States. Neoliberals believe ardently, and some would say rigidly, in free market capitalism. As I shall elaborate, privatization, deregulation, and a narrow definition of public goods have framed how governments approach globalization. Free trade and reduced spending by central governments presumably provide greater freedom to individuals. From this perspective, this is the aim of society. Whenever government intercedes in a manner that restricts choice, then individual liberty is at risk.

Chris Lorenz (2012) has nicely summarized the neoliberal ideology by stating, "The dogma of the free market can best be expressed by a formula: free market = competition = best value for the money = optimum efficiency for individuals as both consumers and owners of private property" (p. 601). Such a dogma has taken hold on institutions whether in LA, Delhi, or Hong Kong. The result has significant ramifications for primary actors within the organizations. Members of the administration, for example, becomes more important insofar as they are the individuals who can create efficiencies and lead the charge up the rankings. Educational organizations are also impacted.

Globalization, Neoliberalism, and Education

Education, in general, and higher education, in particular, are also not immune from the effects of globalization and neoliberalism (Brown et al., 2010; Findlay & Tierney, 2010). Economies cannot be separated from sociocultural contexts in which educational institutions are embedded. Numerous scholars have pointed out how various forces have shaped universities in developed countries. Simon Marginson (2007), for example, has argued that academic governance has been transformed in Australia as the government and universities attempt to position higher education in a global context. David Kirp (2003) has done a similar study in the United States and argued that markets and technology are supplanting traditional academic values. Sheila Slaughter and Gary Rhoades (2004) have critiqued neoliberalism by writing about emerging forms of "academic capitalism" throughout the industrialized world. I have written about the various forms of neoliberal privatization in India as well as how the definition of quality in Central America is in constant tension with how it is defined on the world stage (Tierney, 1994, 1995; Tierney & Sabharwal, 2018; Tierney et al., 2019). Gerard Postiglione and Ailei Xie (2018) have pointed out how the pressures of being "world class" has driven an academic arms race in China and Hong Kong. Peter Scott's (2005) observation is that universities in the United Kingdom are increasingly unable to remain relevant because of erosions caused by the reconfiguration of the labor market.

What seems to be taking place is a myriad of interconnected changes: conventional academic disciplines are falling by the wayside, the traditional role of the academic is being redefined as tenure is being eliminated, research is increasingly corporatized, public funding is decreasing or awarded in a radically different manner from the past, and competition is increasing from education providers that did not even exist a decade or two ago. Coursera, for example, started in 2012 and claims that 40 million students have taken its courses,[1] even though it still has not perfected a business plan and has lost much of its initial luster. While for-profit education providers such as the Corinthian Colleges and Argosy University either have gone out of business or seen their market shares evaporate, other entrants, such as the for-profit Columbia Southern University and the nonprofit Western Governors University, are growing rapidly—in a manner that, according to some, heralds Clayton Christiansen's argument about "disruptive technology" (see Christensen, 1997; Christensen & Eyring, 2011). Christiansen has argued that radical inventions such as the telephone and the internet spring from start-up companies that show enormous growth and quickly force traditional companies out of business. And yet, Christiansen's prediction that half the colleges and universities in the United States will disappear in a decade has proven to be false (Lederman, 2017). Further, during the pandemic, when all of higher education turned to online education, one prevalent comment was that many students preferred in-person classes with other students and a professor. Zoom was an exciting innovation, and then found to be exhausting. Even though the end may not be near, the future is dramatically different from the past. Most observers of higher education agree that the recipe for tomorrow is not based on yesterday's ingredients. All these changes and suggestions for reform work within the neoliberal paradigm, and the pandemic only accelerated these sorts of recommendations as funding declined.

Not unlike the marketplace, academe has seen salaries rise for chief executives of universities—and fall for those who do the labor. Faculty positions are scarcer, and the quest for the "best" students—as defined by quantifiable outcomes such as scores on standard examinations like the SAT—becomes paramount. On the reverse side, issues such as equity or advancing a diversity agenda become less important, and full-time faculty are seen as inefficient.

Students have always been at the center of the higher education enterprise, but recent changes bring even that assumption into question. Whereas a postsecondary degree was once the province of wealthy men, the United States has struggled with equal opportunity since Morrill's Land Grant Act of 1862. India had an underdeveloped tertiary education system as a colony, and although the country has dramatically increased participation rates over the last 20 years at its universities and institutes, the children of the poorest families remain significantly underrepresented (Kumar, 2016; Tilak, 2013). The wealthiest students in Taiwan, Hong Kong, Turkey, and Malaysia always have studied abroad, which speaks volumes about issues surrounding the quality and capacity of these countries' postsecondary systems. Hence, while significant strides have been made for everyone, the challenges of poverty might seem intractable to the pessimist. The likelihood of entry into the labor market on graduation has become harder rather than easier as the twenty-first century progresses, and the democratic role of a postsecondary education has all but been eliminated. Employment was once a by-product of a college education; today, students go to college or university simply to remain competitive (Douglass, 2009).

The Rise of Populism and the Attack on Democracy

One outcome of all these changes is the rise of populist movements throughout the world that have antidemocratic and fascist strains in their strategies and beliefs. A great deal of emergent literature is following changes in Hungary, the United Kingdom, Italy, Greece, and elsewhere in Europe (Furedi, 2017; Hawkins & Littvay, 2019; Mondon & Winter, 2018; Stavrakakis & Katsambekis, 2019; Verbeek & Zaslove, 2016). The obliteration of the Republican Party and the rise of Trumpism in the United States have evoked a great deal of analysis. In India, the emergence of the Bharatiya Janata Party (BJP) and its emphasis on Hindu nationalism anticipated Donald Trump's message to his own constituencies. And even though China has never had a tradition of democracy, its moves are more in the direction of "strongmen" regimes, which has significant consequences for democratic outposts such as Hong Kong.

For my purposes here, I think of democracy as a system whereby a state's citizens are able to participate in choosing and replacing their leaders by election. The idea of democracy that I am working from assumes that human rights are essential; that is, individuals are free to express their opinions without fear of reprisal. As I shall discuss, electoral democracy finds its counterpoint in fascism, which appeals to the masses' need for a leader to solve their problems.

My goal is less to add to the overall literature pertaining to the rise of an antidemocratic nationalist agenda with fascist overtones, but instead to consider academe's role in advancing and supporting democracy. I am asking, What might academic institutions do to bolster and foment democracy and defeat fascism? What sorts of changes need to occur so that colleges and universities model the best practices of democratic life and aid in securing democracy in society? As a recent report from the Brookings Institute noted, "Democracy's fate rests in the hands of people, and securing it begins at home" (Eisen et al., 2019, p. 13). As I elaborate, what concerned me about the Brookings report was that it offered several useful suggestions about how societies might bolster democracy, yet higher education was largely overlooked. Democracy is at the heart of civil society. Robust organizations in a civil society keep democracy strong. These organizations provide citizens with information to make informed decisions, and they are meeting grounds on which we may hash out differences of opinion. Colleges and universities are one of these civic organizations that help preserve and advance democracy in civil society.

The twenty-first century has led to many changes with regard to higher education—both caused by and resulting from globalization and neoliberalism—that are not yet well understood. If academe is to be a progenitor in the advancement of democracy, then we need to consider five changes that have been significant across national contexts: inequality, privatization, identity, academic freedom, and the public good.

Inequality

Wealth accumulation among the richest individuals across the globe continues, even as poverty remains an intransigent problem. During the twentieth century, attempts were made to increase college-going throughout the world, as education was once seen as the route out of poverty. This effort continues globally, whether it is the "college for all" movement in the United States, India's desire to have more individuals attending universities than any other country in the world, or even tiny Sri Lanka's effort to increase its university enrollment by 10 percent a year for several years. The challenge is that, all too often, jobs do not exist for students upon graduation, the skills students learned at the university are irrelevant for the marketplace, or the value of the liberal arts is eliminated such that colleges and universities become vocational schools rather than centers of learning. Indeed, a liberal education in Hong Kong is not only viewed as irrelevant for future employment; the government considers what professors teach in such courses as the groundwork for the protests that have occurred.

The result is that whereas education was once seen as the "great equalizer," in the twentieth century, wealth discrepancy between the wealthiest and the poorest countries, and between the wealthiest and poorest individuals in those countries, continues to grow rather than decline. When the crushing debt burden that many students and their families accumulate is factored in, postsecondary education can be seen as creating greater inequality rather than equality (Auguste et al., 2009).

Who the poor are also varies, not only by race and gender, but also by categories that are unique to different societies. Since its founding, the United States has struggled with issues of equity pertaining to Native Americans, Latinxs, and African Americans. Although racism exists in India and one's skin color is a marker that has the potential to lead to discrimination there, the larger issue pertains to the pernicious influence of caste, which still has a significant impact on the kind of education one receives and on participation and graduation rates from higher education (Pathania & Tierney, 2018). Isabel Wilkerson has written how caste occurs not only in India, but how it is also a force for understanding race in the United States (Wilkerson, 2020). In Hong Kong, caste does not exist and race is an issue on a much smaller scale; inequality has more to do with class, as Hong Kong has no affirmative action system (Kwan & Wong, 2016; Y-L. Wong, 2019; Y-L. Wong & Koo, 2016). Affirmative action has existed in the United States for a half-century and has been under attack for the last quarter-century. India has an extensive framework that includes various castes and indigenous people in its affirmative action system. In all three locations, class frames inequality but does so in different ways, based on additional markers. Education, in all three locations, is still presumed to be a primary vehicle to improve one's social and economic well-being, and increasingly, higher education is viewed as a necessary ticket to the middle class.

Privatization

Private higher education has increased throughout the world. Whether the institution is a for-profit institution such as DeVry University in the United States or Raffles College in Singapore or a nonprofit such as Bilkent University in Turkey or O. P. Jindal Global University in India, one of the larger changes to these countries' postsecondary systems has been the movement away from the monopoly of public systems on tertiary education. To wit, Bilkent is commonly thought of as one of Turkey's best institutions. However, the expansion of private higher education has been remarkable, especially in Latin America and Asia. The private sector serves approximately 80 percent of the students in Japan and South Korea;[2] private institutions enrolled 75 percent of all tertiary-level students in Brazil, and around half of those students are enrolled in a for-profit institution (Knobel & Verhine, 2017). Major shifts are happening in the United States, too. For-profit colleges and universities have existed for over a century, but until recently, they were relatively small companies that offered one specific skill or trade, such as secretarial training, cosmetology, or welding. Now these institutions have vastly expanded their offerings—and their reach. As of the 2016–2017 academic year, 342 for-profit providers participated in federal financial aid programs in California; estimates are that for-profit accredited and unaccredited providers enroll more than 200,000 Californian students (Willis & Allen, 2018). As a result, the very definition of "public" and "private" university has come under debate. The state's obligation to educate its citizens and the recognition of higher education as a public good are under significant reassessment.

What one means by a "public" university and how one defines a "private" university have significant public policy implications (Duderstadt & Womack, 2003; Kaul et al., 1999). One derivative of globalization has been a neoliberal reliance on market initiatives as preferable to government intervention. India and the United States parallel one another, yet in different ways. Both countries have extensive networks of private colleges and universities; in India, more students attend private institutions than public ones. In the United States, however, attendance at a four-year public college or university is now expected to necessitate student loans. The assumption is that the state no longer should provide free postsecondary education to consumers. The same is true to a lesser extent in India, where student costs are on the rise. In Hong Kong, however, the government still largely covers the cost of higher education for the university system and the institutions are overwhelmingly public, although regionally there is a great deal of private, entrepreneurial activity. To get into an elite public institution, however, parents need to be able to pay for private schooling. Public high school education is generally poor, and the wealthy pay for private high school so that their children have the ability to get admitted to a public university or to study abroad.

Identity

Perhaps no idea has been more fraught with contestation in the late twentieth and beginning of the twenty-first century than that of identity. We have changed in ways that are not very comforting. At one point, two large philosophical groups existed with regard to national identity, one of which aimed for assimilation to a universal norm, while the other sought to claim their own unique identities regardless of factors such as race, gender, sexual orientation, religion, ethnicity, differences in ability, and the like. Now, in locations such as Hong Kong, New Delhi, and Los Angeles, all people have differentiated identities, assimilation is seen as impossible (or worse, malicious), and communication across difference is seen as a fool's errand. The idea of intersectionality has fractured identities even more. As poet and civil rights activist Audre Lorde (2009) percep-tively commented in a 1985 lecture to Medgar Evers College, "Some of the ways in which I identify myself make it difficult for you to hear me" (p. 57). She was speaking to black women who found it hard to hear her lesbian voice, and to white lesbians who could not hear her blackness.

The assumption, however historically wrong, in the United States is that immigrants prefer to retain their initial identity and do not want to become American. From this perspective, identity is fixed and unchanging. Similarly, some will argue that Muslims should not be allowed into the country because they are not Judeo-Christian. More conservative white and Christian citizens harken back to a 1950s version of America where the lines were clearly drawn to show who was who.

In India, differences largely are based on religion and caste. For example, those who are born Dalits may convert to Buddhism, but for upper-caste Hindus, however, Dalits will always be untouchables. Muslims may lay claim to a treasured history in India, but to others, that history is to be denigrated and denied, not celebrated. Prime Minister Narendra Modi, in his second inauguration speech, alluded to the fact that minorities "feel" they are discriminated against, thereby suggesting, of course, that they are not. Even different sports can lay claim to a religious identity such that when a sport becomes popular, it is seen as a reaffirmation of Hinduism. From this perspective, yoga is distinctively Hindu and symbolizes an affirmation of one's identity. When a popular Muslim actor criticized the government, many people placed a bounty on his head and called for him to leave the country. Moreover, the newspapers remain filled with marriage proposals stating the caste that a prospective bride or groom requires.

Hong Kong once had an identity at arm's-length from China, but now the rulers in China have all but absorbed the city. The discussion about identity in Hong Kong is a central point of debate but entirely different from what gets discussed in Los Angeles or New Delhi. A Hong Kong identity does not consider skin color or caste based on religion. Cantonese and English were once the primary languages on the island; now there is a push for students to learn and speak Mandarin. Students from the mainland regularly attend universities in Hong Kong, and even though all students may be Chinese, the culture is now very different. Students and faculty are less willing to be forthcoming in class because they fear reprisals for being "Anti-China," and there is a great deal of commentary about students who secretly record professors and fellow students in class and report back to the government. The protests in 2019 led to many mainland students returning home. Some felt worried about speaking Mandarin in the streets. A Hong Kong identity is, in some form, tied up with the idea of democracy. Speaking English was once identified with colonialism and today it has more to do with Hong Kong's democratic tradition.

A nationalist identity was once used to think well of democratic nations. A common platitude about the United States is that we are bound by an "idea"—democracy—and our fidelity to the idea is part and parcel of a national identity. Today, however, nationalism is a synonym for xenophobia. Nationalism in India is not the hope for a secular country but instead speaks to Hindus' desire to place their religion at the core of the nation. In Hong Kong, nationalism to the Chinese government means that the city needs to conform to the central government's definition of identity. Trumpism is a clarion call for returning the United States to a simpler time, when white male dominance was paramount.

Postsecondary institutions play a critical role in the examination of identity. Education brings out in individuals an opportunity for reflection about who they are and how they fit into the grand scheme of things.

An education can create the atomization of identity whereby individuals think of themselves as individuals who identify with a group and have no sense of communal fraternity beyond that group, or whereby claims can be made about a national identity that reaffirms standards and denies those who are different from the norm. Just as the college years have the potential to enable individuals to come to grips with their multiple pasts, there is also the possibility for understanding difference in a way that bridges identities rather than isolates them. Discussions about identity are central to academic life.

I do not think we can simply return to the "good old days," as if the past was a utopia and its re-creation will solve the problems that currently exist. And yet, I also do not think we must enter a brave new world that is entirely void of any historical contingencies. We need to consider how these five ideas have been constituted, reconstituted, and defined today. Of consequence, I am seeking a framework to think about these five issues so that we might have a guide for those of us concerned about how higher education might be used to support a broader demo-cratic initiative in which we lead by example through our own internal policies and actions, and our postsecondary institutions also explicitly work toward fomenting change in the larger society. Although these are broad trends, they obviously are articulated in different ways based on the national identities of particular countries.

As I shall expand on in Chapter 3, I intend to honor individuals' identity, but I equate the struggle for public life with the narrowly defined interests of the group. In a previous work (Tierney, 1993), I talked about how we might build "communities of difference," and I return to that idea in these pages. We have to think about ways in which these issues that confront us bring us together in advancing the democratic project rather than ignoring or refuting it.

Academic Freedom

As I elaborate in Chapter 4, what we expect of academic staff—the fac-ulty—is also changing throughout the world. During much of the twentieth century in the United States, professors were largely autonomous agents able to define the nature of their working conditions; today, the largest number of faculty is part-time and contingent. An increasing number of full-time faculty need a second (and third) job to make ends meet. Research was once a critical component of many institutions and an aspiration for many others; currently, there is more interest in teaching, in general, and online learning, in particular. In all cases, the academic workforce is undergoing seismic shifts accompanied by growing complexity.

There is an odd dualism at work in the United States. The erosion of academic freedom's protector—tenure—has meant that academic freedom is at greater risk today than at any point in its history. Structural reforms to shared governance, tenure, and hiring practices suggest that a sea change in academic practices is afoot, and we see the consequences whether we look at New Delhi, Hong Kong, or Los Angeles.

However, what passes for academic freedom—always a topic of dialogue and debate—is also under reformulation. Ardent supporters of academic freedom have had to rethink its meaning and definition in an era when people invent facts and put forward conspiracies with no basis in reality. To enable discussions about whether the shooting of schoolchildren at Sandy Hook, Connecticut, in 2012 occurred, for example, is not an act in support of academic freedom. I have a wide definition of academic freedom, but its limits have been met over the past few years (Tierney, 2020).

Of consequence, what was once seen as the raison d'être of the academy in the twentieth century—academic freedom—is undergoing significant reexamination and reformulation. Tenure came about to protect academic freedom. If most positions in the academy are no longer tenure track, there's the tacit implication that academic freedom—and relatedly, the search for truth—is no longer a central totem of the academy.

Governments need to respect autonomy; when governments believe that professors are little more than public servants, then what gets said will be constrained and muted. Hong Kong has an academic tradition rooted in the mores of the United Kingdom, where academic freedom and job security were seen as interrelated and essential for academic excellence. Today, however, academics are routinely cautioned not to speak against the state or for independence; if they do, they will lose their employment. The governing board of the universities has exerted its authority in a manner that many see as undermining the power of the vice chancellor and making a mockery of shared governance and free speech. The law that China passed in 2020, ostensibly on national security, has all but eliminated academic freedom in Hong Kong.

Faculty and students have come in for criticism since the Occupy Central movement, and even more so during the prolonged protests that closed campuses in fall 2019. With the first protest, faculty initially suggested that all Hong Kongers should occupy the central area of the city in protest against the encroachment of China on Hong Kong. Students then took over the movement and occupied the center of Hong Kong for roughly three months. One fallout from that activism is that China's central government has taken a much more assertive role in events on campuses and in the city, which partially led to the more extensive protests in 2019 and the passage in 2020 of the National Security Law. The law created a vast security apparatus in Hong Kong and gave China broad powers to crack down on, arrest, and imprison individuals who disagreed with China's various policies. The result is that now if faculty protest, they will be jailed and expelled from the university.

In India, faculty and students face violent attacks when they choose to put forward ideas that run contrary to the established order. The conservative governing party, BJP, has repeatedly condemned universities as allowing anti-Indian discourse. Numerous movies, plays, and books have been banned. Students and faculty have been dismissed and imprisoned. If students or faculty try to discuss the fate of Kashmir, they are likely to face repercussions. The result in many instances has been violence against anyone espousing a controversial view. Dalits and Muslims, in particular, have been targeted. Further, those who wish to give prominence to Hinduism also put forward myths as fact—that Hindus conducted open heart surgery thousands of years ago, for example, or that they invented flying aircraft in the distant past.

The Public Good

A final change pertains to the oversight and financing of public- and private-sector institutions. The state is refashioning its role in relation to the financial support and regulation of public institutions as they become more dependent on external (nongovernmental) funding and more independent from the government agencies that created them. Consequently, how state institutions might be more effectively governed and organized have become key policy questions throughout the world. For similar reasons, private institutions also require new forms of oversight to ensure that consumers are protected (Hentschke et al., 2010; Tierney & Hentschke, 2007).

One might think that a decrease in funding makes a public institution less dependent on state demands. Yet in the United States, as state funding has decreased as an absolute percentage of overall revenue, state regulatory control at public institutions has increased. Meanwhile, over-sight of for-profit institutions has been inadequate and tied up in partisan politics (Angulo, 2016); the Democratic administration of Barack Obama sought to increase oversight, while the deregulation of the sector was a key goal for the Trump administration. In India, fully two-thirds of all students attend private institutions; how these institutions are regulated has become a national conversation because of the subpar quality of the education provided. How Hong Kong's universities interact with the Hong Kong government has become a major topic of debate insofar as institutional autonomy appears to have been eliminated as China asserts greater control with the National Security Law. Although privatization is not a point of discussion in Hong Kong, the autonomy that universities once enjoyed is now undergoing a reformulation as government regulation increases and faculty autonomy is eliminated.

The global move away from the creation, sustenance, and support of a public good reflects shifts with other goods and services. These phil-osophical shifts are such that the state no longer sees itself as a purveyor of public goods. The turn toward enabling the private sector to grow—whether as for-profit institutions in the United States or ostensibly nonprofit institutions in India—suggests that postsecondary institutions are going through a significant change with regard to the state's role in oversight and governance. On the one hand, the autonomy of public universities in Hong Kong is being rethought. On the other hand, the public funding of higher education in the United States and India is largely decreasing, and regulation has become a major topic of debate in both countries (Kapur, 2010; Kapur & Perry, 2015; Tierney & Sabharwal, 2017).

If the role of higher education is to create a more equitable society, the role of regulation necessitates continued examination as a public-policy issue (Salmi, 2011). Both states are increasingly playing a role of oversight and monitoring. India has significant oversight of the public and private sectors, although corruption pervades the system. Just as all prime ministers bemoan the level of corruption in the government, so too is corruption endemic in all aspects of higher education. Regulation is increasingly strict in Hong Kong as China asserts control; the boards of trustees and the senior administrations are less willing to defer to academics or students at the university, and more likely to carry out the desires of the government. Different states in the United States have increased oversight by implementing policies such as Performance Based Funding (PBF), but the positive outcomes appear negligible while the negative outcomes may disadvantage historically underserved students, as well as the institutions they typically attend (Hillman & Corral, 2017; Li et al., 2018; Li & Kennedy, 2018).

Governance within the university systems is also going through significant changes. Shared governance largely came about in the twentieth century in the United States with vestiges of a European influence from the nineteenth century (Tierney & Lanford, 2014). The rise of non–tenure track faculty and the neoliberal environment that prizes the speed that decisions can be made rather than the process of deliberation about issues, has fractured the idea of shared governance (Tierney, 2020). In both India and Hong Kong, faculties think of themselves more as public servants than independent intellectuals who are free to speak out on critical issues in society or at the institution. Deliberation about internal issues that are not politically charged may remain in the hands of the faculty, but informed discussions about the future of the institution are increasingly rare; instead, strategic plans about the future are seen as the province of the senior administration and governing boards. Students in India and Hong Kong have historically had more voice than their counterparts in the United States, but the extent of their power is as much at risk today in Hong Kong and New Delhi as it is in Los Angeles.

The Logic of the Locations

The text highlights the trends that are taking place in three metropolitan areas—Los Angeles, New Delhi, and Hong Kong. I have spent a quarter of a century in Los Angeles. I also have been an Interdisciplinary Research Fellow in Hong Kong for parts of each of the last six years. I had a year-long Fulbright Scholarship in New Delhi in 2015–2016 and returned for follow-up interviews in 2019. The text utilizes data not only from national archives but also from interviews with scores of individuals—students, faculty, senior executives, and policy makers. I am not using these three cities as case studies, which would involve a much more extended discussion. Rather, they are exemplars of what I find taking place, or needing to take place, if we are to protect democracy and defeat fascism.

The kaleidoscopic history of the recent past and current events shaping higher education affords the opportunity to see similarities and differences across metropolitan areas and institutions. Information and stories framed by national data sets have the potential to illuminate trends and hopefully provide material for reflection about what kind of higher education we want to offer in the twenty-first century and what role universities should assume in helping advance a democratic society.

The rise of populism and the demise of democracy is occurring in various locations throughout the world. I have chosen three metropolitan areas in democratic nations (or city-states) to compare and contrast similarities and differences.

Los Angeles

Since World War II, the United States has arguably had the best system of higher education in the world, and California, with its Master Plan for Higher Education, has stood as the exemplar for public support of universal access. Nonetheless, privatization, declining state financing of higher education, and the casualization of academic labor have created questions about the future direction of higher education. With the dramatic increase of non–tenure track faculty has come a reticence of the faculty to speak out on crucial issues for fear that they will be fired. The election of Donald Trump has only increased arguments pertaining to the import and definition of identity. The search for "truth"—once an axiom of academic life—is now derided as fake news. Even though there was no evidence of a rigged election, Trump's claims convinced 75 percent of Republicans that the results were fraudulent.

New Delhi

With 1.2 billion people, India is the world's largest democracy. Although the Indian Institutes of Technology (IIT) are considered centers of excellence, the system is troubled and beset by challenges over funding, regulation, and lack of opportunity for its poorest citizens. The reservation system (affirmative action), the rapid increase in privatization, the corruption that has come along with privatization, and the government's intrusion on campuses have raised equally significant questions about what the country should expect of its tertiary educational system. The rapid increase in offering higher education throughout the country has led to the diminution of scarce public resources and a decrease in the system's quality precisely when these institutions also want to improve their rankings in league tables. The number of degreed citizens needed by the country has become a significant question, as have the rights and responsibilities of faculty to conduct research that, according to some, challenge the assumptions of the government.

New Delhi is emblematic of the challenges that India faces. Home to some of India's most respected postsecondary institutions, the city is also beset with political and social turmoil. Faculty and students are regularly threatened either with sanctions or physical violence for hosting events that the government sees as problematic. Corruption is rampant. The University Grants Commission (UGC) coordinates all higher education activity in the country and is one of the most centralized academic bodies in the world. Affirmative action provides a level of support to members of lower castes but they are still grossly underrepresented, as are women in prestigious institutions such as the IITs (Deshpande & Palshikar, 2008). As I shall elaborate, privatization is a particularly vexing aspect of a system that ostensibly has been devised to support knowledge production but actually does the opposite. Employment upon graduation is often unlikely (Fernandes, 2006). The government also has put forward a vigorous nationalism defined by Hinduism where Islam is often vilified and Dalits (untouchables) are blamed for many of the ills of society.

Hong Kong

Hong Kong's universities are ranked as among the best in the world and have been at the epicenter of democratic reform. Honk Kong University is considered one of the top five universities in Asia and is over a century old; Hong Kong University of Science and Technology (HKUST) is the newest university in the top 100 universities in the world. Today, however, academic staff throughout Hong Kong worry about their ability to conduct research and participate in university governance given the tempestuous relationship Hong Kong has had with mainland China.

Hong Kong is in a troubled situation with the country within which it ostensibly resides. When Britain handed over Hong Kong to China in 1997, Deng Xiaoping developed the idea of "one country, two systems," which seemed to work modestly well. China absorbed Hong Kong, but the city was to be a distinct Chinese region with its own economic and administrative system. Hong Kong was to maintain its own governmental, legal, economic, and educational systems. At the handover, Hong Kong contributed 25 percent of China's GDP; today Hong Kong contributes less than 3 percent of the mainland's GDP. Hong Kong still plays a central role in China's economy because of foreign investment, but its centrality to China has lessened.

Over time, China has asserted more authority in both quiet and dramatic ways. A particular arena of contention has been the universities. Those who claim a Hong Kong identity that is distinct from the mainland run the risk of censure or imprisonment. To speak of some issues, such as independence, is now forbidden. Regulation is high, and autonomy is low. Hong Kong is struggling to define how it is to move forward in these new circumstances, and the universities are at the center of the turmoil (Mok, 2005). Although the Umbrella movement and then the protests of 2019 boasted of being "leaderless," faculty, and in particular, students, played central roles in orchestrating citizens' responses to the government. The campuses became a flashpoint in 2019, and several closed to avoid further mayhem. As they have reopened after the pandemic, the ability of faculty and students to speak out has been curtailed in the classroom and on the campus generally.

I have chosen these three democratic cities because they each face the issues I have raised, and they are also framed by what I have defined as globalization, and relatedly, neoliberalism. One might think that the United States is immune to external forces, or that India's size in general and New Delhi in particular makes it so different from Hong Kong that comparisons are impossible. Hong Kong is a city of 7 million that is struggling to find its way as a democracy within a country that is not, whereas the United States has elected someone as president who many believe threatens the foundations of democracy even in democratic strongholds such as Los Angeles. And yet, all three sites are located in democracies that have had shared assumptions about what it expects of their systems of higher education. Education has been seen as a liberalizing force for society and as a route out of poverty for its poorest citizens. Their faculties have had a protected, even privileged, status, and the institutions have been seen as spaces where the search for truth should be protected and nurtured.

These sites also have had different trajectories. There are obvious differences between the American postsecondary system and the British systems. There also are differences between what takes place in Hong Kong as opposed to New Delhi, given their different paths over the last half-century. However, I have not chosen to explore these cities because of their similarities. Rather, I have asked how three different postsecondary systems in democratic locations have dealt with issues such as the rise of populism and fascism.

Indeed, the forces of globalization and neoliberalism in the twenty-first century have raised significant questions about the nature of higher education in each location (Altbach, 2005, 2007; Beerkens, 2003; Brown et al., 2010). Rather than develop an isolated example, my intent is to use these sites to help understand the ideas I am calling on here. Investigating how each site is grappling with change by way of analyses framed by national data sets within the metropolitan areas of Los Angeles, New Delhi, and Hong Kong aids in understanding that I am not writing of unique changes, but rather of global ones. To be sure, one could isolate data and look only at one country, or, one could only speak with policy analysts about the changes they feel are important. However, in postsecondary institutions located in democratic arenas, higher education is not determined merely by the policies that one or another state agency or administrator finds useful. Comparative research enables us to think of democracy not as distinctly American, or Indian, or Chinese, but rather as an idea.

Organizing the Text

One of academe's more scholarly and important works is Cardinal Newman's *The Idea of a University*, originally published in 1852. Newman's topic was broad—what a university should be—and touched on all aspects of higher education. I intend for this book to be similarly broad. Democracy is a notoriously contested notion, and many might suggest, especially of late, that preparing individuals for the workforce is about as much as a postsecondary institution should or can do. Others, such as myself, will argue that one of the primary purposes of our colleges and universities is to help students think through the thorny aspects of democracy, undertake research that advances the democratic public sphere, and exemplify by example the kind of cultures and structures we wish to have. This is particularly important, as I shall expand on, when we see the development of fascist tendencies in governments and leaders around the globe.

Traditionally, for example, higher education researchers have eschewed classified research based on the assumption that all knowledge that is created should be shared. To speak of the overall import of democracy in the public sphere ought not to suggest that training for jobs is irrelevant.

It is simply a belief that we should not reduce academe to a job training center and little more. It would be ironic to talk about the importance of free speech but work in an environment where it is not protected. Democratic notions of colleges and universities as well as the larger public sphere are predicated on the assumption that we all inhabit multiple social positions, and, as I shall elaborate, we do not have fixed and stable identities. My role as a gay man, as an academic, as a white male—all of these and other such identities—are shaped and changed not only in the environment of the academic institution where I work, but also by the larger social formations at work in society. I also have the opportunity and responsibility within a university to help try to shape the discourse in the larger society so that false descriptions of social reality might be reoriented in a manner that enables a reimagination of the public sphere. Rather than try to tamp down or avoid dissent, we figure out how to enable conversations to occur so that we might understand one another's multiple subject positions and in doing so hopefully enact a reinvigorated public sphere.

In the twenty-first century, I also do not think situating a college or university for democracy is a natural process that simply occurs. Rather, one needs to focus campus energies in a manner that actively engages with the idea of democracy, as well as the contours of fascism. The notion of a public good is largely lost in current society; instead, we have a sense that individuals are the center of existence, and the more we are able to free them from the constraints of the community, the better off everyone will be. From this position, we are all individual agents with no relationship or affinity with one another, especially those with whom we are different. "Leave me alone" is not a phrase that evokes the idea of community—or a university in search of engagement with the larger society. The goal, then, is to reconfigure norms that have been established during my career in academe and think through how we might more productively position universities to be active agents in the promulgation of democracy.

In the next chapter I discuss what I mean by a college or university functioning to promote and enhance democracy by outlining three crises that have settled upon academe. In Chapter 3, I expand on notions of identity and how they shape academic discourse that can either promote or retard universities in advancing democracy. In Chapter 4, I analyze the idea of academic freedom and point out how the rise of social media and technology has made the protection of academic freedom harder, which in turn makes the role of universities as sites of resistance for fascism and progenitors of democracy even more difficult. In Chapter 5 I consider how privatization has grown in each city and examine how tertiary institutions are being positioned in a manner distinct from the idea of a public good. If universities are only focused on jobs, they will become unable to analyze the situations that exist in the larger society.

Chapter 6 considers how we might best respond to fascism and what the implications are for what I have called "cultural citizenship." Chapter 7 concludes by arguing for what universities employing democracy as an organizing framework might exhibit. I am not putting forward a recipe, as if I have created a cookbook. I am trying to think through steps for action for students, academics and our postsecondary institutions.

Thus, I argue that globalization and neoliberalism have created the conditions for the demise of democracy and the rise of fascism. Inequality and privatization are greater, and the public good is more constrained today than in the past. What we mean by identity and the limits of academic freedom are more confused today than at any time in the last century. The conditions, however complex, that we face in the larger society have muted the mission of academe. Universities are different from profit-making companies, and they have held unique positions in the democratic state. They have the potential to shape, not simply the market of the larger society, but also how individuals and groups function and relate to one another in that society. Those of us working within higher education have the potential to reframe discussions and structures in the larger state apparatus. My intent is to help us understand the complexity, analyze why we have been mute when we should be vocal, and suggest how we might offer a more robust response to protect and advance democracy.

CHAPTER TWO

The Democratic Imperative of Higher Education

The University in Crisis:
Hegemony, Legitimacy, and Autonomy

The university in the twenty-first century faces three crises of identity. These crises are evident, whether the institution is in Los Angeles, New Delhi, or Hong Kong. They have been apparent for a while, but they are even more obvious given the pandemic. As opposed to the more commonly discussed crises that garner a great deal of commentary (such as plummeting enrollment and fiscal woes), these crises are challenges that go to the purpose of academic life. In putting forward these three crises, I shall argue that those of us in tertiary institutions need to focus on a scholarship and pedagogy of commitment. From this perspective, intellectuals and the organizations in which they work need to be focused on what I shall define as a cultural politics of transformation. Rather than try to remove themselves from society—or portray the university as a fortress immune from the pedestrian concerns of life—the effort here is for organizations to be centrally concerned with advancing democracy. I am trying to theorize the university in a manner that moves us away from a false neutrality of disinterestedness.

The university helped build the modern nation-state. It trained elites and an increasingly broad middle class through the accumulation of abstract thinking. The university made the case for the democratic project. The faculty in Hong Kong, for example, played a central role in putting forward a modern conception of Hong Kong that was internationally focused. In many respects, Hong Kong was the first global city in Asia. At the birth of an independent India, Jawaharlal Nehru wanted universities to educate the mass of society and achieve scientific excellence with its institutes—none more so than those universities in the nation's young capital, New Delhi. Los Angeles has looked outward to the rest of the country and to the Pacific region and its postsecondary institutions are among the best importers of foreign talent of any organization.

A century ago, a stance of disinterestedness enabled the university to comment on the social mores of society and, through a belief in objective research, bring about change. The democratic state encouraged universities to remain at arm's length from society in order to analyze and improve it, whether the institution was in Hong Kong, Delhi, or LA. However, distance and disinterestedness are no longer sufficient in a world where we are facing a democratic recession (Diamond, 2015). As Henry Giroux (2019) has stated, "We live at a time in which institutions that were meant to limit human suffering and misfortune and protect the public from the excesses of the market have been either weakened or abolished" (p. 27). How did a public and nonprofit sphere that once supported the enlargement of democratic dialogue shift to a defensive posture that has made the university either irrelevant or endangered?

I elaborate in the next chapter about Max Weber's famous adage that intellectuals need to put forward an "ethics of responsibility." Weber walked a fine line between undertaking objective science and delineating the implications of a decision without actually being involved in politics (Waters & Waters, 2015), but he never anticipated the implications of a neoliberal global environment where news and information are instantaneous, and the information ecosystem is characterized by myriad attempts at disinformation. Today, an ethics of responsibility has to consider the rise of the populist movement and how individuals disseminate and utilize information. Hence, my question pertains to what we might do to restore the university's voice, and in turn, reverse the democratic recession. In a globalized world, what is the mission of the university? To answer such questions, we first need to come to terms with the ideological crises that now confront the university.

Hegemony

The first crisis pertains to the university's intellectual role. Throughout the twentieth century, the battle within and about higher education had to do with the production of high culture and the meaning of science. The university was the arbiter of knowledge, and the intellectual scaffolding was largely positivist. As de Sousa Santos (2006) noted, "University knowledge—that is, the scientific knowledge produced in universities . . . was, for the whole of the twentieth century, a predominately disciplinary knowledge whose autonomy imposed a relatively decontextualized process of production in relation to the day-to-day pressures of the societies" (p. 73). The scientific paradigm ruled the day, and how one came to understandings was through the scientific method. Of consequence, the university was the arbiter of knowledge.

The last half of the twentieth century was a battle about the scientific method in many, but not all, academic quarters. Although some of the arguments were focused within natural science departments, the bulk of the contention took place in the humanities, social sciences, and affiliated areas such as education and social work. The popularity of the ideas came and went with blinding speed—deconstruction, postmodernism, queer theory, standpoint theory, and critical race theory, to name but a few—and they each had a particular impact and a particular following, but, other than critical race theory in the social sciences, not much staying power. The underlying tenet of the critiques had to do with the assertion that objective knowledge was impossible. The idea of the impossibility of objective knowledge has remained within the social sciences and humanities. The assumption has been that the observer has a particular stance based on numerous criteria—one's ancestry, class background, sexual identity, and the like. Of consequence was the belief that the search for objective knowledge was a fool's errand. One did not discover truths, as if they were waiting to be found. Rather, the investigator created, or cocreated, these truths. Although the hard sciences seemed immune from much of this debate, epistemological issues pertaining to the sorts of topics chosen, as well as how they were studied, often were open for valid critiques. Medicine tended to privilege studies focused on the male anatomy, for example, and studies of the inner city often looked at people living in poverty in Black communities as reflecting individual pathologies rather than systemic forms of inequality.

For a time, the university's inhabitants were able to have their intellectual cake and eat it too. Those in the hard sciences went about their work, received grants to study all sorts of scientific problems, and on occasion had breakthroughs in the laboratory that improved the lives of individuals and groups, whether from new medicines or new structures.

At the same time, those in the less-hard disciplines were able to point out how different groups had been misunderstood because of this problem of objectivity. Society benefited by greater attention to oppressed people, as well as analyses of how oppression came about, and by whom. Ironically, even those who criticized the scientific construction of knowledge were able to do so within the confines of the organization that defined knowledge. The philosopher of science or the critical theorist could attack the idea of objectivity as an expert even though they were implicitly attacking the idea of experts. The academy protected those who conducted the critiques because of the institution's belief in academic freedom. The result was that the arbiters of knowledge, whether from the traditional or postmodern vantage points, still held their roles.

The crisis that came about was that the hegemony that the university once held was ripped asunder. Universities had been the institution that produced high culture and trained elites through critical thinking and the creation of new knowledge, whether in the sciences or humanities. When the idea of knowledge production began to be questioned, even though it was being done in largely discrete areas, very few analysts questioned what might become of the university. Those who were positivists and trained in the sciences went about their work. Those who were postmodernists and critiqued the epistemological bases of knowledge did so from their academic perch. From either ideological persuasion, most faculty were tenured and free to write, do research, and publish their work without threat of losing their jobs. Eventually what occurred, however, was, at a minimum, a communal questioning of the role of the university, and at the most, an extreme crisis of hegemony. Universities used to be the arbiter of knowledge, but now they communicated that they no longer knew how to define knowledge. Moreover, such a message fit nicely within the framework of neoliberal globalization that had its own problems with objectified expertise.

Legitimacy

The second crisis pertains to how the larger society viewed the purpose of the university. Two changes happened throughout the twentieth century. First, the United States inherited the idea of the modern university from Europe. Until the middle of the last century, the purpose of academic life was to create new knowledge and train students. Training, however, was not vocational. Yes, the United States invented "junior" colleges (aka community colleges) as a way to give specific skills to one segment of the population, but the overwhelming focus, energy, and public monies went to the rest of the academic environment. Faculty did research, regardless of discipline, to understand different phenomena, and they trained students to think. In this regard, Cardinal Newman's epic *The Idea of the University* is an emblematic work; Discourse Five, entitled "Knowledge Its Own End," stated the following about the purpose of higher education:

> It is a great point then to enlarge the range of studies which a University professes, even for the sake of the students; and, though they cannot pursue every subject which is open to them, they will be the gainers by living among those and under those who represent the whole circle. This I conceive to be the advantage of a seat of universal learning. . . . An assemblage of learned men, zealous for their own sciences, and rivals of each other, are brought, by familiar intercourse and for the sake of intellectual peace, to adjust together the claims and relations of their respective subjects of investigation. They learn to respect, to consult, to aid each other. (1852/2015, p. 76)

The implicit assumption was twofold. On the one hand, faculty and their administrations assumed that if they trained students how to think, they would be better prepared to take up positions in society. The view of society until recently had as a central role some sort of involvement in a democratic society. In addition, the assumption was that a literate person with reasonable scientific reasoning would be a benefit to society. Thus, the largest beneficiary of a student's attendance and learning while in college was society. Sure, individuals benefited because they found employment, but that was assumed. Post–World War II America had a surfeit of jobs. Until the late twentieth century, those who worked in colleges and universities did not think of themselves, and the citizenry did not think of the institutions, as vocational centers. Even students who were "pre-med" were learning about the science of medicine rather than simply vocational aspects of the medical field. Some institutions even went so far as to reject the idea of students taking classes to learn a specific skill. Reed College, for example, only allowed a Spanish department to exist so that students might learn Spanish to read Spanish literature in Spanish. Learning Spanish so that one might be a translator or could utilize the language as a skill for a job were not acceptable as primary rationales for a department.

As the larger environment has shifted, however, so has the purpose of the university. Citizens, governments, and students increasingly view higher education as a transport vehicle for jobs. If a university does not train students for gainful employment, then it has failed. Moreover, students may need very specific skills for a job. Such a shift has created the second crisis for higher education. The crisis has resulted not merely in an expansion of career services offices or a greater focus on the cultural capital needed for one or another job. Rather, when the university's raison d'être shifts from what it had largely held for centuries to a vocational purpose, then the institution is facing a crisis of legitimacy.

This legitimacy, ironically, comes about because the university has served the purposes of the larger capitalist structure. The university has never existed to disrupt society but rather is intended to support it. Until recently, the support of society occurred because of what I have defined as the university's ability to be the hegemonic arbiter of knowledge. In the twenty-first century, however, knowledge matters less in terms of a specific menu of pieces that educated individuals have—otherwise known as cultural capital. Given the reach of globalization and the speed with which technology and social media enable information to be conveyed, what counts as knowledge has come to be questioned. Those who use "alternative facts" now question scientific facts—such as those pertaining to climate change. Previously, higher education's responsiveness to the needs of capital and business provided it a privileged status. Today, that same responsiveness brings its legitimacy into question. The mimicry of the marketplace and the precariousness of labor—and within the academy, especially intellectual labor—results in academics as being seen as disposable intellectual objects unless they can train workers.

Autonomy

The third crisis pertains to autonomy. The metaphor of the university as "ivy-covered" painted a picture of a cloistered community removed from society. Shared governance suggested self-governance without interference from the state or other entities. Professors were the arbiters of knowledge. Students applied for jobs and the professors provided letters of reference. In effect, the professors were proxies for what a student had learned. The assumption was that a specific skill set was not what was paramount. Instead, there were intellectual skills that those who taught a student understood, and they alone could determine if the student had mastered the abstract skill. "Bill is very smart" was an assertion by one individual about a student; whether Bill was smart as defined by a standardized test or some other external marker was irrelevant, if not impossible to know.

The implication of such an assumption was that those who made the determinations—the faculty—were indispensable. Otherwise, how would the larger society know if Bill was smart? Such an assumption spoke to the autonomy of the university. Those who ran the institution knew best. As de Sousa Santos (2006) noted, "The institutional crisis was the result of the contradiction between the demand for autonomy in the definition of the university's values and objectives and the growing pressure to hold it to the same criteria of efficiency, productivity, and social responsibility that private enterprises face" (p. 60). The result was that those within the university no longer had autonomous status and were instead part of an interconnected web of relations.

Understanding the Strategic Framework of Globalization and Neoliberalism

All these crises, then, in one way or another center on the rise of globalization and neoliberalism. "Globalization" and "neoliberalism" are not synonyms, but they are intellectually symbiotic. Until globalization surfaced, the assumption was that knowledge was largely produced within the confines of academic offices and laboratories. Academics developed, defined, critiqued, and advanced knowledge. As de Sousa Santos (2016) asks, however, "The idea of a knowledge society implies that knowledge is everywhere: what is the impact of this idea on a modern university which was created on the premise that it was an island of knowledge in a [sea] of ignorance?" (p. 5). It seems that the purpose of an organization that had, at its core, the production of knowledge is at a minimum questioned when knowledge production is diffuse and the arbiters of knowledge are many. Globalization produces avenues for communication that are immediate and without interference of peer review; the result puts the academy in a problematic position. Its hegemony is brought into question, if not rejected; the hegemonic organization once produced abstract knowledge, which is now found to be questionable and irrelevant for a marketplace that privileges content knowledge aimed at meeting the tasks of specific jobs. Moreover, when jobs are no longer in abundance, there is a necessary interdependence between higher learning and the marketplace. These crises, then, came about because of the unexpected rise of globalization, which I referred to in Chapter 1, and the assertion of neoliberalism about how to define the "good" society.

Over the last 30 years, the neoliberal assumption has been that the public sphere should be shrunk and market principles from the private sector should be applied to public and nonprofit institutions. Such assumptions, obviously, have had a significant impact on academic organizations. Henry Giroux has noted in an interview, "As an ideology it [neoliberalism] construes profit-making as the essence of democracy, consuming as the only operable form of citizenship, and an irrational belief in the market to solve all problems and serve as a model for structuring all social relations" (Harper, 2014, p. 1078). The private sector grows, the public sector shrinks, and managerial philosophies from the private profit-making world are called on to streamline decision making and ostensibly improve profits. In order for a bottom line to improve, there needs to be a clear outcome that can be counted and compared to others. As Walton (2011) notes, "The doctrine that things that cannot be measured have no value, has been [particularly] damaging" (p. 21). It is damaging because the worth of a poem cannot be monetized. The value of a student meeting with a professor after class or during office hours not merely to get answers to an assignment, but to engage in thoughtful discussions about an issue raised in class also cannot be precisely calculated. Or, rather, the calculus is that because these activities cannot be measured, they are of little worth. The involvement of a faculty member in the governance of the institution will be seen as a waste of time when it is compared to efforts of a colleague who generates external grants. The Socratic seminar taught by a full-time professor with a handful of students is not as cost-effective as the large online class taught by a part-time instructor. What one learns in either class has to have evaluative outcomes that can be measured by anyone. One assumes, then, that the instructor's knowledge of the material and the ability to assess a student's learning are of little value, and simultaneously of significant cost.

Gainful employment means not merely that students learn skills, but that they are also able to attain jobs that are valued in the marketplace. One does what one needs to do to increase one's monetary worth. The only measure of success is the bottom line—for an organization, a unit within the organization, or an individual. As public support for the public good of education has fallen, the cost of activities comes in for intense scrutiny. Globalization certainly brings into question whether there is not another way to do activities that is more efficient. One asks if there might be another way that is in tune with the pace of contemporary society. A neoliberal framework, however, places a priority on the cost of doing those activities, and it questions whether there might not be a more cost-effective way.

At the organizational level, competition has been taken to new and extraordinary levels. Students (aka customers) always have made decisions when choosing college A over college B. In the twenty-first century, however, institutions spend significant time and resources so that informal decisions about which institution is better are formalized. Rankings come in numerous formats. The University of Hong Kong touts the fact that in international rankings it is one of the top 100 institutions in the world. India has faced considerable embarrassment and consternation that none of its institutions has cracked the top 300. The result is that it invented its own ranking system, and JNU in New Delhi can now say it is one of the country's best institutions. The University of Southern California (USC) and the University of California Los Angeles (UCLA) not only compete on the football field, but also with regard to how they are ranked by *U.S. News & World Report*. Two-year institutions have their own ranking systems, with the result that Santa Monica College in Los Angeles might boast that it is among the best institutions, and California State University at Los Angeles (CSU-LA) will point out that it is one of the "best value" institutions.[1] Smyth (2017) points out how a "specter of fear" now exists that if an institution does not outrank its competitors nationally and internationally, it will lose its competitive edge (p. 14). The result of low rankings is that in a neoliberal environment, scarce public support will be even harder to generate and private resources are made that much more elusive.

My point here is not that capitalism is bad or the enemy of democracy. Indeed, the rise and strength of American universities came about during capitalist eras in the nineteenth and twentieth centuries. Markets can help in certain areas for universities wishing to capitalize on investments or seek new ways to undertake activities. Surely, technology has enabled all organizations, not just tertiary institutions, to be more efficient as well as improved. The result, however, creates concerns not only for the role and purpose of universities but also for how their transformations have influenced the cities and nations in which institutions reside. As Henry Giroux (2003) notes, "In the absence of vibrant democratic public spheres, corporate power, when left on its own, appears to respect few boundaries based on self-restraint and the public good" (p. 161). When university life is framed by simple utilitarian measures that accentuate neoliberalism, universities not only lose their purpose and find themselves in crisis, but the larger society loses a check on the worst tendencies of capitalism. We lose that voice that is able to restrain or question the rapacious appetite of capital. Democracy fails if citizens are not self-questioning, critical, and autonomous, which creates the conditions for the rise of fascism. If such self-reflection is not taught in academic environments, then where will it be learned? If self-reflection and critique are not taught and fostered on a campus, then what is the impact for society?

From the perspective advanced here, the result is that we have not only diminished public goods, but also shrunk the definition of what we mean by a public good and enabled fascist leaders to put forward a very different vision for society. In the United States, no public college or university is fully supported by the state anymore. Institutions such as UCLA get less than 7 percent of their funding from the state.[2] The burden of paying for college now rests on the shoulders of students. Evaluation has become paramount. We evaluate students, faculty, and outcomes. Rankings become important indicators of academic excellence. Cost and the "bottom line" take precedence. If there is a way to decrease costs, then it should be done. The organization can be managed more efficiently and effectively by managers whose primary job is to monitor and evaluate.

From a neoliberal vantage point, the fewer governmental regulations the better, and the market will decide where students should attend college and what they will study. The privatization of public services is seen as a rational response to a market-driven economy. The central goal is to put more capital that is in the hands of the consumer and have less that is shared collectively. The survival of the fittest mentality assumes that individuals get jobs because they are the most qualified. A neoliberal mentality honors the idea of an absolutist form of meritocracy insofar as objective measures will determine who wins and who loses. Any possible structural injustices in the system or biases on the part of individuals are overlooked or seen as minimal rather than inevitable consequences of a capitalist system that privileges some and marginalizes others.

Such mandates cause direct and indirect changes in academic life. Insofar as individuals are irrelevant, to the extent that work can be outsourced more cheaply, the university benefits. The result, of course, is that laborers earn less money but the university is fiscally stronger. Benefits such as health care, retirement, and overtime are diminished, if not eliminated. Similarly, tenure is an expensive proposition because it involves full-time, long-term employment. Non–tenure track and part-time faculty are preferable because the job classification is cost-effective. The savings to the university are clear and calculable. The cuts that occurred during the pandemic were a clear outgrowth of these ideas; universities stopped paying into retirement accounts, for example, hiring was largely stopped, and workers were either let go or furloughed. What is not seen, of course, is the impact on the university with regard to its initial function to search for truth, and for tenure to protect individuals' academic freedom.

The cost of classes and the worth of professors also come into view. Because students will earn more in scientific areas, nonscience classes are less important. Large classes are preferable to small classes. The efficient use of the campus is essential, so buildings should always be in use. Airlines earn revenue when a plane is in flight, not when it is sitting empty on the tarmac. Similarly, a university earns revenue when classrooms have students in them, not when they are empty on weekends or in the summer. One reason why all institutions faced economic hardship during the pandemic was that the campuses were entirely empty for an academic year. The assumption is also that a physical classroom is more expensive than a virtual classroom (although that is not always correct). Ways are thus found to fill classes to capacity as much as possible, and if we can dispense with classes and instead use the internet, so much the better.

Faculty are paid what they are worth—and what they are worth equates with the revenue that they bring into the university. A professor with sizable grants from the National Science Foundation will be paid handsomely; a teacher who trains teachers, less so. The result is an imbalance on campus with regard to academic value (and values). Professors are stand-ins for parts of knowledge—one a chemist and another a historian. In an environment that is run by market rules, in which earnings equate value, some forms of knowledge are valued more than others.

The "Mercantilization" of the Academy

Thus, these crises—hegemony, legitimacy, and autonomy—have hit universities throughout the world because we are in a globalized environment framed by neoliberalism. One of the curiosities of academic life is that institutions, which are insular, are also tied into international networks. In part, these networks occur because the top 250 or so universities train the vast majority of PhD-holding faculty for the thousands of research universities, teaching universities, liberal arts colleges, and community colleges that exist throughout the world. Such a close network of training, in which socialization is likely to be more similar than different, creates likenesses across geographic boundaries. Many countries are also in the throes of neoliberalism and privatization with management practices in the ascendancy.

These crises have erupted at a time where technological shifts have come about that have speeded up time. What once took days or weeks is now instantaneous. The compression of time causes a need for tasks and decisions to be faster. Deliberation is minimized; collegial decision making is less valued than a strong managerial team able to put forward an action plan.

The result is what some have called a "mercantilization of the university" (de Souza Santos, 2006, p. 64). The brilliance of the strategies that have led to these changes is that they appear so rational that they seem matter-of-fact. Strategies are based on ways that place those who disagree in the uncomfortable position of defending the indefensible. If effectiveness is a goal, then ineffectiveness is what the other side wants. If cost containment is a goal, then those against cost containment care nothing about spending other people's money. If a worker can do a job for less money than someone else, then why would anyone want to spend more money for a more expensive worker? If a job is paramount, then college degrees that do not provide graduates with the requisite job skills are a waste of time and investment. If excellence is defined as being at the top in collegiate rankings, then how can someone defend not participating in rankings and trying to do everything to be at the top?

The logic of the neoliberal position almost seems irrefutable, largely because we define the world in a manner that crushes alternative definitions of what counts for knowledge and what matters to a society. All this change, notes Giroux (2014), "contradicts the culture and democratic value of higher education, [and] makes a mockery of the very meaning and mission of the university as a democratic public sphere" (p. 138). The result is that higher education's role for democracy has largely fallen by the wayside.

I am not one who traffics in conspiracy theories, so I do not see a nefarious plot that has existed to transform universities. What has struck me, however, is that I have seen these changes whether I am in Delhi, Los Angeles, or Hong Kong. Globalization and neoliberalism get articulated in localized contexts, but the goals and outcomes are remarkably similar regardless of geography. Faculty are put on trial in Hong Kong for trying to advance democracy, and no one protests. Shared governance falls by the wayside in Los Angeles as faculty find there are more pressing issues on which they will be evaluated. The police come onto campus in New Delhi to monitor and arrest those who speak against governmental policies. The decisions about how to proceed for fall teaching in 2020 occurred largely in administrative offices irrespective of locale. Faculty and students may have proffered ideas about the safety of returning to campus, but the decisions largely rested with the administration, and frequently, financial decisions were determinative.

The result across geographic areas is that our postsecondary sector is now ill equipped to handle attacks on democracy. We strive less today to enlarge the moral imagination and critical capacities of students, and instead focus on marketable skills that will enable students to earn salaries, frequently at two jobs, in order to make ends meet. We are less likely to undertake research that is critical of the societies in which we live and more likely to pursue research that enhances our careers by generating external revenue for the institution. The goal, then, has become to develop knowledge that does not question received narratives and to train students to be docile rather than disruptive. If we are to repair the damage that has been done, then one logical next step is to think about the parameters of democracy. We need to ask where higher education fits in the endeavor of enabling and strengthening democratic institutions and ideas.

Rethinking Democracy

We tend to have historical amnesia when we think about democracy, as if it's a system that has been firmly established and implemented throughout the world for a long period of time. We are likely to think that more countries are democratic than not and that the world is moving, perhaps inexorably, toward greater freedoms, which translate into more democracies. By democracy, I mean a system in which all citizens are able to choose and replace their leaders in regular, fair, free, and meaningful elections. This liberal idea has been constructed around representative democracy, human rights, and a belief in human capital complemented by a strong social safety net. A democracy has formalized, respected institutional mechanisms that translate ideas into public policy that advances the general good of society while also respecting the rights of minorities. In a democratic nation, as Craig Calhoun (1998) has nicely stated, "Public life depends on communities—multiple and diverse—but not on the presumption of or attempt to create a single larger community" (p. 22). This working out of what we mean by multiple communities and how a democracy enables or restricts such groupings in part lies in opposition to a radically defined market-based notion of individualism. A radical libertarian approach assumes that representative government has no communal good; the goal of government is to ensure that individuals are free to make decisions without interference by anyone else. By no means is democracy a perfect system, and certainly in my own country, the United States, we can point to many historical imperfections and failures. Nevertheless, it is widespread assumption that the ability of a people to decide who their leaders are is the best system of governance that has been created. Democracy historically has implied greater freedoms for the citizens of the country with regard to free expression, a free press, civil liberties, and human rights.

In 1974, only about 30 percent of the world's independent states met the criteria for electoral democracy, which amounted to less than 50 countries (Diamond, 2015, p. 141). Democracy then had an incredible 30-year growth spurt, which perhaps accounts for our amnesia. For three decades, we saw a steady rise in the number of countries that changed their governing structure to one of democracy. This increase was a global phenomenon and it was unparalleled. As Yascha Mounk (2018) summarizes, "A quarter century ago, most citizens of liberal democracies were very satisfied with their governments and gave high approval ratings to their institutions; now they are more disillusioned than they have ever been" (p. 5). What happened? Why is democracy less popular today than at the turn of the century?

We are seeing a populist surge that has created an opening for fascists. Interest-based individualism has fueled this democratic recession. Democracies are seen as failing individuals at a time when jobs are harder to come by, and interest-based politics seeks to minimize communitarian notions of the public good. How countries handled the pandemic is also instructive. The United States was seen particularly ineffective, and the interpretation often had less to do with the manner in which Donald Trump conducted himself, and more to do with democracy itself. People did not wear masks because they saw it as a violation of their democratic rights, where democracy was defined as a version of "do your own thing." "Strong-leader" countries such as China were seen to be more effective. In Hong Kong everyone wore a mask.

Around the world, we are seeing populist politicians winning elections by attacking representative democracy and arguing that the government is too weak to protect hard-working, native-born people. The borders of a country have become rallying cries—both to keep immigrants out and to suggest that foreign-lands are dangerous areas marked by terrorism and migrant hordes planning to invade one's homeland.

Established democracies are giving in to illiberal forces driven by popular passions because of the economic forces resulting from globalization and neoliberalism. "Populism," like "globalization," is a confusing term that means different things to different people. Francis Fukuyama (2018) noted that one definition of populism has to do with the definition of "the people" who are the basis for legitimacy: Many populist regimes do not include the whole population, but rather a certain ethnic or racial group that are said to be the "true" people.

Prime Minister Narendra Modi in India has been trying to shift the definition of Indian national identity from the inclusive liberal one established by Gandhi and Nehru to one based on Hinduism. In the United States, President Trump represents populism. He has glorified white men and demonized immigrants from Mexico, for example. Christians are "true" Americans, and Muslims are suspect. The Confederate flag is to be honored rather than viewed as a flag of traitors.

An additional definition of populism revolves around the style of leadership that is exhibited. Rather than a respect for democratic organs such as the judiciary, the "strongman" comes into play, as noted by Fukuyama (2018): "Populist leaders tend to develop a cult of personality around themselves, claiming the mantle of charismatic authority that exists independently of institutions like political parties. They try to develop a direct and unmediated relationship with the 'people' they claim to represent, channeling the latter's hopes and fears into immediate action" (para. 4). Trump's statement at the Republican convention, "I am your voice. I alone can fix it" (Appelbaum, 2016, para. 7), nicely fits this version of populism. A leader can solve problems—no one else can. Modern democracy functions by way of liberal institutions—the legislature, the judiciary, a free press that will disagree with and serve as a check for those in power. The populist sees these sorts of institutions and entities as roadblocks to achieving one's goals. Populist politicians attack the traditional instruments of a liberal democracy and put forward themselves as the solution to what currently ails the country. The rejection by Trump of a free and fair presidential election, and then the insurrection on the Capitol on January 6, 2021 are the most recent examples of populism's impact on democracy.

The result is that for well over a decade we have seen a democratic recession throughout the globe. In his 2016 book, *In Search of Democracy*, Larry Diamond has presented a table of the breakdown of democracy from 2000 to 2014 (p. 84). What is particularly sobering is the fact that since 2014 we have seen a steady march toward less democracy. A slow trend has gained speed. Europe is in the throes of populist surges, which has seen democracy erode in Hungary, Poland, and Turkey and come under assault even in traditionally liberal countries such as France and Germany. Observers originally thought the "Arab Spring" was a struggle for greater freedoms. It resulted, however, in an increase in violence, the collapse of governments, and the rise of more authoritarian regimes (Stacher, 2015). Latin America once had an upsurge in moving toward democratic governments, and now we see the opposite in countries such as Nicaragua and Venezuela (Riera, 2017; Thaler, 2017). We also have democracies without rights such as in Hungary and Brazil (Berman, 2019; Neto, 2017). The military has taken over once again in Thailand (Mérieau, 2019), and voting irregularities in Bangladesh have resulted in an inability to claim the country as a democracy (Ganguly, 2019). Africa remains the most problematic area, but every region of the world has seen a decline in democratic governance. One must be cautious in over-emphasizing analogies, but it is a historical fact that Adolf Hitler came to power through a democratic vote. Hierarchical democracy brings to power people who ostensibly enact the will of the people who elected them. If such elections suggest that traditional organs of democracy such as a free press or the legislature need to be ignored or demonized, then that will be accepted.

There is no single reason for the democratic recession, but surely, in a globalizing world, we have seen a greater concern for making private what was once public. Automation, a shift from manufacturing to services and the rise of the digital economy has made full-time employment harder, a secure future for millions of people riskier, and stark economic differences between the rich and the poor (Autor, 2015; Frey & Osborne, 2017). Under the logic of neoliberalism, the safety net has been weakened, which in turn, has weakened the support for democratic organs because they cannot deliver needed services. The result is resentment and a desire for change.

Neoliberal norms largely have functioned to delegitimize democratic governance. When the market rules and individualism is fetishized to the exclusion of any sense of an obligation to civic community, then democratic institutions will erode. Democracy depends on a communal version of public life where my vote, my opinion, my voice, is as good as yours. The sum is made greater by the parts. When the entities that exist to foster that belief are seen as weak or flawed, then democracy itself is brought into question, if not outright rejected. The result is a resurgence in authoritarianism. In 1995, only 1 in 16 U.S. citizens believed that army rule was a good system of governance; by 2018, that statistic had increased to 1 in 6 (Mounk, 2018, p. 5).

I am putting forward here the idea that neoliberalism is not just a neutral economic system as if one is a shopper in an economics grocery store. Barbara Tomlinson and George Lipsitz (2013) have pointed out the following:

> Unimpeded capital accumulation requires extensive ideological legitimation. Neoliberal practices seek to produce neoliberal subjects through a social pedagogy that aims to naturalize hierarchy and exploitation by promoting internalized preferences for profits over the needs of people, relentless individuation of collective social processes, cultivation of hostile privatism and defensive localism based on exaggerated fears of difference (p. 4).

The result is a mobilization of anger against vulnerable populations such as Muslims in India or immigrants in the United States. Failure is an essential ingredient. When someone fails, it is the individual who has failed—or it is other individuals who do not deserve to be in the country who have forced failure on an individual. Because failure is etched into the framework of neoliberalism, the time becomes ripe for a strongman to come in and upend democratic norms. Democratic notions, such as voting, are seen as weak and flawed; centralized control, such as what is now emanating from mainland China toward Hong Kong, is seen as preferable to democracy.

In the United States, a man was elected president who was clearly more comfortable working with dictators in Russia and China than America's traditional allies in democratic nations such as Canada and France. Equally troubling was Trump's full-throated attack on the news media, which he labeled "fake news," and his disdain for traditional organs of democracy such as the judiciary. He largely rejected traditional democratic norms, painted his rivals as enemies who should be in prison, labeled some in the Nazi movement as good people, aimed for a narrowing of civil liberties, and was not fully committed to constitutional norms. Stephen Levitsky and Daniel Zeblatt (2018) believe that what has happened elsewhere is a precursor to what is taking place in the United States. Congress remains unable to pass a budget; bipartisan legislation is an artifact of the past. The periodic shutdown of the government and the assertion by the president of executive privilege, irrespective of what the law stipulates, are additional signs of the weakening of democracy.

The same points can be made about India and what is taking place in Hong Kong. India has had a conservative government, which has authoritarian tendencies akin to what has been seen in the United States. Prime Minister Modi has claimed that his opponents are enemies of Hindus and has fostered an environment in which critics of Hinduism have received death threats or been victims of violent attacks (Faleiro, 2019). When Hong Kongers are asked to speak about their identity, they inevitably will talk, like most individuals, about food, language, and culture. Nevertheless, as I mentioned in Chapter 1, they also speak about a commitment to democracy as the core principle that separates Hong Kongers from the Chinese. In addition, they fear that since Hong Kong has become part of China, the erosion of democracy has been consistent (Ramzy, 2019a). These are the issues that drove the uprising in 2019; they have only become more severe as China tries to destroy the idea of "one country, two systems" and bring Hong Kong into the fold.

The takeaway from the overall situation is a concern about basic freedoms throughout the world. As Larry Diamond (2015) concludes, "there is a growing danger that the recession could deepen and tip over into something much worse. Many more democracies could fail" (p. 153). President Trump has laughingly spoken with admiration that his authoritarian counterpart in China has been successful because its president, Xi Jinping, does not need to bother with democratic elections and can stay in office far longer that the term limits in the United States allow (Shepardson, 2018). The case ought not to need to be made in the United States about the benefits of democracy, but there is a significant segment of the population who now place market values over democratic engagement. The insurgents question the benefits of democracy. They have suggested that only a strong president, such as Trump, is able to put into place those strategies that will ensure economic dominance.

All surveys point out that a significant segment of society remains committed to democracy, but the rise of what has come to be known as the populist right has given people cause for concern. In the United States in 2014, confidence in the Supreme Court had sunk to 30 percent (Mounk, 2018, p. 100). The appraisal of politicians is largely negative, and the approval ratings of officeholders is at historic lows. In a democracy, more often than not, individuals will express exasperation when the opposition's party is in power, but the democratic recession has brought about, not just disagreement with an individual or party, but a loss of trust that the organization or instrument for democracy can function.

Robert Reich (2018) has nicely summarized the benefits of democracy:

> The genius of a system based on political equality is that it does not require us to agree on every issue, but only be bound by decisions that emerge from the system. . . . Some of us want stricter environmental protections, other more lenient. We are free to take any particular position on these and any other issues. However, as political equals, we are bound to accept the outcomes even if we dislike them. This requires enough social trust for us to regard the views and interests of those with whom we disagree as equally worthy of consideration to our own. (p. 35)

Not only do we need trust, but a democracy also requires participation. Alternatively, without trust, individuals will not participate. If there is an upside to the authoritarian actions that are occurring in Hong Kong, Los Angeles, and New Delhi, it is that there has been a remarkable increase in protests and civic-minded movements. The Occupy Central protest in Hong Kong lasted for three months and involved several thousand individuals; the protests against the government expanded to literally millions of people and lasted for months. The Women's Marches in Los Angeles and elsewhere numbered in the hundreds of thousands, but Trump still received well over 74 million votes in his losing reelection bid. BJP's restrictive policies brought about continuous protests and critiques on social media and in Delhi's newspapers, but Modi was overwhelmingly reelected in 2019 and then issued a government-led fatwa against the citizens of Kashmir.

Martin Luther King's well-worn statement that "We will have to repent in this generation not merely for the hateful words and actions of the bad people but for the appalling silence of the good people"[3] has been put to the test over the last several years. The enormous power of the state requires a vigilance and steadiness that make it difficult for people with families, jobs, and multiple tasks simply to maintain a modest lifestyle. A march that lasts a day or a protest that lasts for months are certainly impressive and inspiring, but ultimately they alone will not bring about a revival of democracy.

If we are to see a resurgence of democracy, then we need a language of community that celebrates commonalities and honors differences; we need a respect for democratic agencies that put forward opinions that force us to question authority but maintain respect for the integrity of the process. As Calhoun (1998) notes, we need a "language of public life that starts with the recognition of deep differences among us and builds faith in meaningful communication across lines of difference" (p. 32). We need the ability to comment on flaws in our systems without either assuming everyone must agree or that if we disagree the end is near. We need, in effect, to build communities of difference.

Higher Education's Conflicted Role in Advancing Democracy

We arrive, then, with a double problem for higher education. On the one hand, those in universities face the crises of hegemony, legitimacy, and autonomy. On the other hand, universities now exist in an increasingly fascist environment where professors frequently are disdained, academic knowledge is derided, and social facts compete against fictitious facts. The pandemic made the situation even more absurd when wearing a mask became a political statement rather than one about public health and safety. The message to derive from all these points is that universities have a crucial role to play in combating the retreat from democracy.

Francis Fukuyama (1992), a neoconservative, coined the idea of "the end of history" a generation ago as he predicted that democracy was here to stay. He now not only acknowledges that he was sadly mistaken, but also analyzes how populism has taken hold in countries across the world. Fukuyama (2018) made an important point when he said, "It is not possible to beat something with nothing" (para. 24). His argument has been that simply being against Trump, or against BJP, or against integration with

China is not enough to bring about change. Those of us who want to see a new social order need to paint a picture of what that world entails. Academics have the ability to portray what a new society can look like, not through whimsical thinking, but based on empirical work. Those of us who subscribe to intersectional notions of identity can work to ensure that different people are neither erased nor confined to the margins. A community of difference is one in which we come together to understand how we are different and unique from one another, but also struggle to create a more inclusive community.

Too often, the citizenry has come to think of disagreement as if we are on a cable news show. We either all agree with one another and are comfortable, or we shout at one another. Academic life has to be a model for how to have reasoned arguments and debates in which individuals can disagree and not be shouted down or talked over. At the same time, we have to engage in arguments that are factual and not invented out of whole cloth. Academics have facts readily available in all disciplines. And yet, we have largely failed to take the argument to those with whom we disagree. Our largest concerns erupt when a controversial speaker descends on our campus; we should care more about making our case known to the larger public and modeling how we want arguments and discussions to go.

Perhaps James Baldwin (2016) suggested the clearest rules for engagement when he said, "We can disagree and still love each other unless your disagreement is rooted in my oppression and denial of my humanity and right to exist." Baldwin is arguing here, I think, for a large arena in which disagreements might occur. We have room to debate climate change, for example, and by way of facts, defeat arguments that are spurious and ill-informed. Where we draw the line are at certain arguments that always have been with us but have now taken a more public turn with the rise of social media and a particular strain of populism. That is, Holocaust deniers and their ilk always have been a microscopic part of the general populace, but they were largely on the fringes of society. Their beliefs were not merely odious but had no basis in historical fact. Unfortunately, as I elaborate in Chapter 4, in the twenty-first century the ancestors of these individuals are able to generate a sizable following on any number of topics. Barack Obama was not born in the United States and he is a closeted Muslim aimed at overthrowing the government. The elementary school students at Sandy Hook, Conn., and the high school students at Parkland, Fla., were not shot dead; the events simply did not happen. According to some in right-wing media, Hillary Clinton ran a pedophile ring out of the basement of a pizza parlor in Washington, D.C. These sorts of stories get at where Baldwin was drawing the line.

Postsecondary systems have both an inward and an outward role to play in advancing democracy. They can make a better public argument and take issues out into the public arena. What about within a college or university? What might be possible on our campuses? Lolich (2011) has pointed out how we need to rethink the neoliberal framework for students:

> The language used in the government's discourses creates a new way of being a student whose main objective is to become a valuable economic agent. This new identity is defined as an independent and self-caring individual. . . . When new conceptualizations of what it means to be human appear, they can shape and influence behavior as people change and adapt to fit these new labels. What is worrying is that there is no place in this definition for relationships of love, care, and solidarity. (p. 276)

The point, of course, is not that students should be unable to have skills that enable them to find fulfilling jobs. However, in a democratic society we are aiming for citizens who find fulfilment in ways other than simply in the marketplace. Globalization has increased anxiety, and those who support neoliberalism have used that anxiety to become hypersensitive to the requisite skills needed to fill ever-decreasing numbers of jobs, usually without benefits or support systems for health benefits and retirement.

Academics have a twofold purpose. We need to be able to point to what a good, or a better, society entails, and then discuss what that means for active citizenship in a democracy. I am not arguing for a society where individuals simply sit around and talk all day. The caricature of academic life is that we are a disengaged debating society about esoteric topics. Richard R. Nelson and Nathan Rosenberg (1993) counter this narrative in their analysis of national innovation systems: "The modern industrial laboratory and the modern research university grew up as companions. Universities play an extremely important role in technical advance, not only as places where industrial scientists and engineers are trained, but as the source of research findings and techniques of considerable relevance to technical advance in industry" (p. 11). We tend to emphasize the entrepreneurs who created their invention in their basement or garage and went on to become billionaires. I certainly do not dispute that such geniuses exist. We also need to get our stories straight, however, and recognize the wealth of creativity that takes place on campuses.

In addition, such an observation raises the second point. We not only need to make the case about what an alternative to neoliberalism is for the larger society so that a more engaged discussion of the strengths of democracy might take place. We also need to mirror that in how we engage with students on our campuses. Far too often we have reduced students to economic agents, attempting to meet their needs by building climbing walls and dining halls to cater to their every whim, or we have said that we must focus simply on job skills and let every other sort of engagement fall by the wayside.

Of course we want to understand "customer" preferences. Who can argue about whether to serve healthier meals than the mush served in the dining halls when I went to college? However, we tend to obsess about consumer preferences and forget our obligation to treat the range of needs that a student has. We should acknowledge that our task is deeply personal and critical for a rejuvenated democratic public sphere.

When we work from a position of engagement and put forward a notion of a community of difference, we recognize that students need to be treated in a different manner. The manifold groups with whom the university interacts also need have different forms of interaction with individuals on campus. I am suggesting that universities have all too often unquestioningly mirrored society rather than be its fountainhead for change. Hamer and Lang (2015) have made the point that "universities function instrumentally as employers, landlords, business partners with consulting agencies and other private firms, and corporate entrepreneurs through such activities as licensing" (p. 898). The result is all too often, claim the authors, a stance that reflects and reproduces the racism and other forms of structural violence that pervades society. The false notions that academics should be outside society and work from a disinterested standpoint, and that all failures fall back upon the individual, have helped create precisely the sorts of crises I mentioned earlier.

This sense of disengagement overlooks how often this stance has been anything but disengaged. I appreciate that all research at all times is not necessarily ideologically tinged and politically motivated, but we also need to recognize that some work comes within an ideological frame-work. Alcoholism was once within the purview of theology departments because it was a moral failing. Homosexuality was in the domain of psychology departments because it was a mental illness. Literature was defined as that which existed in Europe. Art was Western. Moreover, as Tomlinson and Lipsitz (2013) have pointed out, "Scholars have never been simply neutral observers of racial projects, but rather socially and historically situated thinkers and writers who often unwittingly produce the concepts and categories upon which racism depends" (p. 18). Hence, we need academics to not only maintain a focus on empirically based research that offers facts on crucial issues of the day, but also retain a questioning focus on how we construct our issues and problems. And equally important, we need a greater sense of engagement with society as it now currently exists.

Giroux (2009) speaks to my point here: "Intellectuals who inhabit our nation's universities should represent the conscience of American society because they not only shape the conditions under which future generations learn about themselves and their relations to others and the outside world, but also because they engage pedagogical practices that are by their very nature moral and political, rather than simply technical" (p. 14). It is vital to recognize the dualism in which academics are engaged. They connect the larger society with the challenges that confront society. They also work within the university in trying to unsettle and equip students with the skills not simply to gain a job, but also to become critical intellectuals able to challenge and work for the transformation of society.

Bourdieu-the-obscure (2000) actually raised similar questions by asking, "Can intellectuals, and especially scholars, intervene in the political sphere? . . . What role can researchers play in the various social movements?" (p. 40). The challenge for all of us is that in the search for truth, we are supposed to be disinterested; such an idea drove Weber's notion of an ethic of responsibility. When we interject ourselves into the political arena, we shed that which gives us authority if we turn from scholar to politician. One obviously needs to be careful in all our undertakings; academic life trains us to labor by ensuring that we quote correctly, analyze a formula accurately, stick to the data to inform our findings. I appreciate that our desire to "get it right" frames our hesitation to speak in the public sphere. We need to recognize, however, at least three issues that arise with our concern for accuracy.

First, by standing at a distance from the community, by inference, we are implying that those who are not so careful as ourselves are somehow lesser, or anti-intellectual. At times, we are explicit in our condescension for those who may not have as much formal knowledge as we do. At other times, we are so absorbed in our own work that we inadvertently convey disdain, but that is how others see us. Second, we hesitate to speak until we are able to communicate our ideas with certainty. The challenge in an age when news comes out instantaneously is that the tempo of academic discourse appears out of touch with how the larger community receives and integrates information. Third, we are versed in how to communicate our work to other academics rather than the larger community.

These sorts of challenges create hurdles for the academic. We want to indict anti-intellectualism, but we also do not want to be accused of intellectualism. "Critical reflexivity" states Bourdieu (2000), "is the absolute prerequisite of any political action by intellectuals. Intellectuals must engage in a permanent critique of all the abuses of power or authority that are committed in the name of intellectual authority" (p. 41). Reflexivity enables us to at least attempt to analyze ourselves rigorously rather than simply dismissing others' findings because they lack academic knowledge.

What I do not think is viable during a democratic recession is to remain aloof from the challenges that confront us, hermetically sealed from the problems that exist on an everyday basis. The task ahead of us right now is extremely urgent and exceptionally difficult. It is urgent because populism is rising rapidly and democracy is on the decline. It is difficult because we may have the knowledge but not a mastery of the communicative vehicles currently available. Yet it seems to me that academics have a critical role to play in the current environment, unlike at other moments in recent history. We can highlight when facts are wrong or when the knowledge we have informs the debate. Scholarship with commitment is a different stance from what we have done in the past and positions the university in a distinctly different light. Engaging in scholarship with commitment suggests that the disinterestedness of the past now is coupled with a concern for immediate action. Scholarship with commitment suggests that, rather than disinterestedness being the greatest value of the academic, the preservation and enlargement of the democratic public sphere are our greatest concern.

I am suggesting a new articulation of the university. As Sotiris (2014) has argued, "The university is not simply a venue or forum of ideas, it is a complex articulation of practices and strategies" (p. 11). By acknowledging that the university is. or can be. an ideological weapon to preserve particular domains of power, we open up the potential for a new conceptualization of the university and those of us who work within it. Crises can be moments of chaos and pain, but they also have the potential to bring forth a renewal of civic purpose and inner meaning. The university, in this light, is trying to reimagine the state in a manner that moves us away from the most constricting forces of neoliberalism and toward a greater sense of communal belonging. Simply writing abstract texts or calling for change is not enough.

I acknowledge that there is a certain self-satisfaction for scholars who persuasively call for more public funds for universities, when the chief beneficiaries will be those very academics. I also do not wish to suggest that many of the real market challenges that exist for different organizations are not real, or that they do not exist. Declining enrollments are a matter for concern at some institutions. The needs of the larger environment in terms of training skills are important. COVID-19 created economic chaos for virtually all institutions, private or public, two-year or four-year, residential or commuter. However, what seems critical right now is to confront these multiple challenges rather than simply try to absorb them and move on to the next challenge. What we need are strategies to defend, reimagine, and transform universities so that they are better able to meet the needs of the larger public sphere.

I have posited that globalization and neoliberalism have framed universities and countries in unhelpful ways that have led to this rise in populist fascism. Globalization is not something that can be wished away, as if we were able to return to a Luddite past, absent technologies and communication strategies that have become commonplace. We also ought not to assume, however, that our current circumstances are rigid and unable to change. De Sousa Santos (2010) has noted:

> The only efficient and participatory way to confront neoliberal globalization is to oppose it with an alternative, counter-hegemonic globalization. Counter-hegemonic globalization of the university-as-public-good means that the national reforms of the public university must reflect a country project centered on policy choices that consider the country's insertion in increasingly transnational contexts of knowledge production and distribution. (p. 5)

De Souza Santos is putting forth a dualism that enables us to acknowledge that globalization is a societal social fact and we cannot simply wish it away; however, the neoliberal façade that surrounds the changes that have taken place can be resisted—and the university is the logical choice for that resistance to be developed, fomented, and enacted.

To put forward an alternative to what we currently have is a demanding political project for anyone, but particularly academics. I want us to reject the idea that only those within the academic monastery are capable of envisioning new futures for that portrays the intellectual yet again divorced from and above the masses. I also want to move forward with a sense of optimism that not only can we formulate a democratic project for the twenty-first century, we can work with others to make these changes happen. Far too often, we have reinscribed notions of power that privileges the work of the intellectual. Moreover, we just as often have claimed that the university is unable to change.

To respond to the current situation, we must recognize the forces aligned against intellectuals who assume a public posture. The state has used the university to secure its location of power. If the university puts forward an alternative to neoliberal globalization, then those who have benefited the most from the reduction of public goods and the privatization of public sectors are likely to be troubled. However demanding academic life can be, we also have the ability of not having to engage with those with whom we disagree. The university can be an echo chamber in which one might be challenged about a theoretical proposition, but it does not have the rough-and-tumble of everyday politics. If we engage in the manner that I am suggesting, we will not only be extending our reach, but we also will have to figure out ways to speak across difference, rather than simply maintain academic discourse for the privileged few. In sum, the elitism of the university, that which has enabled it to speak from "on high" and has enabled it to be an honored and useful organization for the maintenance of the state until now, is what we currently need to counteract.

I seem, then, to be putting forward an impossible dualism. We speak because of our knowledge. We reject that knowledge. We speak with the authority of the academic, but we reject that authority. We seek our colleagues' analysis of our ideas because of their intellectual history, but we now look for others who have no intellectual history. I appreciate the difficulty, but also point out that the university has a historic legitimacy that at least gives it the potential for beginning such a dialogue. We are able to put forward alternative ideas that affirm our standard definitions of knowledge, but we also try to move in a new direction based on the changed circumstances that are upon us. The reinvigoration of civil society seems, of necessity, to necessitate the university to be involved in some fashion. What that fashion is, of course, is in part what this book entails. What is increasingly clear is that for those of us in academe to function as if we are on an island away from the storm is useful for neither the university nor the larger society.

There will be forces aligned against a democratic agenda such as I am suggesting. However, the university, with all its flaws, is one of the few remaining institutions in which the sorts of dialogue I am calling for is even possible. At least the potential exists that social problems can be carefully articulated and discussed and critical dialogue can take place. Again, oddly, while the university has inherited the crises that have raised questions about our mission, there is also a space that has been opened for critical engagement. The result is that there is a great impetus to try to neutralize the university and silence it. Who needs an organization, much less a public one that partially survives on public monies, that is going to raise uncomfortable questions and put forward answers that will lessen the power of the powerful? As Stanley Aronowitz (quoted in Giroux, 2014) nicely put it, "The system survives on the eclipse of the radical imagination, the absence of a viable political opposition with roots in the general population, and the conformity of its intellectuals who to a large extent are subjugated by their secure berths in the academy" (p. 152).

Surely, a history of defeat and an inability to find one's voice are not going to be reversed overnight. The challenge is one that academics first need to imagine and then enact. Curiously, because of the erosion of tenure, and the lessening of traditional benefits, we are now able to recognize that the "secure berths" in the academy are no longer so secure. What we need to do, then, is no longer consolidate power, but question it, disburse it, enable it to be taken. I am assuming that envisioning a better tomorrow enables us to begin thinking about what we might do today. Rather than focusing on what divides us by way of our identities, I am trying to think through what unites us during a time of reduced social welfare and the battering ram of a populist message from leaders who tell us, "Only I can save you." Instead, we need to reimagine a public consciousness and the organic intellectual that seeks communion with those in the larger society.

Understanding the Environment for Democracy in Three Cities: The Value of Keeping One's Head Low in Hong Kong

Hong Kong, with an estimated 7.524 million people, is currently in the throes of redefining its relationship to China, or more correctly, China is redefining the relationship.[4] More than Los Angeles or New Delhi, the larger environment of Hong Kong is striking at the heart of academic identity. The University of Hong Kong (HKU), founded in 1911, was the first tertiary institution on the island. Not unlike many institutions a century ago, most faculty were hired to teach, and there were no aspirations for the university to be "world-class." The university relied on public funding, and the faculty largely came from the United Kingdom.

The elaboration and expansion of a higher education system, beginning in the 1950s and largely taking place during the 1960s and 1970s, was not particularly different from what one might have seen throughout much of the developed world. More universities opened to accommodate more students, and research became an important function. The oldest university, HKU, received recognition as a very good institution and one of the best universities in Asia.

The most significant difference in Hong Kong's gradual—and then rapid—increase in postsecondary institutional capacity had to do with the larger environment in which it existed. Until the United Kingdom handed over Hong Kong to China in 1997, the universities were part of the British system of higher education. Universities were public and largely supported by state monies; students still pay very low tuition in comparison with U.S., Australian, and U.K. universities. The faculty were largely British but, over time, took on an international presence. The student body was largely traditionally aged Hong Kongers who were accepted after high-stakes examinations. Instruction was in English. Students were trained for middle-class jobs, largely in Hong Kong, and research was predominately focused on Asia and located in the social sciences, although a medical school has been a fixture of HKU since its inception (Lanford, 2016).

China's assertion of "one country, two systems" is a work in progress that has seen gradual change in how Hong Kongers see themselves, and how those in universities see their role. When, in 2020, China enacted a "National Security Law," whose enactment was presumably a fait accompli, the democracy movement in Hong Kong, including on its campuses, came to an end. All universities change over time, and they are dependent upon their environment for how their missions are enacted and worked out. Academic freedom, for example, was not much of an issue in the first half of the twentieth century, but it took on importance as the twentieth century ended (Postiglione, 2017). What academics can say and do, and how students should comport themselves on campus, have changed, not only because the environment has changed around them, but also because the students have changed. Students were once predominantly from

Hong Kong. Given the willingness and ability of international students, especially from mainland China, to self-fund their postsecondary studies, however, a proportional increase in international students in Hong Kong's UGC-funded institutions proved extremely controversial and fired up an already-tangible resentment about immigration (E. Wong et al., 2019). Although the language of instruction remains English, the flavor of campus life changes when one group of students predominately speak Cantonese (the language of Hong Kong), and the group from the mainland speak Mandarin. English is generally a second language, and students talk among themselves in their own vernacular; the result is that there is a distinct grouping of students based on national and local identity.

Students from Hong Kong are generally more political, and they largely desire to do what the alumni have done—gain middle-class jobs in Hong Kong, buy a home, and stay close to one's family. Most Chinese students intend to go back to the mainland and begin their professional life. The challenge for Hong Kong's students is that housing prices have placed that middle-class life out of reach, and the ability to earn a wage that enables one to live a comfortable life in Hong Kong is becoming impossible. The reason why housing and jobs have become so difficult to obtain is that rich people from the mainland have driven up prices by buying second homes. S. Y. Lee (2016) has persuasively argued that Hong Kong's elite class sees massification as a tool for alleviating unemployment, wage compression, and other social concerns, yet they lack the will to increase public investment in higher education so that increased social mobility and greater equity can be achieved.

At Hong Kong University there is a large sculpture commemorating the violence perpetrated by the Chinese government on the protesters in Tiananmen Square in 1989. Although students and the administration over time had conflicts not different from struggles on countless other campuses, the handover to China has created an environment that exacerbates tensions and causes many professors and journalists to self-censor (Chan & Kerr, 2016; Fong et al., 2020; F. I. F. Lee & Lin, 2006; Petersen & Currie, 2007). Most recently this self-censorship has become imperative. With the passage of the law in 2020, some faculty and students who were seen as pro-democracy were arrested. Obviously, one can never be certain what someone intended when a decision is made, the dual paths that Hong Kong and China have traveled on since the handover from the United Kingdom is not that difficult to understand.

China sees Hong Kong as an integral part of the country. Just as with Tibet and Taiwan, the government may acknowledge certain differences but an independence movement is anathema. The result is that even the most benign discussions about independence are not countenanced. Booksellers who sell literature calling for independence have been abducted, and books about sensitive topics such as what happened at Tiananmen Square are not allowed (Bandurski, 2017). Candidates who have run for the legislature and do not claim fidelity to the Chinese government are held in contempt and not allowed to take their seats. Those who supported democracy have resigned en masse from the legislature (Kaeding, 2017; Leung, 2019). Television shows or movies that are sympathetic to independence are not allowed. Visitors or foreigners who advocate for human rights, much less independence for Hong Kong, are refused entry by immigration authorities (Grundy, 2019; Lum et al., 2018; Mahtani, 2020). Even a professor who takes photographs of the protests in Hong Kong may be denied reentry (Lum, 2020). And the culmination is that today protests of any sort are no longer countenanced.

As a British colony, Hong Kongers certainly had a fraught relationship with the United Kingdom. One also may interpret Britain's negotiations with China as weak and flat-footed. Nevertheless, there is a certain nostalgia today for what Hong Kong was, or was becoming, as opposed to where the island finds itself today. The definition of identity is never neat and tidy. All groups have certain cultural aspects that are likely to resonate with personal definitions of a culture. Food and language are obvious cultural markers. Southerners in the United States pride themselves on their regional cuisine, just as Korean Americans are likely to talk about their food with delight and pleasure. Language, of course, sets people apart. Nevertheless, these kinds of cultural significations are surface-level markers. How one gets to the meaning of one's identity is a complex and complicated issue that defies easy generalizations.

Today in Hong Kong a great many people will talk about democracy, free speech, and an independent judiciary as differences in their identity and their counterparts from the mainland. I am not sure Hong Kongers would have claimed this as part of their identity before the handover. Since that time, however, the differences between the two groups have been clear and stark.

One hour by bullet train from Hong Kong are the rapidly growing cities of Guangzhou and Shenzhen. They are not unlike the rest of China, but their proximity to Hong Kong makes the differences clear. Many more newspapers, magazines, and books are banned in Guangzhou and Shenzhen than in Hong Kong. Many Western-owned social media sites, such as Facebook, are not allowed unless one figures out which virtual private network (VPN) to employ to get around the censors. Television and movies have to make their way through the censors. Although many in Hong Kong will say that local news outlets such as the *South China Morning Post* (*SCMP*) have much less freedom than mainstream competitors in the United States, *SCMP* certainly has a great deal more latitude in what it reports than newspapers in Guangzhou or elsewhere on the mainland. Many observers now fear or even assume that Hong Kong will face the same fate as Guangzhou and Shenzhen.

The result for the universities has been significant. Again, when the handover happened, there was not a seismic shift from one day to the next. Universities also have mimicked their counterparts throughout the globe. Rankings are more important. Research is more important. A presence on the international stage is more important.

Significant differences also exist with their international counterparts. Public universities in Hong Kong receive the vast majority of their funding from the government. Students pay comparatively little to attend university. Issues of equity with regard to the poorest individuals on the island—largely immigrants from Nepal and the Philippines—is not particularly a point of significant discussion. How to deal with students from the mainland is a topic of conversation in ways that it is not in most other locations (B. Yu & Zhang, 2016). Research funding is microscopic in comparison with the United States, but not that different from their Australian counterparts. Most funding comes from federal agencies that support research projects, and there is virtually no support from either private foundations or philanthropic donors.

The most significant dynamic for tertiary education in Hong Kong today, however, has to do with working out the relationship of the island with the mainland and, of consequence, the universities. Discussions about independence can be theoretical and practical; the reality of such an event also has something to do with how people see the topic. The thought that California might claim independence from the United States has recently become a topic of conversation, but the possibility of cessation happening is so far-fetched that no one feels threatened by such conversations. As I will elaborate, the independence of Kashmir from India is not theoretical; such conversations either in New Delhi or on any of Delhi's campuses will inflame passions. When Quebec argued for independence in Canada, although individuals were passionate about their opinions, no one banned the conversations. When Ireland claimed independence from Great Britain a century ago, the leaders of the independence movement were put in prison. Catalans have been able to argue for independence from Spain, but when they claimed independence, the government cracked down and arrested the leaders of the movement.

China is not unlike Great Britain in regard to Ireland in the early twentieth century. It will not tolerate any sort of conversation about independence; indeed, the impetus for the National Security Law resulted in part from Hong Kongers wanting to discuss independence and refusing to pledge allegiance to the China. Thus, when two professors called for a protest in the central part of Hong Kong they faced criticism and the universities came under a harsh light for allowing such "hooligans" to claim academic freedom to put forward their ideas. Both professors were also sentenced to 16 months in prison on "public nuisance" charges (May 2019). Virtually all groups within the universities are unsure of how they should respond to the challenges that currently exist in Hong Kong. In 2019, concerns about the city's unique status came to a head when the Hong Kong government proposed an extradition bill that would have allowed Hong Kong residents suspected of criminal activity to be transferred to the legal system of mainland China (F. Lee, 2020). Ostensibly, the idea seemed straightforward. If someone from the mainland was suspected to have committed a serious crime such as murder and was in Hong Kong, there was no mechanism to have the individual returned to China. An extradition law would enable the person to be brought back to justice. The fear, however, was that the wording of the proposal was so broad that people who had spoken out against various Chinese proposals would be extradited to China for no crime other than speaking their mind.

Hundreds of thousands of individuals demonstrated against the extradition bill on Sundays (Ives, 2019), and tensions became even more heated when an armed group of 100 individuals attacked a group of protesters, journalists, and lawmakers in the Yuen Long train station after an evening protest on July 21, 2019. The police response to the attack was widely viewed as inadequate (Ramzy, 2019b), and protests became much more violent over the ensuing months, with a great deal of violence and bloodshed (E. Wong et al., 2019).

The pandemic at first halted protests as everyone sheltered in place. The pandemic also created the space for President Xi to implement the

National Security Law. By the time Hong Kongers were allowed back on the streets, such protests were met with a strong show of force. Democracy's supporters seemed to have been defeated in the streets, in the legislature, in the judiciary, and on the campuses.

The trustees of Hong Kong's universities also have asserted their authority in a new manner. They once were in the background of the university, but now they are seen as enforcers of the mainland's ideas and ideology. Although some boards have a few elected positions from the faculty and staff, they are largely outnumbered and their impact is relatively minor. The vice chancellors and their senior administrative staff are increasingly accountable to the mainland, and they face harsh criticism if they appear to support student or faculty protests. The faculty are largely compliant and focus more inwardly on their own work than on what they believe is good for the university or the academic profession.

The wild card has been the students. Traditionally, students have had more voice and power than students in Los Angeles, but not so much as in New Delhi. Students were the leaders of the Occupy Central movement and played a central role in 2019, but they also have paid the price for their activism. The leaders of the student movements spent time in jail and still face harassment from the government. Benny Tai, one of the professors who received a 16-month jail sentence for encouraging the protests, was praised as a "voice of restraint" (Khan, 2019), but he ultimately lost his job at Hong Kong University after being released from prison. Other student leaders have protested to the board about administrative policies only to face trial and imprisonment and/or a fine (Rauhala, 2017).

The interesting point about life in Hong Kong right now is that the meaning of democracy is a major point of discussion and contention. Most observers believe that voters desire a greater voice in appointing the legislature and chief executive, as well as a discussion about what the status of the island should be vis-à-vis the mainland. Virtually everyone, however, believes that the likelihood of greater voice and more fulsome conversations about the future of Hong Kong is not going to happen.

These conversations and actions are unlikely to occur not only because of the fear of a backlash from the mainland, but also because of the island's current economic environment. The consequences of globalization are that jobs are more difficult to find and wages do not keep pace with the cost of living for the common Hong Konger (Stevenson & Wu, 2019). Although the economic pressures of the university are less than in Los Angeles or New Delhi, they still exist. Academics are expected to compete with one another on the international stage. Rankings matter; thus, the number of articles one publishes and the number of juried conferences in which one presents a paper matter (Tierney & Lanford, 2017). Election to international societies and greater international renown make a difference.

At the same time, competition has increased. The consequences of neoliberal globalization are that whereas in the past, HKU and one or two other universities in Hong Kong stood alone as the Asian "jewels in the crown," there is much greater competition today. According to most ranking systems, China has seven institutions in the top 200 universities in the world.[5] The willingness of the Chinese government to pour significant resources into higher education—and scientific disciplines in particular—has resulted in the ascendancy of Chinese academics in prestigious associations throughout the world. Several other countries—including Japan, Korea, and Taiwan—also are involved in the global competition, which translates into even more requirements for Hong Kong's universities to improve their performance.

Who has time to worry about issues of identity or academic freedom, much less democracy, when day-to-day existence in one's personal and professional lives are so taxing? Most recognize that the university could play an important role in shaping the dialogue about democracy and the future of the island, but the message they have gotten is to keep their heads low, concentrate on their work, and they will make it through another day.

The Enduring Struggle for Identity in New Delhi

All modern cities, obviously, were once barren patches of land or peopled by a few streets that enabled individuals to congregate as they bought and sold goods. New Delhi, however, is particularly hard to imagine insofar as the city has 22 million people today and was inaugurated less than a century ago. The helter-skelter nature of the streets, houses, businesses, government offices, and street vendors provides a feeling of a city on the move, or at least not yet settled. And yet, New Delhi, sitting adjacent to Old Delhi, affords one a sense of history, of a crossroads of ancient empires, religions, and people.

As the home of the government, New Delhi also provides a sense of modern history. At one end of the boulevard is India Gate that symbolizes the transfer of power from a colonizer—Great Britain—to a former colony that overnight became the world's largest democracy. At the other end sits the legislature. Down the road is the home of Nehru, where he gave the address that rallied the nation and inspired the world on the night of 1947: "We have a tryst with destiny" (quoted in van de Wetering, 2016, p. 53). What more inspiring words could be said of a nation shackled by a colonial empire and endeavoring to move forward to create a secular nation where all religions would be tolerated?

Further down the road is the spot where Gandhi was assassinated by a Hindu extremist in 1948. Up the street is Indira Gandhi's modest residence, where she lived when she was prime minister and where she was assassinated one morning in 1984 in her garden by her Sikh bodyguards. Reportedly, 3,000 Sikhs died in Delhi's streets when Hindu compatriots rioted and sought revenge for the murder of the prime minister (Burke, 2012). Gandhi's son, Rajiv Gandhi, could have stopped the rioting but instead responded, "When a big tree falls, the earth shakes" (Singh, 2007).

The other feeling one gets in New Delhi today is from the climate. Delhi has overtaken Beijing, Shanghai, and Calcutta as the world's smoggiest city. On a smoggy day in Los Angeles, the air quality index (AQI) might be 75 and there will be a great deal of griping. Hong Kong's smog index now will approach 150 on a bad day, and Hong Kongers will claim that it is all because of the pollution from the mainland (even though their shipping is the major cause of pollution). A 2019 study by the World Health Organization found that New Delhi is the most polluted capital city in the world due to a toxic combination of construction, the frequently employed practice of crop and garbage burning, and vehicle and industrial emissions (Bhardwaj, 2019). Therefore, New Delhi's BPI index can be 500. It could be higher, but there are no higher ratings. The smog has gotten so bad that for at least a few days during the winter the government will cancel classes so that schoolchildren do not have to go outside. Planes regularly cannot land at the city's airport. During the pandemic the sky cleared and children saw a blue sky for days on end for the first time in their lives. As the lockdown ended, the pollution returned, and perhaps as an apocryphal sign, a plague of locusts descended on the city.

The city defies easy characterization, and not unlike its Hong Kong counterpart, politics, democracy, and identity dominate life. Nehru's Congress Party controlled the first decades of the new country. The most recent government has been led by Narendra Modi of the BJP party. BJP was long a fringe element that sought to accentuate the importance of Hinduism to India and relegate other religions, especially Islam, to the sidelines. Its intellectual progenitor is Hindutva (or, Hindu nationalism), which speaks of the import of Hinduism in India; the man who assassinated Gandhi was a member of the group. He has become something of a cult figure among the most strident members because Gandhi sought reconciliation and understanding among all religious groups.

The complementary aspect of BJP and Modi is that he is seen as an economic reformer. He has made a decided move away from the socialism that defined the early decades of the country, and he has tried to lessen the regulations that strangled free enterprise. Corruption is endemic in all aspects of daily transactions, and Modi has tried to put rules in place that make corruption harder. He has made little progress, and the country has experienced little economic growth, but he has put forward such a convincing message that BJP won a resounding victory in the most recent national elections.

All religions face modern interpretations and challenges on one aspect of their beliefs or another. For Hinduism, the largest concern revolves around the caste system, which lodges individuals into a particular caste based on one's past. Dalits, formerly known as untouchables, are the poorest people in India. Gandhi has come in for criticism because he accepted Hinduism's basic tenets, which results in a miserable life for Dalits. For those who see the unbearable poverty and discrimination that Dalits face, Hinduism is anathema. Nehru made B. R. Ambedkar, a Dalit who, remarkably, earned his PhD and studied with educator John Dewey, the chair of the committee to write the country's new constitution in 1950. The constitution outlawed castes, but the caste system has persisted.

For a Hindu, one cannot simply wish away one's caste. A Hindu who is a Dalit may convert to Buddhism or any other religion, but according to the tenets of Hinduism, the individual will always remain a Hindu, and by inference, in the caste in which they were born. Those who are untouchables face considerable discrimination, for the assumption is that anything they touch will be impure. Obviously, having relationships across castes is impossible, but Dalits also may not touch the same utensils, eat the same food, or even participate in the same sports for their sweat might get on a Brahmin or someone of another caste. The violence perpetrated against Dalits remains horrific, and the discrimination remains still in place.

Women face similar problems. Although the situation is improving, gender parity by no means exists, and women are still subject to harassment and sexual violence. Women are particularly at risk if they marry outside of their religion or marry below their caste. Casual dating or fraternization, as one might see in Los Angeles or Hong Kong, are rare, and women are equally unlikely to be on a street by themselves after dusk. The irony, of course, is that a prime minister has been a woman, and some of the country's most prominent intellectuals and authors are women, but their abilities tend to be seen as aberrations rather than the norm.

All of these issues, the entire complexity of India, frames how to think about higher education because higher education touches on each topic. The universities have gender-segregated dorms; men can stay out after dark, but women have to be in the dorms by sunset. An affirmative action program aims to increase representation in India's colleges and universities by lower caste individuals, indigenous people, and women. Just as corruption is endemic in society, so it is in all aspects of higher education. Reports abound of students cheating on tests or paying someone to take their exams. Some students are "nonattending" because they never set foot in a classroom yet get a grade for coursework (Tierney & Sabharwal, 2017). Teachers get paid but do not teach classes; administrators made deals to bolster their salaries. A great deal of the corruption exists, not because individuals are necessarily wealthy, although that can be the case. More often, however, individuals are simply trying to generate enough income to survive.

New Delhi has some of the country's most prestigious and oldest institutions. The Indian Institutes of Technology (IIT) are regarded as the premier universities in India, and Delhi's IIT is one of the best. As with their IIT counterparts in the rest of the country, the Delhi IIT gets the lion's share of government funds; IITs and their counterparts (Indian Institutes of Management [IIMs] and the National Institutes of Technology [NITs]) have only 3 percent of total students but they receive 50 percent of government funds (Sharma, 2018). Nevertheless, the IITs remain severely underfunded. Only 3 IITs are ranked among the top 200 universities in the world by Quacquarelli Symonds, and they are all in the 150–200 range. The Center for World University Rankings does not have a single Indian institution in the top 400. A generation ago, China decided to improve its postsecondary system. At least a full 4 percent of its GDP has been earmarked for higher education since 2012 (State Council, People's Republic of China, 2019). The result is that the amount of revenue that China spends on one of its research universities is equivalent to what India spends on all of its universities combined. Every Indian campus I have visited is in dramatic need of repair. The buildings are run-down, and landscaping is nonexistent. Faculty salaries also are not sufficient to support a family's basic needs, especially in the nation's capital, New Delhi, where rents can be expensive.

India also recognized the importance of increasing the number of students who might attend a college or university. The government also knew that it lacked the funding to build new campuses. The result was an odd combination of private colleges wedded to public institutions; for-profit institutions are not allowed, but profit is the motive for many of the private institutions to exist; private colleges ostensibly have more freedom to act than public institutions, but they actually have less because of the regulations created by the University Grants Commission (UGC). Online education is on the rise even though those who can benefit from this kind of education are unlikely to have a laptop or interconnectivity.

As noted, the UGC, because of India's size and love affair with bureaucracy, plays an outsized role in higher education, much like the Supreme Court plays in the larger society. Delhi, a city of 20 million people, has no governing board for its 27 universities, 176 colleges, and 98 stand-alone institutions (Ministry of Human Resource Development, 2018). Vermont, a U.S. state of approximately 624,000 people,[6] 1 university, 4 state colleges, and 14 state-chartered independent colleges has three governing boards (Vermont Higher Education Council, 2019). All decisions filter through the UGC from the appointment of faculty and vice chancellors, to the hours that dorms stay open and what kind of events may occur on a campus. Private institutions are as highly regulated as public institutions, and in some respects even more so, because they have an additional layer of reporting requirements to the public institution with which they are affiliated.

What is remarkable in a system that is chronically underfunded, where academic staff are underpaid, and any sense of out-of-class engagement that regularly occurs in Los Angeles (and to a certain extent in Hong Kong) is absent, is that India regularly turns out prominent intellectuals in the sciences, social sciences, and literature. Nine Indian citizens have won Nobel Prizes, and two British Nobel laureates were born in India. In 2019, Abhijit Banerjee, an economist at the Massachusetts Institute of Technology, won the Nobel Prize for economic sciences. India has a long tradition of valued historians and novelists who have gained prominence throughout the world. Unfortunately, many, although not all, of these prizewinners work at institutions outside India, not merely because the working conditions are better in terms of pay and facilities, but also because of the political interference from the Indian government.

Indian students also have an extremely strong work ethic. Unlike in Los Angeles and Hong Kong, where students are able to enjoy themselves outside classes, students in New Delhi tend to work at all hours. Of the three cities, the students in New Delhi have the poorest facilities, as well as the least mentoring or support. The poorest students are dramatically poorer than their counterparts in Los Angeles or Hong Kong. Unlike in the other two cities, where there is a great deal of discussion about "cognitive" and "noncognitive" variables and how to support students in and out of class, in New Delhi there is virtually no support outside class, especially for Dalits. Many of these students literally walk on a campus for the first time when they arrive for fall term to start their first year. There is no "Dalit support center," and other students may shun Dalits in the eating halls and on the playing fields. And yet, they do remarkably well on test scores and employment.

India's students are also more activist than either students in LA or Hong Kong, and those in New Delhi are the most activist. Some faculty also tend to speak out. Over the last several years, as the Modi government has sought to advance a Hindu agenda, the campuses have been centers of protest and discussion.[7] The internet, similar to what is being done elsewhere, is being used to put forward untruths and lies about the sorts of activities that are taking place on Delhi's campuses. Frequently, Hindu activists will threaten and harass students and faculty on or off campus for something an individual or group is reputed to have done. Discussions about Kashmir are particularly provocative, but any number of other topics can bring about controversy. A movie that promotes homosexuality, a group of Muslim students who cook beef in their dorm room—the cow is sacred in Hinduism—or a discussion about a controversial book are all incidences that have triggered a backlash.

India is a country consumed by the struggle for identity. Nehru and Gandhi sought to advance a nationalist identity that was deeply secular, even when the country was born by the tragedy of partition. Gandhi sought to honor and celebrate all religions; Nehru tried to focus more on a national identity, not unlike the founders in the United States. At the moment, a secular notion of identity is absent, and instead many people are retreating to their religious affiliations. The colleges and universities are flash points because they largely serve to put forward a nationalist and secular identity.

Identity and academic freedom also crisscross one another. As I mentioned in Chapter one, scientific meetings have had presentations that assert that open-heart surgery occurred thousands of years ago in the hands of Hindu physicians. Hindus purportedly flew airplanes thousands of years ago as well. Clearly, these points are absurd, but one risks retaliation if one suggests they are not fitting arguments for academic discourse. The result is that India is at a crossroads—except that the country always seems to be at a crossroads as it struggles to break free of the grinding poverty that besets its people. India is an ambitious country. India's leaders and citizens alike want to assume what many people see as India's rightful place as a country accorded respect as the world's largest democracy. Delhi is the epicenter of the issues on and off campus. And yet, the universities frequently seem peripheral to resolving the arguments even though individual students and faculty often risk their lives to put forward ideas pertaining to the future of the country.

Higher Education in the "City of Dreams"—Los Angeles

When the University of Southern California started in 1880, Los Angeles was a city of less than 10,000 people. By 1920 the city had exploded in growth to over 570,000. Today, with more than 4 million citizens within the city limits and over 18.7 million in the Greater Los Angeles area, Los Angeles is the second largest city in the United States, and one of its most diverse. Approximately half of the population is Latinx, and the estimates are that roughly 1.37 million undocumented individuals live in the region (Hayes & Hill, 2017).

California and its cities are considered the home of the "resistance" to President Trump. With less than 25 percent of the legislature, the Republican party has been decimated in the state, and even more so in Los Angeles. Since 1961, Los Angeles has had only one Republican mayor. Although the challenges that the Trump administration has created are manifold, the largest issues that confront the city are local. The cost of housing has made homeownership unaffordable to the middle class and out of reach for the working class. Due to the high cost of living in southern California, homelessness has been on a sharp rise in Los Angeles County. From 2010 to 2017, the number of homeless people increased by 42 percent, from 38,700 to 55,000 (Neighborhood Data for Social Change, 2018). The schools are in crisis. In 2019, the teachers went on strike and demanded a variety of structural changes—smaller classes, a nurse on school grounds, academic counselors—but the agreed-upon changes have made a minimal difference in the quality of schooling. Supported by billionaire benefactors, charter schools have exploded in growth, and they have had variable influence. The school board hired as school superintendent—the sixth in ten years—a businessman with no previous educational experience.

Los Angeles also has been a major site for the Black Lives Matter movement. People have protested the murders of unarmed Black men, and numerous groups have called for reducing the budget of the Los Angeles Police Department (LAPD). In 2020 the Los Angeles Unified School District reduced the budget for policing in schools by 25 percent. Numerous calls have been made on campuses in LA to reduce policing and break off relations with LAPD.

Although the Trump administration influenced all of the country with its foreign affairs gaffes, coarsening of the public discourse, and economic policies that increase income disparity, for Los Angeles specifically there have largely been two areas of immediate concern, climate change and immigration.

The city has the worst pollution of any major city in the United States. Although the pollution levels do not approach that of New Delhi (or Hong Kong), they are hazardous, especially for senior citizens and children. The loosening of environmental restrictions will only make pollution worse. Further, the state of California, and particularly, southern California goes through increasingly hazardous weather patterns of torrential rains or long periods of drought. The result is land that has a great potential for wildfires or mudslides. Although earthquakes are always a hazard, the likelihood of a tremor that obliterates the city is once every few hundred years. However, severe droughts that cause major forest fires and mudslides that eliminate areas of the city are now annual events.

Immigration is both a strength and a concern. Los Angeles is a city of immigrants. A vast swath of the population views the diversity of its citizens as a strength, and this is one of the reasons they choose to live in LA. From the inordinate variety of food that is available to the deep cultural histories of different populations, Los Angeles affords its citizens a range of cultural learning and knowledge rare in most cities. The Supreme Court has made clear the sorts of rights to which undocumented individuals are entitled—free medical care, education through high school, legal support, and the like. The state has provided additional support, such as in-state status for attendance at a postsecondary institution.

Those rights that derive from rulings of the Supreme Court presumably should have some sort of financial support provided by the federal government. If a state chooses to expand on rights—such as in-state tuition—then of course the state should bear the cost. The reality, however, is that more often than not, the bulk of funding that is provided to individuals comes from the city and state where they are located. Immigrants to Los Angeles, many of whom work at essential jobs that others do not fill, and frequently hold two or three jobs to make ends meet, also fall at the low end of income earners. The result is that the financial cost of immigration to the city is significant, especially at a time when the federal government is reneging on policies that have been in effect for over a decade. The Trump administration's policies are raising the cost to immigrants and the city due to harassment and the unduly strict enforcement of immigration laws by the attorney general's office. There is no evidence whatsoever that an immigrant population commits crimes, for example, at a higher level than the domestic population. But because of governmental policies that make earning a living wage difficult, the cost of immigration to the city is significant.

The postsecondary system is heavily influenced by its environment just as in New Delhi and Hong Kong. The state of California has a typical network of postsecondary institutions one finds in most cities in the United States. There are 114 community colleges, 23 campuses in the California State University (CSU) system, 10 campuses of the University of California, and approximately 80 private nonprofit institutions. In total, 26 percent of postsecondary students in California attend a private institution, and the for-profit branch awards 60 percent of all postsecondary certificates (Johnson & Mejia, 2016). The majority of students attend the state-supported community colleges, with approximately 2.1 million students enrolled during the 2016–2017 academic year.[8] At the same time, the CSU system is the largest four-year system in the country with 484,300 students during the 2017–2018 academic year.[9]

Several of the largest Cal State Universities are located in the Greater Los Angeles region, including the three largest campuses in CSU Fullerton (40,439 students), CSU Northridge (39,816 students), and CSU Long Beach (37,065 students).[10] Unlike the community college system, which has students of all ages, 73.8 percent of CSU students are within the "traditional" age range of 18 to 24. The CSU system also has a lower proportion of Latinx (40 percent), White (23.6 percent), and African-American (4.1 percent) students, but a higher proportion of Asian students (16 percent). Nonetheless, the CSU institutions still afford opportunity to many students, as approximately a third of CSU students are the first in their families to enroll in higher education.

Many of the issues that trouble higher education in Los Angeles have to do with the policies of neoliberal globalization in the United States. Students who attend a four-year institution now are likely to go into debt to get a degree. Whereas the famed "Master Plan" of California in 1960 assured students that a place awaited them in the postsecondary system that was free (Marginson, 2016), the reality of state and federal support has changed. Not only have the costs of higher education gone up; the decimation of higher education as a public good means that students now shoulder the burden for their education.

California's failed tax policy—Proposition 13—came about because the taxes on a person's house were rapidly increasing as the value of the house was increasing. Home owners could not afford the taxes and mortgages for their homes because the taxes were rising faster than their income. The result is a policy that destroyed state revenues for public services, especially schools. Whereas California's public schools were once among the best in the nation, they now rank toward the bottom. Teachers went on strike in Los Angeles because class size approaches 45 students/class. The counseling to student ratio should be, at most, 1:250. In Los Angeles, however, it's 1:682 (Kim, 2019). Every school is supposed to have a nurse and a librarian; most schools in Los Angeles do not. There is a great deal of argument about whether every student needs to graduate from high school and go to some form of a postsecondary institution. However, there is general agreement that not enough students are graduating from Los Angeles high schools and heading to college to meet the person-power needs required over the next decade. Around 39 percent of the students who enter a CSU campus are not prepared to take college-level courses, and no more than 62 percent graduate with a BA or BS within a six-year time frame (Gordon, 2019; Koseff, 2017).

The wealth of cultural diversity makes Los Angeles and its campuses stronger. However, the crushing poverty that many individuals face because of tax policies and a reduction in public services makes for a very difficult time for the postsecondary sectors. Too many students graduate from high school unprepared for college. At least 40 percent of first-year CSU students need a remedial class in math or English composition before taking college-credit coursework (Legislative Analyst's Office, 2017; Mangan, 2017). The lack of funding has created gigantic entry-level classes for the CSU and UC systems precisely at a time when students need the most support. Out-of-class learning may not be of concern in New Delhi, but educators in Los Angeles know the sorts of supports needed by first-generation students, and they are largely unavailable. Although the campuses are in better shape than those in New Delhi, deferred maintenance on public campuses is over a billion dollars, and there is no plan for how to acquire those resources.

Obviously, the pandemic impacted the city and all postsecondary institutions. Although the mayor of Los Angeles and the Governor of California initially received high marks for leadership during the crisis, the economic consequences were severe. The University of California system were close to a billion over budget as the fiscal year ended. USC furloughed staff, reduced salaries and stop providing retirement benefits in order to try to balance their budget. The CSU system canceled in-person classes for the academic year, and UCLA and USC offered a blended model. The recovery would be slow and gradual, and the state was not in a position to provide much economic relief.

Although issues of academic freedom certainly roil a particular campus from time to time, the sorts of challenges that faculty and staff face in Hong Kong and New Delhi are largely absent. Individuals do not worry about Los Angeles's relationship to the state or country, so faculty do not feel pressured about what is safe to talk about or whether they may protest a particular measure. Certainly, a great many controversial topics exist, especially in the Trump era, but the threats of violence or censorship pale in comparison to what takes place in New Delhi. There is a concern on all campuses right now about the nature of what one may say or how one should act when it comes to cross-cultural issues. A growing, if still insubstantial, literature on microaggressions has raised questions about how students of color and other groups (e.g., LGBTQ, women, the disabled) are forced to deal with frequently unintended insults and slights on a daily basis in the classroom and on campus (Pérez Huber & Solórzano, 2015; Sue et al., 2007). The "Me Too" movement has raised questions about what the appropriate relationship should be among any number of individuals, but in particular professors and students. Again, what may have been an unintended comment or action can be interpreted as harmful, hurtful, or inappropriate. What once may have been allowed has finally come to be seen for what it is—harassment or abuse that forces those most at risk into a vulnerable position, which not only impacts learning but also creates a hostile environment.

The challenge is that there is no roadmap for action, no clear set of rules that makes college campuses learning laboratories for how to act in a manner that fosters learning and does not marginalize anyone. As I discuss in Chapter 4, there are those who will claim that their academic freedom is circumscribed because they cannot say or do what they once said or did. Academic freedom, however is not the liberty simply to blurt out whatever comes into one's mind. Nevertheless, core values such as academic freedom need to be discussed and possibly reformulated. Los Angeles has long thought of itself as a modern city trying to work out the next innovation rather than look to the past. The "city of dreams" is a city of reinvention rather than history. The campuses of Los Angeles are at the epicenter of the reinvention as the city struggles to move into the future.

Whither the Democratic Imperative?

Universities always have been unique cultural organizations for a city. Whether in Hong Kong, Los Angeles, or New Delhi, however, they have until recently stood apart from the rest of the city. Some might say that their separation has been driven by a smug attitude of privilege suggesting that academics have not wanted to dirty their hands in the rough-and-tumble of urban life. An alternative, and more traditional, view might be that those in the university have needed distance to observe and reflect on the problems under investigation. Until recently, all institutions have been the purveyors and arbiters of knowledge. As I have argued, however, that hegemony is finished, and a crisis of legitimacy exists at the same time that the support of the institutions has circumvented their autonomy. Institutions, even those removed from society, are impacted by the environments in which they exist. I have put forward the notion that we currently face a democratic recession, and universities have a challenge in front of them. What might they do to speak more forcefully against a variation of populism that is antidemocratic? What might those within the university do to work more forcefully in creating in their own communities an ethic of responsibility based on difference rather than similarity? In the next chapter, I elaborate on the issues of identity that I touched on here in order to help us think through the role of the university in either bolstering or repressing one's identity in order to foster civic society.

CHAPTER THREE

Identity Matters

Communities of Difference

Notions of identity circumscribe academic life today, just as they do on a larger level in ways mentioned in the previous chapter in New Delhi, Hong Kong and Los Angeles. Identity, however, was not always front and center in the academy. As with the democratic recession, however, we tend to think that people's identity is how they have always defined themselves when in actuality the idea is relatively new, both in the academy and in the larger society. Stereotypes of a group may have existed—Jews acted one way and Christians another—but how an institution was supposed to respond to these groups was with neglect and exclusion rather than in a way that was proactive and informed. One also supposedly did not step outside of one's identity.

Obviously, times have changed. Individuals internalize and proactively identify as a member of one group or another. The rise, strength, and vibrancy of the women's movement, race-based networks, LGBTQ groups, and the like have taken hold on college campuses in a way that could not have been predicted a half-century ago. Black Lives Matter is arguably the largest protest movement the United States has even seen, and there are groups on virtually every college campus.

Stereotypes and gross generalities always have been present in the larger society, but those in the group itself largely did not put forward their own unique identity that demanded consideration and particular policies. Assimilation was the policy of the early twentieth century. Native Americans had their children sent away to boarding schools so that they might "assimilate." The gay rights slogan, "We're queer, we're here, get used to it," highlights the coming of age of a group that once tried to hide their identity for fear of what might happen if people found out. Conversion therapy assumed that homosexuals could change into heterosexuals, and that by doing so, they would be better off. Beginning in the 1970s, however, those in the LGBTQ movement affirmed their identity and said they did not need to change. Society did. The disabled fought for their rights, not to be "abled" since they could not be, but to be able to have productive lives on their own terms rather than being shuttered at home.

Postsecondary institutions have been at the center of discussions about identity because many students are trying to figure out where they fit in the larger world. In some respects, we might locate the more recent academic discussions of identity in Erik Erikson's notions of the self in the 1950s. He named something that most individuals did not realize they went through—identity development—and something they did not know was bothering them—an identity crisis (Erikson, 1968). Erikson could not have predicted how his ideas might germinate. By the twenty-first century, it is fair to say that many individuals on college campuses think that a major challenge for adolescents is to come to terms with how they define themselves and efforts of society—and the academy—to affirm, deny or harm that identity.

The idea of identity now revolves around what has come to be known as identity politics. We realize that the answer to "Who am I" is neither simply an existential religious question nor something found in the recesses of one's psyche. What one needs to come to grips with is the interplay between the inner self and the larger world's social rules and norms.

Satya Mohanty (1997) has written usefully about the epistemic status of cultural identity. As he notes, "Whether cultures are inherited or consciously and deliberately created, basic problems of definition—who belongs where or with whom, who belongs and who doesn't—are unavoidable the moment we translate our dreams of diversity into social visions and agendas" (p. 202). This sort of question was generally not envisioned prior to the 1980s. Merit-based admissions policies in the early twentieth century may have been partially enacted to demonstrate that an institution was not biased against Jews. Affirmative action came about in the 1960s to see if more African Americans (and subsequently Latinos and women) might be admitted to the academy. Yet none of these sorts of policies envisioned that one's identity was somehow going to shape and change the structure and culture of the academy. The academy was going to change them. The assumption was that different sorts of people did not change academic life; they changed to meet the norms of the academy. The identity of who taught students was irrelevant, or implicit. Liberals might have advocated for more women and people of color to assume faculty positions, but there was no question whether a White male instructor could do a good job teaching a student who was different from himself. A professor taught a subject, not a student. Equitable treatment meant everyone was treated equally and one's identity was irrelevant. The student needed to master the material whether the subject was chemistry, history, or law. Who the student was mattered not at all in the mastery of the material.

Curiously, many of the recent arguments about identity go back and forth between essentialist and social constructionist notions, often simultaneously. Identity is fixed and stable, or it changes based on temporal, cultural, and individual beliefs. A gay person does not choose their identity; sexual orientation is not a lifestyle choice. A person neither can be recruited to be gay, nor changed with reparative therapy. And yet, some will say that at birth children are neither a boy nor a girl and that we must wait until they are old enough to claim their identity.

The epistemic status of cultural identity goes to the heart of the current challenges that frame academic life. What we label and call people (e.g., homosexual, gay, queer, transgender, cisgender) in part reflects changing notions of group and individual identity. "Colored" changed to "Negro" and then "Black" and "African American" as the named became the masters of their names. The clinical referent of sickness with the term "homosexual" changed to "gay" as the liberation movement worked for equality within a traditional framework. When AIDS arose and individuals died because they could not get needed services within that traditional framework, then "queer" politics arose, not to work within norms, but to disrupt them. Grammatical accommodations that tried to accept that a "president," a "doctor," and the like may not only be a male but also a female gave way to "he/she" and eventually "they" constructions: "If an individual works hard, then he/she can become president." Transgender individuals, however, transcended traditional gender binaries so someone now may opt to be called "they," even if by traditional notions the term is grammatically incorrect. Someone has light black skin and does not identify as African American as a child because his parents are from Cape Verde. Nevertheless, when he gets to school his teachers think of him as Black; when he goes to college his White fellow undergraduates think of him as Black, and his Black colleagues do not. One's identity is now front and center, no longer implicit but instead claimed by the speaker and argued over by the larger community.

The language of difference was not merely a simple linguistic switch, but also suggested that one's standpoint framed how one viewed the world, and in turn, how the world viewed the individual. My view of my self was neither less than those in the majority nor in need of repair. African Americans ought not to need to conform to the mores of the larger culture. Their views of that world were neither irrational nor unenlightened. Standpoint theory highlighted how women, gays, and others viewed the world, and that their experiences had shaped their views and how they defined situations (Khwaja et al., 2017). If their positions had an autobiographic standpoint, then surely everyone else's positionality needed to be defined as well. Members of a particular group had a precise burden and a privilege. Individuals from a group understood the group; outsiders did not. The result is that those in the group now had to define their world to others, but they also became the arbiters of truth. The work of a White man who once studied Native Americans as an exotic culture did not do so from a privileged scientific position but instead from a standpoint imbued with racist privilege.

Initially, most in the academy did not understand the implications of the epistemic status of cultural identity. As I noted in Chapter 2, the twentieth-century university adhered to a notion of scientific knowledge whereby the trained professional—the academic—was the arbiter of knowledge. If a patient went to a doctor, the individual who offered the diagnosis was not the patient. When an anthropologist went to study a distant tribe, the natives were not the ones who made sense of their lives. By the late twentieth century, however, the idea took hold that not only did the patient and native have something to offer, but they also knew as much as, if not more than, the trained clinician.

Eventually, we came to understand that one's standpoint was not a singular notion of one's identity, but rather plural and intersectional (Gee, 2000; Walby et al., 2012). A person was not merely a woman or not merely African American, but both. The identity of a lesbian African American was different from that of a straight African American female or a lesbian White woman. White women could not speak on behalf of Black women because they did not understand their intersectional identity.

The discussion of identity continued to go back and forth between a realist notion of experience and one that was constructed as scholars continued writing about the topics. Racism existed—it was real. Gay people always have existed. Women are different from men. Those who are disabled are differently abled. One person is different from another in real ways.

However, how one experienced that racism, sexism, disability, or homophobia was through the lens of one's individual identity. Gradually, the postmodern notion took hold that the entire social world, and in many ways the natural world, was up for grabs. My interpretation of reality mattered. Post-positivist realism seemed to want to have it both ways. A social world existed in which injustices were real and could be named, but they could not be named objectively—from a distanced standpoint.

Reality existed. Police subjected African Americans to more abuse than Whites, women were paid less in the workplace, and the disabled experienced discrimination because of who they were. These were not simply socially constructed categories—they existed in the "real" world. The protests in 2020 that erupted after a Black man, George Floyd, was murdered by the Minneapolis police emphasized the import of identity in daily life and the challenges that Black people face in the United States in the twenty-first century. Hence, the cultural radicalism of the postmodern framework largely had been rejected, and yet we have not come to terms with what to put in its place. We know that fixed categories are unstable and changing; we also know that the world is not entirely up for grabs. Moreover, we have come to believe that those who can best interpret the world are those who are of it because they have epistemic privilege. In anthropological jargon, emic, rather than etic, perspectives have taken center stage (Beals et al., 2019). Understandings within a culture are closer to reality than those imposed on the culture by the scientist.

How can one reject essentialism and social constructionism? How does one determine what is real? Post-positivist realism does not provide a fulfilling answer insofar as the response is contradictory: An objective world exists, but my vision of the world mediates that world. An objective world cannot exist if my interpretation of it will differ from yours. And yet, through interpretation and mediation of that world, we are able to grasp its meaning. Michael Hames-Garcia (2000) points out, "Post-positivist realism sees that there are different ways that knowledge can be constructed and seeks a dialectical mediation of experience with the understanding that theory-laden and socially constructed experiences can lead to a knowledge that is accurate and reliable" (p. 109). Such an argument may not be as far gone as postmodernism, but it is also a rejection of the scientific method. Two individuals view a situation; one has epistemic privilege and the other does not. The individual with epistemic privilege is to be believed.

Although there is much to agree with in the realization that the world can be mediated by the social and cultural experiences of individuals who are from various social groups and identities, we have arrived at a point in time when such a view has brought about a standoff on academic campuses. My identity defines how I see the world. If someone else has a different view of the world, then they are seeing the world incorrectly and there is little need for communication across difference. Identity not only frames my world; it is impossible for you to understand the world I inhabit and a useless undertaking to try to understand the "Other."

To make our understanding even more complex, identity has a double meaning. As Fearson (1999) points out, "It refers at the same time to social categories and to the sources of an individual's self-respect or dignity" (p. 2). Identity is not only social markers such as race, gender, sexual orientation, or class, but also a host of other societal characteristics. I have been an academic for a quarter of a century and part of my identity is defined by my work; such is not the case for many individuals, at least explicitly. Although I was raised as a Catholic, my religion is largely peripheral to my identity today. For a friend who is a devout Muslim, religion is central. Religion may not appear to be central to a man I know in India, but for his wife it is fundamental because of the societal and cultural pressures that Islam creates for women. By relationship, of course, then religion is also fundamental for the man. Identity frames the idea that social categories are essential to how individuals, groups, and ultimately society make sense of the world. Identity is not simply a psychological characteristic.

Some might think that a focus on identity is little more than late-night gabfests that might be of interest to college students with time on their hands, that it does not really impact either the university or the larger world. Such an assumption is wrong, and that is why I am focusing on the term here. One issue that has arisen with our focus on identity is what I think of as epistemic closure. If one's standpoint defines how one sees and interpret the world, and if the interpretation of the world is up for grabs, no amount of "neutral" information can change one's opinion.

I previously outlined the crises that confront the university. The legitimacy of knowledge and the academic who defines knowledge come up for questioning, if not rejection, when one's identity is the arbiter of knowledge. In the extreme version of epistemic closure, a Black student is unable to learn from anyone other than a Black professor. If I learn about the world from particular sources of knowledge and they inform me that the Koran calls for the annihilation of Christians, then as a Christian I will see the necessity for a Crusade in the defense of my religion. One only learns from one's self or the extensions of one's self. Difference is neither celebrated nor honored, but instead rejected. Curiously, such an assertion is increasingly accepted by those who are fundamentally at odds with one another, those on the radical right or left, those who are fundamentalist Muslims or fundamentalist Christians.

Epistemic closure also leeches into other areas. If what I believe defines what I know about my identity, then what stops me from defining other issues in a similar fashion? I know something to be true based on my belief as a woman, or as a gay man, or as Christian. If my belief structure is framed in such a manner, then what stops me from believing that my children need not get a vaccine because I have read online that vaccinations are not only unnecessary but actually harmful. When we reject the legitimacy of knowledge in one area, we open ourselves up to rejecting it in all areas.

Jonathan Haidt (2016) has argued that those who advance the notion of epistemic closure are after something fundamentally different from what has been thought of as the traditional notion of the university. He allows that individuals may have several personal goals—the accumulation of wealth, social justice, and happiness, for example—but the telos of a university has to be "truth." He argues that a singular focus on truth is not only an optimal, but actually a necessary, condition for a university. Truth, by Haidt's reckoning, rejects epistemic closure. One does not find truth through identity; who one is plays no role in determining the truth of an issue.

We can recognize the fine line we walk when we subscribe to notions of epistemic closure, but we also are troubled by claims to truth by climate change deniers, or those who feel that a particular group needs to be annihilated. If a university is supposed to be on a quest for truth but consistently undervalues or obscures the contributions and qualities of women, then isn't one or the other notion mistaken? Such a question is fundamental for an organization such as a university. If I go to my doctor, I may believe him when he tells me what to do to avoid kidney stones, but when he opines about where to hike in the Dolomites, I may dismiss it. We all have the ability to sift through professional advice and casual opinions. An organization after the search for truth, however, is different.

We argue within the academy about various facets of knowledge, but, at some point, we promulgate, not merely opinions, but social facts. When some social facts are questioned, however, then we begin to question how credible the organization may be on any social fact.

Let us appreciate that, in part, identity revolves around the simple question "Who am I?". Context matters. When I am abroad, part of my answer turns on nationality, but if I am home citizenship may not arise. Again, obviously being from the United States frames my identity even if I am not aware of it. An African American is more likely to claim identity as a Black person than a White person will. More recently, however, White nationalists are making claims to a racial identity that only fringe groups once made. Does that make race less of a marker for White people yesterday but more tomorrow? Why has one's Whiteness become such a marker today?

Similarly, a gay person is more likely to say they are gay, whereas a straight person is less likely to claim a sexual orientation. A current norm in a college seminar is to ask students what pronoun they want to use. Those students who are most confused by the question are the ones whose sexual identity has been so obvious to them that they have never asked themselves the question. A boy becomes a man and always employs "he" or "his." That simple pronoun is never questioned, and he never recognizes that the person sitting next to him may prefer the use of "they." A student who is undocumented may not realize their citizenship status until they learn they are not eligible for financial aid.

Of import is the realization that identities change over time. Although some people may have accepted, however secretly, one's homosexuality a century ago, many others did not even have a word for defining same-sex attraction. In the twenty-first century, the meaning of gender has changed so much that great variety exists that is increasingly viewed as normal. With these changing definitions of gender, identity has changed as well. To be of the working class once did not provoke economic insecurity or anger about one's social status; today, the working class is increasingly troubled by the ability to save for the future and provide for one's children. A man who labeled himself a coal miner in the 1940s identified in a way that is entirely different from his counterpart in the twenty-first century. Coal mining was once a decent job that provided an income for a family. The job was passed from father to son. Today, the work does not enable many individuals to earn a comfortable income, and the health-related dangers give many pause to having their children follow in their footsteps.

The result is that identity is not just a static social category but also an ever-changing and fluid notion that points to one's role in the world. Identity helps define an individual's sense of truth.

Conversely, when truth is no longer objective but instead is radically subjective, based on the epistemic status of one's identity, then what do we make of the role of the university? Traditionally, the university had the opposite role. Rather than enabling hyperindividualism, the institution sought to inculcate a collective communal identity. Faculty were supposed to help individuals think beyond their subject position, and the creation of an "educated mind" had nothing to do with identity. What the faculty had not understood was that an objective truth was one that largely adhered to the status quo and maintained the hierarchies that existed. Blacks entered the academy, but they needed to think and act like Whites. Women were to be like men. Gay people originally had to accept their mental illness or eventually accept their essential differences, which made marriage or child rearing impossible. Nevertheless, our adherence to science at least provided individuals with a sense of a dominant understanding of right and wrong. How, then, do we determine right from wrong in a world that suggests that identity is central and group cohesion a fool's errand, and what are the implications for a world that is seeing the rise of fascism and the downfall of democracy?

Building an Ethic of Responsibility in the Twenty-First-Century University

I mentioned in the previous chapter Max Weber's (1917/1958) famous adage that intellectuals need to put forward an "ethics of responsibility." Today, an ethics of responsibility has to consider the rise of populist movements and how individuals disseminate and receive information. I appreciate that we cannot, and do not want to, turn back the technological clock. We accept that the university's intellectual hegemony is gone. Nevertheless, what might we do to restore and reinvigorate the university's voice, and in turn, reverse the democratic recession? In a globalized world, what is the mission of the university? To answer such questions, we first need to come to terms with what identity suggests for higher education, in light of what I have been arguing.

I am not sure about Haidt's assertion that an organization can have but one telos. Haidt's rejection of what he calls "viewpoint diversity" is understandable for someone whom we might have labeled a positivist at one point. From this perspective, there is a singular understanding of the world that is based on science. Why would we be unable, however, to pursue "truth" from this perspective and also be concerned with social justice? Religious institutions, surely, have sought truth and a multitude of other concerns, one of them often being social justice. Cardinal Newman's (1852/2015) "idea" of a university was multifaceted and was a mixture of faith and science. Until recently, universities sought to help students struggle with the great questions of the world but also tried to provide a vocational skill so that they might be employed on graduation. Vocational training was not something ancillary or hidden, and certainly had little to do with Haidt's notion of telos.

I appreciate Haidt's concern for the seeming abandonment of telos, but I am puzzled by his assumption that our focus has to be a singular goal or else we shall fail. Chad Wellmon (2018) has pointed out that "higher education leaders across the country [in the late nineteenth century] cast this dual mission of truth and the public good as the defining purpose of a distinctly American university" (para. 6). When higher education came of age in the 1880s and 1890s, we were moving distinctly against the idea that truth, as defined through a strictly religious mindset, was what a college or university ought to pursue. A singular devotion to a religious ideal gave way to a distinctly American definition of purpose. True, professors were still tasked with seeking "truth," but the purpose of higher education revolved more around the idea of a public good. Learning was not simply for one's mind or soul, but also for involvement as a citizen. We learned skills that equipped us to participate in a democracy and to obtain gainful employment.

I raise my concerns about a view of the academy as focused on a singular version of telos because not only is that an incorrect solution for the future, it is also an incorrect view of the past. I appreciate those who have a concern about the diminution of a larger social good of the university, but before we define the purpose of the institution, we should not invent a past that never existed for the modern university. In India, modern universities always have played a dual role in trying to reach scientific excellence and also serve as a focal point for protest and communication about the challenges that society faces. Even the search for scientific excellence was, on the one hand, focused on basic science and, on the other, on training students for employment in a country desperately in need of an indigenous professional class. Hong Kong, as well, has tried to conduct basic research but also to intellectually challenge the framework for citizenship. The ideal was not simply on a search for "Truth," but also what citizenship means for students born in a Hong Kong that now was part of China.

Telos void of context is a curious notion that conjures up the idea of a monastic institution removed from society. The portrait of the monastery is one of stasis that does not change regardless of the monks who come and go. Such a view is overly romantic and historically uninformed. Further, even the view of a static monastery does not align with post-secondary institutions. Our universities have not been such institutions for well over a century, and Newman's classic treatise of the nineteenth century would have rejected such a portrait. The Land Grant Act, which was enacted during the Civil War, also enabled institutions to be created that were not based on an ideal of telos, but more focused on practical training. The GI Bill was aimed at supporting returning soldiers so that they could gain a college degree, and through that education, a job. Hong Kong created a university of science and technology a little over a half-century ago that prides itself on reform and change; India has committed to creating online learning in a manner that is decidedly different from the portrait of a monastery.

My point here is that the mission of an institution is never settled. If anything, what we are doing in our universities should be a primary question that we continue to ask ourselves. Universities are not profit-making entities where the goal of profit is easily enough understood, and what they sought yesterday they will continue to seek tomorrow, as long as the enterprise generates revenue. The processes will change, but the goals will not. There are base-line data points for a college or university, to be sure. An institution has to balance its budget, bring in students, support graduate students, and the like. Such points, however, are simply markers aimed at organizational efficiency, even when dealing with the impact of the COVID-19 pandemic. What matters is the substance of what gets taught and learned. The challenge for us today, however, revolves around notions of identity and community and how these definitions define what we should be doing.

As individuals, we also assume roles that, in part, account for what we think of as our identities, that are distinct from, but related to, core identities such as race and gender. I am a professor, and I teach students. A friend is a mother and involved with her children's upbringing. The fellow who just fixed my toilet has been a plumber for over 20 years. The airplane pilot is also the daughter of a rabbi. Each of these vocational and personal roles are part of our identities, and they help shape who we are and what we think. Indeed, they were once how we thought of identity. They may shape critical interactions in some arenas, and not at all in others. The mother and plumber have domains of expertise and interest where I am likely to defer. What the mother wants for her child, or what the plumber suggests should be done with the toilet are areas that I am likely to accept. Child services may question a mother, and the plumber needs certification to be a plumber. However, all of us may enjoy baseball and root for different teams, but we most likely would not define one's identity as a baseball fan, or that fandom based on one being a mother, a plumber, or an academic.

In academic life, however, one's identity has clear markers and others that are not so clearly delineated. I may approach a classroom as a father, or coach of my daughter's baseball team, but ultimately what enables me to teach a class is that I am a professor, not that I am a parent, a Dodgers fan, or an amateur gardener. What about that I am also gay and able-bodied and Anglo? The challenge for us today is to consider when individuals assume the identities of professor and student what that means. Where do we defer or define that person's abilities because of those titles, and how do other characteristics of identity come into play?

We ought not to forget how we have arrived at the present moment with regard to identity politics. The norms that existed were not simply "norms." They also privileged some and confined others to the margins. African Americans, women, and gays for one reason or another, were on the sidelines in a democracy that subscribed to the fairy-tale notion that "all men [sic] are created equal." We fought a Civil War to ensure that all "men," irrespective of race, were equal participants in the democracy, and then, immediately after that war, we ensured by laws and practices that the former slaves would not be equal because of their race. We celebrated a phrase about equality that omitted 50 percent of the country because of their gender. One's sexual orientation was normal for many and a moral and psychological failing for others until the twenty-first century.

Of course, we should not overlook the progress we have made. African Americans are more equal participants today than a century ago. A Black man became president of the United States. Women have the right to vote, and a woman almost became president of the United States. Gays and lesbians now have marriage equality. A gay candidate for president was given serious consideration. Surely, any group that has been marginalized is going to develop a set of ideas about itself in a manner that frames group identity and, consequently, how a member of that group thinks and acts.

For centuries, Dalits, or untouchables, were condemned to fierce discrimination because they were Hinduism's outcasts. They were confined to the margins of society, forced to do the worst forms of labor, and assured of living in unspeakable poverty because of how the religion defined who they were. Their identity defined them; it was unchangeable and not debatable according to the tenets of religion. Even Gandhi supported the caste system, although not the violent discrimination that Dalits faced. When India became an independent nation, the government outlawed castes in the constitution, but a great deal of violence and discrimination have remained in place. The affirmative action policy that has been created has helped to overcome the prejudices that still exist, but Dalits are still among the poorest citizens in India and still face horrendous acts of discrimination and violence.

From these forces of oppression, a sense has developed first of the burden of one's identity, and then of its strength. From the 1960s onward, individuals have come together under those aspects of their identity that they share in order to find solidarity and work toward their group's improvement. There have been many successes. Nevertheless, those groups who have faced historic discrimination still have not achieved parity with those in control in many areas. Blacks earn less than Whites. Dalits still are underrepresented in higher education. Those Filipino and Nepalese immigrants to Hong Kong still live in impoverished homes and are unable to send their children to school.

The criticism of identity politics is understandable in terms of what has occurred in the country as well as on our campuses. However, those who call for the end of identity politics and a return to a civic notion of community seem barely to acknowledge why we have focused on identity. I appreciate calls for community and shall make a related argument, but I do not think we can do so without the understanding I am offering here.

Identity, however, is under attack. "When," argues Andrew Sullivan (2018), "elite universities shift their entire world view away from liberal education as we have long known it, towards the imperatives of an identity-based social justice movement, the broader culture is in danger of drifting away" (para. 2). Mark Lilla (2018) extends this line of thinking by calling for a return to a collective identity, saying, "This will require a reorientation of our thinking and engagement, but above all, it will mean putting the age of identity behind us. It is time—past time—to get real" (p. 17). William Eggington (2018) understands how groups have come together under the banner of identity but bemoans "the cultivation of isolated identities" (p. 4). Relatedly, Francis Fukuyama (2018) folds concerns about identity under the idea of "the politics of resentment" (p. 7). He points to its creation as the actions of those of us on the left, and he argues that the problem with identity-based politics is that we are not building "solidarity around large collectivities" and instead unfortunately focus "on ever smaller groups being marginalized in specific ways" (p. 90).

I do not think these arguments are going to be very successful. The larger community—the very community that all of these authors claim we ought to join as we drop our membership in the identity-based clubs—has hardly been very welcoming to those of us on the margins of society. Black Lives Matter has come about, not because of some fantasy about police violence, but because of documented evidence about how Blacks are shot by police and others almost at random, and at a significantly higher rate than Anglos. The "Me Too" movement arose because of how women have been treated in the workplace and at home. We still have a sizable number of people in the United States who do not want to allow gay people to marry, and they do not want to have to serve them in restaurants or bake cakes for their weddings. In India and Hong Kong, gay marriage is still not allowed; homosexuality was removed as a crime in India only in 2018. Women continue to face fierce discrimination in India. Immigrants in Hong Kong are barely counted in headcounts of national population.

Further, as we have learned more about identity, we also have seen a further splintering of identities, as Eggington suggests. These splinters, however, have arisen largely for the same reasons that the larger group identities developed in the first place. Transphobia can be just as pronounced in the gay community as the straight community. Trans people spoke up and worked on behalf of a different articulation of their identities in large part because their needs were not being served by the gay community. Intersectionality is not a further fragmentation of a group to bemoan, but the recognition that different people have different needs and different ways of seeing the world. The women's movement has long been troubled by White women leading organizations where those who are women of color feel marginalized and their needs ignored. Why would Dalits assume that Brahmins and all other castes would support them when they have a thousand-year history documenting the opposite?

What those who bemoan identity-based politics seem to overlook is that the issues that motivated a coming together around notions of identity remain of concern today. That is, they may tend to say that the organizations that created change a half-century ago were useful but are no longer needed. Such an argument might be premised on the idea that the problems have been solved or at least largely ameliorated. A second argument might be that larger, communal-based organizations will now serve the needs of everyone, and the weaknesses of a singular focus on identity can be eliminated. Unfortunately, the first assertion is fallacious and the second is based on trust. Although people of color, for example, may face less discrimination today than they did a half-century ago, there is ample evidence that they still are not treated equally. The creation of identity-based groups is in large part based on a lack of trust. Few believe that a larger group will work for the equal rights of those who face discrimination based on one's view of history. The United States has had a vice president who believes that gay people should not be allowed to marry, even though the Supreme Court has said the opposite. Why would I trust the vice president to speak up on my behalf?

The issues we face on college campuses pertaining to identity warrant attention. Two recent ideas that have come in for criticism and seem to pertain to identity-based politics are trigger warnings and microaggressions. The twin ideas are related but distinct, and I elaborate on them at length in the following chapter on academic freedom and free speech. Nevertheless, a short definition is in order here. Trigger warnings are what students request—or demand—if someone is going to assign a reading, video, or lecture that may be upsetting because of the content (Bellet et al., 2018). A great deal of information in the humanities and social sciences can trigger uncomfortable feelings, but even the natural sciences are not immune. Dissections of mice in a lab or discussions about how the world evolved are potential triggers for some. A professor who casually and repeatedly makes religious references could be a trigger to those who have faced trauma while attending church.

A microaggression is frequently unintentional (Sue et al., 2007). A professor may state in class, for example, that he was surprised that a female student knows a lot about the Super Bowl, that an African American student's favorite author is Shakespeare, or that a poor student is a connoisseur of fine wine. The professor may not have overtly been trying to put the student down, but that is the way the student may have interpreted the comment.

Those who disdain identity-based politics have all sorts of issues with trigger warnings and microaggressions. The scientific evidence that trigger warnings or microaggressions inhibit learning is currently thin. We are teaching students to avoid controversy. Students have become "snowflakes," who cannot stand the heat. Academic life should be about wrestling with ideas, not avoiding them. Proponents of microaggressions simply want to shut down viewpoints with which they disagree, and frequently those viewpoints are conservative. One cannot support microaggression and academic freedom. One cancels out the other. Rather than train students to be victims we should enable them to become critical thinkers with agency. We are encouraging students to engage in "emotional reasoning" (Lukianoff and Haidt, 2015, para. 18) rather than critical thinking. We are creating safe space where students are emotionally safe, but intellectually fragile. We are kidding ourselves and our students that, by avoiding difficult dialogues on campus, we are creating change in society (Fukuyama, 2018).

There is a degree of truth to the various explanations. I want students to be critical thinkers. I want to be able to entertain difficult dialogues in my classroom and on campus. I want a variety of viewpoints discussed in my classroom. I want to ensure that students who have opinions that diverge from the majority are able to be heard.

Curiously, many of those who want to move away from identity politics also have the same concerns about the rise of populism and the election of populists around the world. Their diagnosis of how individuals such as Trump came to power is by way of identity-based politics. They suggest that the intense focus on one's identity came at the expense of a cohesive group sense. Race-based groups or those who support gay marriage gave stimulus for an alternative formation—White groups, or straight groups, or male working-class groups. Those who support Trump and others have given rise to a nationalism and populism that returns the country to a narrow conception of what it means to be a citizen of a country.

We are on the horns of a dilemma. Critics of identity-based politics make two thoughtful points. On the one hand, they point out how the focus on identity has come at the cost of a larger sense of group cohesion and identity. On the other hand, they point out that the response by those who have fostered the current nativism is to adopt their own brand of identity-based ideas and policies. Based on their logical analyses, they then suggest that those who have found comfort in identity-based politics ought to move away from that stance and more toward a nationalist framework. The leap of faith that they demand seems illogical. Why would a group that has been marginalized pin their hopes on the group that not only historically has marginalized them, but now has reinforced that marginalization with populist rhetoric? The proponents of collective identity seem to be laying the onus on those who have focused on identity-based groups—and looking to them to change.

Consider, for example, Mark Lilla's (2018) lament: "We must relearn how to speak to citizens as citizens and to frame our appeals—including ones to benefit particular groups—in terms of principles that everyone can affirm" (p. 15). Fair enough: I certainly concur with the idea of the statement. But then, in a footnote, he says, "It is a sign of how polluted our political discourse has become that any mention of the term citizen leads people to think of the hypocritical and racist demagoguery that passes for our debate on immigration and refugees today" (p. 15). Again, I agree with his footnote, but if my parents are immigrants or refugees, why would I give up my identity-based politics because some well-intentioned White man tells me to do so?

Eggington (2018) concludes in his book, "Through all this the left failed to see that while winning the battle over identity, it was losing the war over community" (p. 4). Lukianoff and Haidt (2018) ascribe identity politics and its ramifications to the rise of a "victimhood culture" (p. 210) that is based on identity politics. What the authors seek is "dignity culture." They go on to explain dignity culture:

> People are assumed to have dignity and worth regardless of what others think of them, so they are not expected to react to strongly to minor slights. Of course, full dignity was at one time accorded only to adult, white men; the rights revolutions of the twentieth and twenty-first centuries did essential work to expand dignity to all. (p. 209)

Again, the "of course" in the statement is what many of us who are involved in identity-based groups, or what they might call "victimhood cultures," will find humorous. I know next to no one in the gay community who honestly believes that a queer "revolution" would have happened without what Lukianoff and Haidt are ascribing to victimhood culture. These community-based scholars seem to be blithely ascribing achievement of "full dignity" almost to centrifugal force; rights happened because their time had come. When individuals ask for a leap of faith, they have to demonstrate more understanding than most of the authors are doing here.

At the epicenter of these discussions is the university. To be sure, a free press is central to shed light on nefarious acts that occur in society. The judiciary can provide security and justice for those who are being harmed. The university, however, has the potential to play a role for both sides of this argument. The communalists see how civic culture can be nurtured through teaching and learning. Those who call for identity-based politics believe that a hyperconcentration on microaggressions and individual difference will enable safe spaces for learning.

Lilla (2018) points his finger at academic liberals:

> You would have thought that, faced with the dogma of radical economic individualism that Reagan normalized, liberals would have used their positions in our educational institutions to teach young people that they share a destiny with all their fellow citizens and have duties toward them. Instead, they trained students to be spelunkers of their personal identities and left them incurious about the world outside their heads. (p. 60)

One might agree with Lilla's general ideas if he were less hectoring and more informed. Student volunteering certainly has remained high. The sorts of conversations he is calling for are more likely to occur in the humanities and social sciences than in engineering or business. Unfortunately, students arrive on campus with a predilection for majoring in engineering, business, or the sciences. Humanities and the social sciences are shrinking; I do not celebrate those choices, but training students to be "spelunkers" or world travelers is going to involve a great deal more than simply assuming that all of academe moved toward one viewpoint in lockstep.

What Lilla derides as "aimless self-expression" (p. 104) was in part what the academy has long done—help students think through the question, "Who am I?" The answers to that question may not be what the communalists have wanted, but it is also not a rejection of what the twentieth-century university did. Lukianoff and Haidt also call for the rejection of what they term "emotional reasoning" (p. 259), and it is the same sort of focus that Lilla derides. Eggington (2018) gets to the heart of the matter by reminding us of Allan Bloom's *Closing of the American Mind*. "Education," Eggington writes, "has ceased to be the means by which our community transforms itself into a citizen" (p. 90). Bloom got it wrong, he contends. Campus liberals were not closing "the" mind of America's youth; we were "splintering into a thousand different individual selves, sorting into ever more specialized explorations of identity and into gated communities that could only see value in what would give those selves a competitive edge" (p. 90). His lament at least considers a larger society that has placed its own constraints and expectations on today's students.

I appreciate the concerns that the collectivists raise. We are in a tendentious time on our campuses. I entered academe as an assistant professor in 1986. I have never seen our campuses as fraught with conflict. A large part of the problem emanates not from within the institution but from external events. China's desire for more control over Hong Kong reverberated on campus and pushed faculty to call for a nonviolent protest. At the basis of that protest, again, were questions of "Who am I?" Are students unique in Hong Kong and distinct from mainland China? Or are they merely living in another Chinese city, the way we might think Chicago is not that different from Los Angeles? The rise of the Modi government in India created tension on campuses between what people could and could not say, or watch, or teach. The repression of texts and speech obviously are always context-based. One might suggest that Muslim students, or Dalits, or women, were being overly sensitive about their identities, that they should reject their fragility, but the attacks came about based on their identities.

Trump and his followers, perhaps more than any other individuals, have impacted American universities on several levels. Lukianoff and Haidt (2018) point out that students used to be the leading proponents of an expansive definition of academic freedom, but, in less than a decade, they have switched and now seek limits. The influx of speakers such as conservative provocateur Milo Yiannopoulos at UC Berkeley seemed aimed more at incitement and self-promotion than thoughtful debate, and campus activists pushed back. The past is also now a determinant of the present; if an administrator made a foolish mistake a generation ago and appeared in a high school yearbook in blackface or wearing a stupid costume that is insensitive, then their job today will be at risk. What one writes on Facebook—or tweets without the filter of waiting until morning to ensure whether the message should be sent or deleted—runs the risk of having a message go viral on one or another website. Such mistakes can cause a conflagration that could result in the loss of employment.

Perhaps the greatest impact has been on those of us on the academic frontlines who deal with students in the classroom and in our offices. The overwhelming majority of colleagues I have encountered always try to be respectful to one another and their students. However, in today's classroom, one can never be sure how to provoke thoughtful conversations on any number of topics. Even extraneous comments before or after class can be misinterpreted—perhaps not even by the recipient of the message, but someone else who walks by when a teacher is conferring with a student. The result is that faculty are now extremely careful about what they say and do. Caution, of course, is good and prudent, but if caution causes us to avoid conversations we think we should be having, then we are meeting the needs neither of the identity-based proponents nor those who desire a broader discussion. We need to step back and think through the kind of society we want and what that portends for the academic organization. Are we really correct that ultimately this is a forced choice, that we must focus either on identity or on community?

How We Got Here:
Reconsidering Critical Theory and Postmodernism

I have previously called for cultural citizenship in the academic community (Tierney, 1993). What I have portrayed up to now in this chapter is an "either-or" dichotomy. Either one focuses on singular (or intersectional) identities or one aims for the larger community. The assumption is that we cannot do both at once, and, by focusing on identity, we have given up on a communal focus. The risks are self-evident. A focus on identity excludes some individuals, just as it includes those who are of a particular identity. The result is that discussions and events are circumscribed by an identity-based ideology that suggests we have nothing in common with the other and, indeed, we cannot understand the "other" and certainly cannot speak for him/her/them.

    Such a point is particularly important for those of us concerned about enabling democracy to flourish. If we only hold self-encapsulated discussions framed by identity politics, then there is no concern about the larger community. If we eschew a concern for identity, then those of us on the historic margins will find ourselves resigned to the periphery. Populist notions of identity that drive fascism speak of the "other" as the problem, whether they are Muslims in India or in the United States. Identity politics in New Delhi and Los Angeles run the risk, however, of an absorption with the identity-location of particular groups rather than a concern for the larger issues that frame democracy. If there is no "I" in "we," then there is no point of conversations about what we want for society. Curiously, Hong Kongers seem to be concerned precisely with these issues: how do we enable all the people of Hong Kong to affirm their identity and devotion to democracy? China seeks not merely to stifle that voice but eliminate it in favor of an allegiance to the mainland.

The recent intellectual roots within the academy of a focus on identity pertain to critical theory, critical race theory in particular, and postmodernism. Although we make much less vocal use of the ideas of critical theory and postmodernism today than a generation ago when I started writing on the topic, the frameworks are what drive our current dilemma. Critical theory, with its origins in the 1920s and the Frankfurt School, seeks to understand the oppressive aspects of society in order to generate societal transformation. The assumption, in part, has been that structures existed, not in a rational and neutral manner, but in order to constrain individual emancipation and advance the power and privilege of the wealthy. Critical race theory moved these ideas further by pointing out that critical theory largely overlooked the cultural aspects of constraint, in general, and the racial aspects of individuals within these structures, in particular.

The work of Pierre Bourdieu (1986) has been useful in highlighting the cultural aspects of constraint. His ideas pertaining to cultural capital, social capital, habitus, and field help us in understanding how education functions and what it does to constrain individual mobility and liberation. Cultural capital, the intellectual accumulation of goods largely through the networks developed by social capital, frames a person's habitus. Although individuals have the ability to enjoy some mobility (similar individuals with the same social networks and capital accumulation may not have the same trajectories), the constraints provide for very little mobility. All this activity occurs on a field. Educational institutions comprise one of the primary fields of constraint. Bourdieu's overarching framework was good at enabling researchers to come to terms with the cultural aspects of oppression, but it was less helpful when understanding a course of action one may call upon to enable change.

Critical race theory focused explicitly on race, but its import extended in several directions, such as analyses of gender and sexual orientation. Simply put, critical race theory emphasized that constraints frequently were racialized in society in explicit and implicit ways. Analysts also viewed how the academy frequently overlooked race in its analyses, or they placed racial and ethnic minorities in a particular light, as if the work was objective when in reality it was not. The same sorts of work then developed about gender, sexual orientation, disability, and other key aspects that we frequently ascribe to identity.

As this work developed, one's stance, or standpoint, came in for analysis. If the object of study could not be neutral, then, of necessity, the individual doing the research also was not neutral. Such a stance was at odds with much of the reigning intellectual ideas of the twentieth century. Logical positivism had defined the scientific method and helped aid the rise of the modern American university. The assumption was that the scientific method, which can be verified by scholarly investigation, was true knowledge and could be expressed in logical form. Anything other than the ability of the scientist to prove "his" thesis within the confines of the antiseptic laboratory was simply an unverified assertion. Such a stance, naturally, assumed that the researcher was irrelevant. The reproduction of scientific tests mattered, not in terms of the identity of the individual, but in terms of the conditions of the experiment.

Critical theory, along with critical race theory, exposed theory as an ideological undertaking whereby the scientific method came in for criticism and, for many, rejection. Although the goals of one's research remained explanation and, to the extent possible, prediction, the larger issue was to explore and then expose how social and ideological systems have constrained human mobility and restrained individual freedom. Ideological constraints passed on from generation to generation were curiously also socially constructed in the moment. That is, each generation created ways to interpret the world. And yet, the structures of oppression remained, and would remain, without a critical understanding of how these structures functioned and were articulated in the larger society. Macroanalyses of societal constraints and microanalyses of how processes have limited human emancipation became central.

Postmodernism took things one step further. Not only was the scientific method rejected, but the ability to understand across boundaries became impossible. How one sees the world was intricately tied to the multiple identities of an individual. Hence, the process of attempting to understand across boundaries was a fool's errand. From a postmodern perspective, we will never be able to achieve agreement about the nature of either truth or oppression. The scientific method was discarded, but also eliminated was a critical stance that sought to understand the structural conditions of oppression. Neither rational logics nor the power of persuasion existed, and metanarratives about how the world functioned were not to be a goal of research, but instead interrogated and exposed.

The idea of difference became a central organizing topic. All signifiers were intellectual creations because the world was a solipsistic social construction that occurred within the identity of an individual and made sense to the person, but not necessarily to anyone else. Argumentation, in which the goal was to put forward one's ideas in the hopes of convincing someone else, became an impossibility because there was no foundation on which to ground one's analysis.

The result of these contradictory ideas, a generation after they took hold in the academy, have contributed to the tensions we currently face. I do not in any way blame those of us who put forward these concepts, because the ideas hold intellectual value in terms of how to think about the world and our role in it. And yet, when one argues that one cannot understand reality or that the only one who can make sense of that reality is the individual who operates within it, then we place academic life—and those of us within it—in a tenuous position.

Individuals operate from their subject positions and will interpret the world differently based on that position. If understanding cannot be gained across difference, then having White teachers teaching Black students or Asian American students learning from Latino faculty would be problematic. Even when we interrogate oppressive structures, cultures, or situations, we are fooling ourselves if we pivot from, for example, queer oppression to Black oppression. Oppressive structures function differently, and considering them all together is, at best, mistaken and, at worst, an assimilationist attempt to paper over differences when they should be accentuated. The postmodern "grand narrative" has been destroyed, and in its place is individual identity whereby we are cordoned off from one another in the academy and in society. One can reasonably make the claim that, with the rise of Black studies, queer studies, and the like, also have come those who promulgate White studies, or men's studies, in an attempt to claim their identity because it has been fractured. Now that it is under attack, what was once the structuring format of academic and societal culture is nothing better (or worse) than other identities. Of consequence is the rise of yet another focus on identity.

Developing a Community of Difference

What might be a way out of the dilemma? I have long thought that a central focus of academic life ought to be the exposure of conditions of power that lead to the subjugation of individuals, groups, and countries.

Thoughtful work can be done from a critical perspective that enables reflection about how to proceed and create the conditions for empowerment.

Postmodernism enables us to tie micropolitical processes with macropolitical structures and frameworks. Where we have erred is the assumption that not only is understanding across difference difficult, it is actually impossible. The individual, then, is both a subject and an object that gets expressed on a cultural terrain that is contested, redefined, and resisted. Thus, we have a degree of praxis that enables us to overcome the structural straitjacket that some see as impossible to remove. Praxis, however, is a strategic approach that optimally we can create in our academic institutions to create coordinated change. Rather than assume that understanding across difference is impossible and ought not even to be attempted, I am saying that if we are to get out of the current conditions in which we find ourselves, we must try. Academic work must, especially at this juncture, seek a greater relationship with society. We need to help point a way out of our current dilemmas, rather than simply bemoan or, worse, exacerbate them.

Herbert Gans (2002) has eloquently noted what I see as the work ahead:

> Public intellectuals (i.e., the scholars, critics, and others who speak to the general public on topical matters in which the public may or should be interested) play a crucial role in modern society. They are not only a bridge between intellectuals, academics, and the rest of society, but they also offer society at least a sampling of intellectual commentary on issues of the day. (para. 1)

The public intellectual is vitally important not only for the larger public, but also at home on campus. The culture of the academic institution is a site of production and contestation; we should not bemoan our fate, but instead should welcome it. Where we fail is not when we engage in difficult dialogues, but instead when we reject them, or sidestep them to avoid controversy. I appreciate wanting to dodge tough conversations. Who wants to hurt others, or to put oneself in harm's way? However, we have to be involved in a dialectical relationship with one another not simply to be a public intellectual concerned about the welfare of society, but also in order to become what I have termed elsewhere a "culture citizen" (Tierney, 1993, p. 141).

From this perspective, academic life is contested terrain that, of necessity, involves a politics of difference and coalition building. Rather than assume either that we can speak for other identities or that understanding across difference is impossible, we seek to honor identities that are different from our own. Identities are respected, not by assuming we can amalgamate differences, but by engaging in dialogues of respect and understanding. I am not interested in enabling one group to speak by silencing others or assuming that if I speak for you, then all is right with you. Rather, we need to begin from a position of misunderstanding and not take for granted difference.

It warrants repeating that the ideological crises that I raised in Chapter 2—hegemony, legitimacy, and autonomy—were justified concerns. The attacks on the university had a degree of legitimacy, and if we are to be more involved in bolstering democracy, we need to forthrightly deal with these issues. We cannot go back and try to reassert academic dominance. We can, however, accept difference as an organizing framework for the institution and be the organizing entity for enabling difficult dialogues. We can be better at pointing out fact from fiction and at admitting when we do not know. We can improve community relations so that the borders between academe and society are broken down. Legitimacy does not have to come through authority or mystification.

I am not offering a panacea, and I do not see what I am suggesting as a middle ground—as if we need to meet identity somewhere in between a radical, postmodern construction and an assimilationist, communal one. Rather, we need to create new intellectual geography that enables us to acknowledge that we need an organizing framework that brings us together in our differences. William Eggington (2018) notes, "If we are to solve the catastrophes facing the world today—from the rise of fundamentalism to the rise of the seas—we can only do so by learning to come together as a community of equals" (p. 224). I do not think that by calling for the reinvention of civic community we need to reject the critical work on identity that has taken place over the last generation. We simply do not need to remain wedded to versions of identity that reject at least trying to converse across differences.

Indeed, that has to be the work of the university. It was what we have tried to do, in half steps, with considerable failure but also some degree of success, over the past century. As I mentioned earlier, Dalits are more involved in Indian higher education today than ever before. Hong Kong has been a site for discussing the challenges that exist with forging a new relationship and identity with China. Los Angeles is ground zero for trying to work through how we think of American citizenship and the rights and responsibilities we all have not only to ourselves, but to one another. The question turns then on what the role of the university should be if we seek to build what I have been calling a community of difference. What should be the organizing concept on which we construct the idea of the university?

CHAPTER FOUR

Understanding Academic Freedom and Free Speech on Campus

What Counts as Knowledge

Heretics have always been with us. I will discuss in detail in a subsequent chapter the role of the university in advancing knowledge, but I recognize the role academic freedom has played, or can play, in analyzing the heresy. Galileo used his telescope to posit that Copernicus was right and the earth and other planets revolved around the sun. Galileo's initial steps toward building a scientific method brought him into the crosshairs of a church founded on belief rather than empiricism. By the seventeenth century, a great many individuals had been martyred for their beliefs. The Inquisition found Galileo to be a heretic in 1633, and he died in 1642 under house arrest. One believed doctrine, tautologically, because it was doctrine. To raise questions about one doctrine brought into question the underlying structure of the church. An argument can be made that Galileo's work set the stage for the university's role in determining truth that was not necessarily founded on belief.

We have moved far afield from institutions such as the University of Pisa, where Galileo attended and taught. The university began in 1343 as a secular, public university. Professors taught the common courses of the time—theology, law, medicine. The scientific method, which Galileo and his colleagues were beginning to invent, did not have a place in the university. When the church held the trial and found him to be suspiciously like a heretic, no one in the university came to his defense. No one said that his academic freedom was at risk or that he should be protected. His colleagues had no institutional support to enable them to speak their minds. Why would someone risk his job for a heretic?

Perhaps there were those at the University of Pisa who felt like those in Hong Kong today. Perhaps there were those who quietly supported Galileo and his ideas, just as in Hong Kong there are those who supported Professors Benny Tai and Chan Kin-Man in the Umbrella movement, and others who support protests against the National Security Law today. Galileo's quiet colleagues did not want to risk having troubles of their own if they came out to support him. Or perhaps they were like faculty in India today, who defer to the government about what can and cannot be taught or investigated. Rather than the university as the arbiter of knowledge, it is the government and church that decide. Or perhaps they were more like my colleagues in the United States who do not wish to make a misstep and be accused of upsetting their students or confreres, so they simply stayed quiet as Galileo faced his persecutors.

The challenge then, as now, is how to adjudicate whether an assertion is at least fallacious, if not heretical. In Galileo's time they would not have thought so, but the task was relatively easy. Was the accused heretic guilty of going against scripture? With Galileo's assertions, the church hierarchy certainly thought so and the matter was put to rest. It took the Roman Catholic Church 350 years to admit it had made a mistake. The conflict between reason and dogma, science and faith, is one of the great exemplars of why society needs universities as arbiters of knowledge proclamations—and not governments or religions. Because individuals believe something does not make it so.

Yet how does society distinguish between heresy and truth, between fake facts and real ones? Those of us in a democratic nation have made the decision, over time, that clarifying truth and belief is critical for making sense of, and improving, the world. We have acknowledged that much, but not all, of what one does as a job depends on prior knowledge that needs to be incorporated into one's skill set, and not belief. We also have made the complex case that belief can comfortably coexist with scientific truths. Concomitantly, we have argued that an understanding and appreciation of beauty is of merit.

The assumption is that there are truths about which the scientific method will be the arbiter. The scientific method, however, cannot teach us about beauty or immortal truths. We have the humanities to help us think through such matters. The professional schools equip us with skill sets that inform our work.

Academic freedom and free speech touch on all these matters within the university. For example, abortion and homosexuality are extremely controversial topics, about which one's beliefs and science can collide, rather than overlap. Debates about these issues are contentious and frequently end in a stalemate with neither side believing the other. And yet, at least we ought to be able to discuss the matters. In Galileo's day, discussion was not possible—an Inquisition was.

We also need to recognize that academic freedom and free speech also speak to issues of power. For Galileo, the speaker lacked power to define reality and was punished for it. In the twenty-first century, we also have individuals who are powerful enough to define reality. As I will elaborate, for some individuals their claims of trigger warnings and microaggressions have to do with the power to define classrooms, academic institutions, and identity. When we only look to the legal parameters of speech, we too often overlook the motivations of speakers and ignore the power relations that are at work. Hence, while I tend to have an expansive interpretation of permissible speech, I also cannot ignore those power dynamics that are at work, and need to empathize with those who feel, and often are, attacked. And empathy cannot simply be a feeling; we have to create the conditions in the classroom and on our campuses that enable people to learn. When someone is marginalized and we fall back on the easy assertion that speech is preeminent, we fail to meet our pedagogical responsibility.

Universities serve a role, not merely as a means to enable us to come to decisions about contentious issues, but as a forum for discussing these issues. The atmosphere ought to be different on a campus than in a courtroom. Issues are decided in a courtroom as well, but there the "evidence" is based on the accumulation of facts that is void of experimentation and communication. Academics are more discursive; we have learned over time that our discursiveness needs to have two kinds of freedom—free speech in some instances and academic freedom in others.

The social role of the university has been that of arbiter in a manner related, but distinct from that of a courtroom. The legal process determines right from wrong and, if someone is guilty, what the penalty is to be. A democratic nation in part bases itself on the assumption that every citizen can weigh evidence and come to a decision about a person charged with a crime. A jury of one's peers is a legal cornerstone, and another cornerstone is the belief that experts are able to judiciously interpret the law for us based on their impartiality in order to render an opinion.

The university, especially the modern university, has had a distinction made about the import of knowledge. That is, academic freedom arises because society is saying that a democratic society needs a neutral forum where ideas can be battled out to determine what to believe. The jury of one's peers pertains to academic peers. The concept of peer review, at the university, in our publications, presentations, and determinations about tenure, ostensibly is about the worth of one's findings.

If we were to eliminate academic freedom, and to go further and state that an extreme form of free speech should occur within the university, what might be the consequences? We would lose the goal of trying to gain knowledge through neutrality and objectivity. I certainly appreciate the knee-jerk response that research is not value-free, and a great deal of evidence exists about how research has either misrepresented or overlooked crucial information, especially about those of us who have historically been on the margins. The failures of value-neutral research ought not reject the goal of undertaking such work. That is, what we have attempted to do with an overriding ethos of academic freedom is try to come to terms with phenomena in a way that Galileo attempted but was not allowed to do.

When we eliminate academic freedom either by fiat or fear—one by legislative decision and the other by academics unable or unwilling to defend their colleagues—we lose a key principle of the modern democratic state. Without the modern university and its challenges to live up to its fealty to academic freedom, one key component of democracy is eliminated. I am not sure what we see as its counterpart—other than the ability to decide what we want to decide based on belief rather than evidence. Thus we return to the time before Galileo.

An extreme version of free speech also moves us in the opposite direction of what we have come to think of as a bulwark of democracy. Free speech on a campus has never been framed to mean that one should be able to blurt out whatever he or she wants. If the organization ostensibly is after truth, then those who fabricate ideas or develop conspiracies are in another arena. Even on social media, we are seeing limits placed on hate speech. Again, I am putting forward only those sorts of ideas that once were confined to those who said the Holocaust didn't happen. Today we have many more such notions that strain credulity and have no place in a higher place of learning.

The modern university has played a critical role in the advancement of the democratic state. I am neither glorifying nor romanticizing such a role. I am fully aware of the shortcomings and failures that universities have played. These failures have little to do with academic freedom or free speech. Indeed, they usually occur, over the last hundred years, when the faculty have not lived up to the values that we have espoused. The faculty's silence in the United States during the Joseph McCarthy era, when the state made ridiculous charges against their colleagues, is but one example. Clearly, our foot dragging on enabling equal rights for women and people of color is the most obvious example of academe not living up to its espoused values. Similarly, Black Lives Matter on campuses is not some rogue group in search of special rights; it exists to highlight the inequities Blacks face on campus, and to propose solutions.

The ability to categorize all these failures, however, ought not over-look the successes that have been made or the realization that the failures are not because of our fealty to academic freedom and free speech. Our challenge, then, is not to look the other way as attacks on central values are made, but to think through how we might be more straightforward in espousing what we believe and how we intend to safeguard those beliefs. In what follows, I offer various ways that issues of academic freedom and free speech arise on campus and how we might think about them.

Academic Freedom in Context

In 1947, for a convocation address at an Indian university, Jawaharlal Nehru stated, "A university stands for humanism, for tolerance, for reason, for the adventure of ideas and for the search of truth. It stands for the onward march of the human race towards even higher objectives. If the universities discharge their duties adequately, then it is well with the nation and the people" (Madani, 2019, p. 1). Nehru's assumption was that a fundamental component of academic life was the search for truth, and that such a search benefited society. At the heart of that search for truth has been the ideal of academic freedom.

The modern conception of academic freedom is largely thought of as originating in the beginning of the twentieth century in the United States, although its roots go back to the German university and Immanuel Kant's conception of knowledge. American professors, many of whom had received doctoral training in Germany or the United Kingdom, returned to the United States in the late nineteenth century to participate in the great expansion of the modern research university (Rudolph, 1962). Cornell, Johns Hopkins, and a pantheon of other institutions wanted professors, not merely to teach students, but also to conduct research that would be of intellectual merit. Teaching was not to be focused on memorization of received wisdom; instead, learning was about the search for truth. One institution of immediate acclaim was Stanford University, founded by Leland and Jane Stanford in memory of their son, Leland Jr., who died of typhoid fever. The university admitted its first students in 1891.

The Stanfords intended for their university to be an institution where the intellect was revered and the search for truth was paramount. They found their man to lead the institution in David Starr Jordan. Jordan came from the University of Indiana and was widely regarded as a thoughtful public intellectual. He defended the right of the faculty to give voice to the wide spectrum of ideas, and he wanted students to grapple with their education rather than simply receive rote lessons from a disengaged faculty. Governor Stanford supported Jordan's conception of faculty by saying, "I wish to leave you entirely free in your selection of professors. I cannot advise you. Must exercise your own judgment as to forces needed" (Elliott, 1937, p. 326).

As the first president of Stanford, David Starr Jordan set about hiring those faculty who would help put Stanford on the intellectual map and mirrored his views about knowledge production, teaching, and learning. Stanford was to be the Harvard of the West; it had the revenue to build a dynamic campus, and Jordan had the intellectual firepower to hire professorial heavyweights. One of those heavyweights was Edward Ross, a liberal economist. Jordan hired Ross in 1893. They knew of one another from their time together in Indiana. Jordan and Ross were ambitious scholars who worked to enable the young university to rise to prominence. They both were liberals, although Ross was a socialist and Jordan was not, and they also shared a belief quite common among many educated Californians—eugenics.

In 1901, a series of events occurred that gave rise to the idea of academic freedom. Former governor and senator Leland Stanford died. His wife, Jane Stanford, was the sole trustee on Stanford's board. Today Edward Ross would be considered a public intellectual. He wrote scholarly articles and also spoke in public settings, and he published articles and op-eds in the popular press. He was secretary of the fledgling American Economic Association (AEA), and, as a Progressive, an avowed advocate for the working man.

Joan Wallach Scott (2019), an ardent historian of academic freedom, writes that "Ross quickly incurred the wrath of the founder's widow by supporting socialist Eugene Debs, advocating municipal ownership of utilities, calling for an end to Chinese immigration, and defending the free silver platform of the Democratic party" (p. 43). Apparently, according to Scott and others (such as Hofstadter & Metzger, 1955; Mohr, 1970; Veysey, 1965), Jane Stanford was incensed by Ross's writing and attacks on her husband and called for Ross's dismissal. In 1900, Jordan finally fired him. Seven additional faculty members resigned in protest. The AEA undertook an investigation of the incident and decided that a professor's academic freedom had been violated. The result was the creation of the American Association of University Professors (AAUP) by John Dewey and Arthur Lovejoy, one of Ross's colleagues at Stanford who had resigned in protest.

The case has all the ingredients of a good melodrama. A poor professor speaks out on the rights of workers; the eccentric wife of a railroad baron demands his dismissal. A craven president accedes to the power of the wealthy board of trustees. The result is the birth of an organization that protects faculty rights; the faculty, in turn, fight for the common person.

Melodrama may be good for afternoon TV, but it is not good for intellectual engagement. By way of historical analysis, I offer a different interpretation of the Ross case that is more complex, yet critically important for the problems that confront us today. To be sure, Jane Stanford's initial problems with Ross began in 1896 when Ross worked actively for William Jennings Bryan and the free coinage of silver, as well as for the socialist Eugene Debs. Ross's speeches on behalf of Bryan and Debs sparked a debate that has yet to be settled. At what point do the public utterances of a professor need to be separated from the identification of an individual's profession? "No one has the right to speak for the University in any matter of opinion," wrote Jordan, "but each man as a private citizen is perfectly free to take any stand in politics he may choose" (Elliott, 1937, p. 336). Ross, however, seemed to be speaking, not as a private citizen, but as a Stanford professor. Nevertheless, Ross was neither sanctioned nor penalized for his work on behalf of the presidential candidate, and he remained at Stanford. He was a popular teacher, well respected by his peers, and seen as an intellectual giant.

I disagree, however, with the suggestion that what led to Ross's firing were his views on economic reform. The real issue that led to Ross's dismissal pertained to his racial views, which Jordan shared. Although Ross was definitely on the side of labor and a socialist, he was also a eugenicist, like his friend David Starr Jordan. At the time, eugenics was a popular idea in California and on its campuses. Eugenics is the discredited idea that certain genetic groups are inferior to others, and, in order to maintain the quality of superior races, inferior genetic groups needed to be excluded by any means necessary. "The theory that races are virtually equal in capacity," wrote Ross, "leads to such monumental follies as lining the valleys of the South with the bones of half a million picked whites in order to improve the condition of four million unpicked blacks" (Menand, 2001, p. 383).

On May 7, 1900, here is part of what he said that led to Jane Stanford calling for his dismissal:

> The Oriental can elbow the American to one side in the common occupations because he has fewer wants. To let this go on, to let the American be driven by coolie competition, to check the American birthrate in order that the Japanese birthrate shall not be checked . . . is to reverse the current of progress, to commit race suicide. . . . We are resolutely determined that California, this latest and loveliest seat of the Aryan race, shall not become, if we can help it, the theater of such a stern, wolfish struggle for existence as prevails throughout the Orient. (Ross, 1900)

Jane Stanford read the speech in the newspaper and then wrote to President Jordan: "I am grieved to the depths of my heart. . . . This movement . . . is but a repetition of the old prejudice against the Chinese, and a repetition of "Kearneyism" when a reign of terror pervaded our city. . . . The teaching of violence is inconsistent with the Founding Grant" (Bromberg, 1996, p. 116). "Kearneyism" was named after a popular orator and nativist California labor leader who consistently spoke on behalf of removing Chinese and Japanese laborers from American shores. Ross followed Kearney's line about the dangers of immigration and the threats to the purity of the Aryan race. They had a significant following, and Ross gave an academic patina to an otherwise horribly flawed intellectual argument.

Although many can rightfully claim that Jane Stanford tried to run the university as a matriarchy, Stanford was also coeducational when many institutions were not, and the university welcomed students from various social classes and racial and ethnic groups when other colleges remained rigidly White and mostly upper class. The founding class had 15 nationalities. In 1891, students protested that they did not want Chinese and Japanese workers in the dorms because the food would be contaminated. Jane Stanford rejected the students' complaint as vulgar and uninformed.

Ross, however, argued against letting in, in his words, "coolies." He tried to demonstrate scientifically the supremacy of the White race and did not want them to contaminate Stanford's students.

My purpose in going back to the roots of academic freedom is to consider two questions: How has academic freedom traditionally been defined? And how does that definition hold up today? I am not trying to create an alternative melodrama in which a valiant old lady stands against an unscrupulous mob. And yet, when I read Ross's statements and writings, I equally reject the heroic portrait of a professor who used eloquent words in defense of the working class and therefore needed the protection of academic freedom. If Ross used those words on a campus today—and, unfortunately, they could still be used—many of us would define that language as hate speech. A eugenicist certainly could not be hired as a professor at a research university today, much less be appointed as its president. Certain ideas are not simply out of fashion, but entirely discredited. We do a disservice to the idea of academic freedom, however, when we mistake the concept for the ability of individuals to blurt out whatever they like on a campus.

Academic freedom refers to the freedom of the professor to search for truth in and outside the classroom. For over a century, those of us in higher education have largely supported the idea that universities need academic freedom for excellence. In order for it to be supported, the structure of tenure exists so that someone will not be dismissed simply because of their controversial views. Academic freedom endures because individuals continue to have such views. If everyone agreed with what a professor had to say, then there would be no need for academic freedom. However, when an individual speaks out in ways that may be discomforting to the administration or external audiences such as legislators or politicians, then the import of academic freedom becomes evident. Thus, if a professor is speaking on behalf of the workers and a trustee takes offense, then the workers have been supported by the system put in place to protect academic freedom. Today, Ross's words still would require the protection that tenure provides to ensure that academic freedom exists. However, many people would question his language and wonder if he should be protected. What are the limits of academic freedom in the twenty-first century? Are there ideas or language so noxious that an individual should not be able to think or utter them in the confines of the academy?

In the classroom and in one's research, the idea has revolved around scholarly judgment. Academics debate ideas in their search for truth and ultimately determine which ideas have merit. The assumption is that those who are versed in a topic are the best judges of what counts as knowledge and what should be taught in the classroom. One might have hard-fought debates within a disciplinary paradigm, but the idea is that scholarly arguments determine the worth of an idea; what gets discussed in a classroom is not voted on in order to determine right from wrong.

The second important aspect of academic freedom is that the professor is able to speak on any number of topics while on campus as a professor. I might not be versed in the scientific values of vaccines, for example, so it might be a mistake to claim academic freedom to teach whatever I want about the matter in an accounting class. I could, however, sponsor a talk on campus that addressed the issue with regard to the recent pandemic, even if the topic were controversial and the ideas were not within my specialized realm of knowledge. I could host a discussion by someone who is an "anti-vaxxer" or by someone who adheres to the scientific literature on vaccines.

Academic freedom is also an organizational right for individuals. As I will elaborate, the framework is distinct from my First Amendment rights. I have the right to speak on controversial topics as a citizen in public settings. When I employ academic freedom, however, I am not calling on rights as a citizen, but as a professor. The argument has been made that society is stronger when we have a group of individuals involved in the search for truth, and that search needs to be unhindered. Hence, academic freedom gives the academic the right to search for truth wherever it may be, and tenure is the structure that supports the search.

But what of today? How do we think about academic freedom at a time when the social context in which higher education exists has changed and attacks on truth and facts occur on a daily basis?

Hong Kong and the Threat to Academic Freedom

In late 2014, two professors, Benny Tai Yiu-ting and Chan Kin-man, and a Baptist minister, Chu Yiu-ming, called for a peaceful demonstration to protest the lack of democracy in Hong Kong. This act of civil disobedience, which paralyzed downtown Hong Kong for 80 days and came to be known as the "Umbrella movement," was a call for more democracy as China began to assert its dominance over the former British colony. The goal to "Occupy Central with Love and Peace" attracted thousands of supporters, many of them university students. Any movement will include diverse interests, and presumably the goals of the students were not identical with those of the initial organizers, but the overall objective of creating a greater democratic voice is what united everyone.

The Chinese government did not accede to any of the demands, and the protesters eventually went home until an organic protest began anew in 2019. Since that time, the mainland Chinese government has asserted greater control over Hong Kong, and hopes for more democratic engagement by the citizenry faded until 2019. In fall 2018, a trial began for Tai, Chan, and seven others charged with conspiring to cause a public nuisance. In spring 2019, they were found guilty and went to prison for periods of up to 16 months in a maximum-security prison (May, 2019). Chan Kin-man retired from his university when he went to prison. Benny Tai, a tenured professor of law at the University of Hong Kong, lost his job when he was released from prison. The board, with the compliance of the institution's leadership, fired Tai for speaking out on behalf of democracy. Some of the faculty signed a letter of protest, but it came to nothing.

Shortly after these nine leaders went to prison, events escalated. The extradition bill that China wanted provoked protests by thousands, then hundreds of thousands, and ultimately millions of Hong Kongers (Wu, Lai, & Yuhas, 2019). To Beijing's surprise, democratic candidates swept an election in which 7 in 10 eligible voters cast a ballot (Bradsher et al., 2019). Students led the protests, and campuses became flashpoints for demonstrations (Silver, 2019). Classes were canceled, and any semblance of normalcy either for the island or the universities evaporated. No one could have predicted these events, and the actual outcome is still unclear, although the Chinese government seems intent on ending the special status that Hong Kong has had. The idea of "one country, two systems," appears dead. Hundreds of thousands of Hong Kongers continued to jam the streets on weekends and demand that their voices be heard, even through the 2020 coronavirus outbreak, but such protests have faded. In fact, anger about the Hong Kong government's perceived reticence to close the border with China in response to the coronavirus outbreak has caused some Hong Kong residents who were previously pro-China to support the protesters (Pinchin, 2020). Then, in 2020, during the midst of the pandemic, Chinese president Xi introduced legislation that passed without opposition, eliminating the idea that Hong Kong could govern itself in a manner different from the mainland. Carrie Lam, the hand-picked chief executive of Hong Kong (akin to the post of mayor), immediately backed the legislation, as did a majority of the presidents of the island's universities. Students and citizens protested, but it was a fait accompli. One implication is that academic freedom in Hong Kong is now dead.

Neither Tai nor Chan, who were associate professors at the University of Hong Kong and the Chinese University of Hong Kong, respectively, received strong support from their institutions. Their actions would be sanctioned even more severely today. Indeed, they would be arrested and imprisoned if they dared to speak out on behalf of democracy. Moreover, throughout the protests, the universities were not seen as places where discussions could be held or as think tanks for reform. Tai and Chan were faculty in good standing at their universities, yet no one spoke up on their campuses. The silence was especially troubling because the leaders of these universities had chosen to speak out on other issues. In 2017, the vice chancellors of 10 universities in Hong Kong issued a statement condemning slogans on student message boards calling for independence from the mainland (Grundy, 2017). And yet, these same vice chancellors stayed silent about Tai and Chan, saying nothing about the rights of faculty to speak out on crucial issues of the day by calling for nonviolent protest. The boards of trustees of the professors' institutions said nothing when they were imprisoned, and HKU's board fired Tai after he was released. The faculty said virtually nothing. Professorial associations from across the island said nothing. One need not be surprised, then, that when President Xi put forward his legislation in 2020, the universities were not sites of resistance led by their boards, presidents, or faculty.

When the protests began in 2019, the universities were involved peripherally; students may have met to organize for a protest, but the university was not a center of action. Because of the central involvement of students, however, universities soon became targets, both as protection for the students and as locations to monitor by the police. On November 12, 2019, police arrested several students on the campus of the Chinese University of Hong Kong, claiming that the campus was being used as a "weapons factory" (Smith & Lamb, 2019). In response, student protesters barricaded the main bridge to campus with bricks, tables, chairs, and other pieces of furniture. They also prepared gasoline bombs and flaming arrows, while setting up a makeshift medical center in an athletic building near the university track. The resulting conflict between riot police and student protesters, in which no fewer than 70 students were injured, would become known as the "Battle of CUHK." Hong Kong police would later report that they shot 1,567 canisters of tear gas, 1,312 rubber bullets, 380 bean bags, and 126 sponge-tipped rounds in a futile effort to reenter the Chinese University campus (Cheng, 2019; Chung et al., 2019).

Five days later, on November 17, a new battle between police and student protesters flared up under similar circumstances at the Hong Kong Polytechnic University. The scale of the battle at Hong Kong Polytechnic was shockingly even greater. Within two days, Hong Kong hospitals were overwhelmed, as approximately 200 people were being treated for various injuries suffered on the Polytechnic campus (Leung et al., 2019). The chief editor of the *Global Times*, a state-run newspaper located in Beijing, called for the police to use live ammunition on the student protesters (Wong et al., 2019). By November 20, approximately 1,100 individuals had been arrested and charged with a variety of crimes, including suspicion of rioting and possession of a weapon (Napolitano, 2019; Yu et al., 2019).

Chan and Kerr (2016) have succinctly stated, "Academic freedom in Hong Kong is under real threat" (p. 9). Most observers of higher education in Hong Kong will point out that these threats began with the handover of Hong Kong to China in 1997, and that attacks on academic freedom have less to do with what occurs in countries such as the United States and the United Kingdom and more to do with universities in countries with oppressive regimes. The attacks on academic freedom in Hong Kong have gone on for two decades.

In 2000, for example, Robert Chung, an academic at the University of Hong Kong who did opinion polling research, displeased the chief executive of Hong Kong by tracking the politician's declining popularity. The chief executive, in turn, pressured the vice chancellor of the University of Hong Kong to tell Chung to stop polling. A brouhaha ensued, which Chung ultimately won, but the stage had been set (Petersen & Currie, 2008). From 2000 until the call to Occupy Central, other attacks on academic freedom occurred (Chan & Kerr, 2016), and faculty gradually got the message that public utterances jeopardized one's job. The breaking point appears to have been the very public call for greater democracy and the resultant actions. Since the beginning of the Umbrella movement, professors have been told to monitor their comments both in and out of class. Students also have been imprisoned for their advocacy of independence from China.

Prior to the protests of 2019, academics in Hong Kong believed they were learning a dual lesson: speaking out accomplishes nothing, and such talk endangers one's career as well as liberty. When Hong Kong became part of China, no one was entirely sure what "one country, two systems" actually entailed in practical, day-to-day terms—either for the city or its universities. Over time, however, the implications have become clear, and the citizens have finally risen up in protest. Those who seek autonomy for the island from China will face harassment, perhaps imprisonment, or they may even disappear, as was the fate of some booksellers in Hong Kong (Palmer, 2018). As of 2019, however, massive protests have raised questions about the future. Very few people seriously believe that Hong Kong could be independent, but its relationship to China had been in question. Since the handover, many believed in the phrase, "one country, two systems." Presently, however, at the universities, faculty assume that those students from the mainland who are in their classes will inform on them if they criticize China. A conference that might discuss the independence or increased autonomy of the city will not be countenanced. Prior to 2019, discussion even among one's colleagues needed to be carefully framed in terms of what one can and cannot say. After the legislation's passage in 2020, those discussions would not even be countenanced.

"We practice self-censorship," one young academic told me prior to the protests of 2019. "We know nothing will change, so why risk speaking out?" said another. Others confessed they feared losing their jobs if they spoke in support of their colleagues. Since passage of the new legislation in 2020, many have taken themselves off social media and deleted their virtual private network (VPN) accounts. The prosecution of nonviolent protesters is not simply an effort to try an individual for a crime. The bigger message is that individuals ought not to speak out, because if they do, they will face a lengthy trial and possibly jail. Some individuals who have employed academic freedom in speaking out have been removed from their posts; others have not been promoted or encouraged to retire early. The coercion and attempts to silence people finally became unbearable and led to the massive, weekly protests of 2019. The outcome is quite unclear.

For example, Chin Wan-kan is a former assistant professor of Chinese at Lingnan University. He published a book entitled *On the Hong Kong City-State* in 2011, and he has been outspoken in his support of autonomy for Hong Kong. After the Umbrella movement protests in 2014, the president of Lingnan University advised him to change his ways because his work brought dishonor to the university. In 2016, his contract was not renewed. Most doubt that such an act would occur today because of the protests that would ensue. But no one is really sure what would happen because the demonstrations have been huge and protesters appear unwilling to give up.

The past, however, provided clear examples to individuals about how they should act. In 2014, a search committee recommended to the vice chancellor that he appoint Johannes Chan, a well-respected former dean of the law school, to be pro-vice chancellor for human resources. In an extraordinary measure that was a key factor in the vice chancellor resigning his post before the end of his term, the board turned down the request. Over 300 articles had been published against Professor Chan in the media by agents of China. Chan had supported Professor Tai when he talked about the importance of democracy in Hong Kong. Chan subsequently went up for an extension to his retirement age, which is ordinarily approved for an individual of his stature; the request was denied.

The governance of universities also has become politicized. At one point, the governing board was a largely ceremonial post, and senior administrators and the faculty oversaw the activities and strategic plans of the institutions. The chair of the council had been the governor of the city, and when the handover occurred, the chair became the chief executive of Hong Kong. Although part of the Occupy movement pertained to the direct election of the chief executive, nothing has happened. The chief executive largely remains a position appointed by the Chinese government, even though the individual is actually "elected" by a small circle of approximately 1,200 individuals. The protesters want direct elections, and presumably a greater say in who serves on the universities' boards.

Over the last decade, however, the appointment of members to the boards of the universities has become increasingly politicized. The council chairperson, who is beholden to China, has become much more involved in the decisions of the universities. The council now makes decisions, whereas similar decisions were rubber-stamped in the past, and they put forward their own agendas, which are largely supportive of China and frequently at odds with those of the faculty. It is not far-fetched to believe that some sort of change is in the offing. Equally plausible is a crackdown by the Chinese government that makes even the mildest of protests impossible.

Observers often point out that even though Hong Kong's academics have seen their freedoms restricted over the last decade, they still have much more autonomy than their peers in China—until passage of the legislation of 2020. The observers have made a good point; however, in a report about academic freedom in Hong Kong, Kevin Corrico (2018) stated, "These trends suggest that elements of academic control in place elsewhere in China are gradually being incorporated into the Hong Kong system, threatening the city's academic freedom and thus its universities' reputations" (p. 1). Many observers, however, note that global rankings do not consider ideas such as academic freedom. The result is that China does not factor academic freedom into its overall assessment of academic quality—and even finds it irrelevant, as well as contradictory, to what the country actually wants to achieve.

The challenge is in determining where one looks for guidance. In the People's Republic of China, academics have very little academic freedom, so one assumes the recent legislation will erode academic freedom in Hong Kong. Criticism of the Communist Party remains a punishable offense, and there are various topics that have been deemed "sensitive" and off-limits for academic inquiry. Some journals that are deemed political have been banned, and individuals practice self-censorship.

Hong Kong, however, had been ruled by the United Kingdom. Its version of academic freedom, prior to the handover, was closer to that of the United States. Scholars had been free to criticize the government and investigate topics on any issue that they desired. In 1997, Hong Kong became part of China after lengthy discussions and debates around what has come to be known as the "Basic Law." Articles 34 and 137 state that "Hong Kong residents shall have freedom to engage in academic research, literary and artistic creation, and other cultural activities" and "educational institutions of all kinds may retain their autonomy and enjoy academic freedom." Such statements seem to make clear that academic freedom will be respected. However, the interpreters of the Basic Law have the power to interpret the document however they see fit. The result is that academic freedom is defined in a manner that is in keeping with China's version of the ability to conduct research, and at odds with how John Dewey and his colleagues initially defined the term.

To say Hong Kong is in flux is an understatement. What used to be considered the norms of academic freedom were increasingly overridden, criticized, or at least internalized in a way that suggested to academics that they should keep still. In an interesting article, Chan, Tang, and Cheung (in press) wrote:

> A "new normal" appears to emerge in terms of the professional practices of Hong Kong's academics. Problematically, participations in civic and social movements, especially those not in line with the government and national agenda, are judged as unprofessional and going beyond their professional duties [with] regard to research and teaching. . . . [Now], new

governing practices seem to be normalized, having not taken any resistance and protests into account. Their voices being unheard, busy Hong Kong's academics start to adapt to the new normal and see many kinds of resistance to the powerful as futile endeavors. While the role of academics as public intellectuals is under siege, there is also polarization in view of issues which are easily taken in the dichotomy of pro-democracy verses pro-establishment/national interests. Universities fail to function as a place where the truth is pursued, deliberated, and defended.

The sobering analysis suggests that the future of academic freedom is up for grabs, and the opponents of faculty being able to undertake work wherever they see fit are poised to impose their will on academic life. Ironically, I might point out that as of this writing, these authors remain free to express their opinions. At what point, however, does such work destroy academic careers and, by inference, the quality of autonomous universities in Hong Kong? In part, this is what the struggles in the streets have been trying to address.

New Delhi: Kashmir, Texts, and Movies and the Undermining of Academic Freedom

In winter 2016, a cultural program was held on the campus of Jawaharlal Nehru University (JNU) in the heart of New Delhi. JNU, which is largely a graduate institution and has 8,000 students, is thought of as one of India's best institutions. The faculty and students have the reputation of being politically progressive and vocal in opposition to the current government of Narendra Modi. There is also a vocal minority of students who are members of Akhil Bharatiya Vidyarthi Parishad (ABVP), a conservative organization closely allied with the Rashtriya Swayamsevak Sangh (RSS), another ultraconservative group.

The event was organized by the Democratic Student Union and initially approved by the administration. The ABVP protested, however, whereupon the administration canceled the event. The students nevertheless went ahead with what they defined as a cultural program. The program's purpose was to commemorate, through poetry, music, and art, the death of Afzal Guru, the terrorist convicted of bombing the Indian parliament in 2001. The organizers also talked about the ongoing struggles in Kashmir, the rights of the people in the region, and the importance of self-determination. Kanhaiya Kumar, the president of the Student Union, attended the event in support.

Three days after the event, the vice chancellor let the police enter the campus and arrest Kanhaiya Kumar for sedition. Many in the country believed that speakers crossed a line by talking about Kashmir in a manner that suggested independence. In the ensuing years, as the situation in Kashmir has grown more fraught and the government more conservative, what one says and does on campuses has become more circumscribed.

The actions on and off campus about Kashmir had been front-page news for months. Those on the right condemned the protest. The Home Minister of India stated, "If anyone raises anti-India slogans, tries to raise questions on the country's unity and integrity, they will not be spared" (Rook-Koepsel, 2019, chap. 5). Some people argued for violence against anyone who spoke against the country; others said the university should be shut down—that such events should never be allowed at a public university. The High Court judge who granted bail to Kanhaiya said that "the entire JNU campus suffers from some unpatriotic and anti-national infestation that requires cleansing through pro-active policing" (Tierney & Sabharwal, 2016, p. 15). Others suggested that Kanhaiya's arrest and the ensuing outcry are yet another attack on academic freedom.

India is a democracy, but its definitions, for example, of what counts as sedition differ from other democracies, such as the United States or Canada. The sorts of movies and books that get censored in India reflect an environment that is more conservative than in the United States. For example, the movie *Aligarh* depicts a relationship between a male professor and a (male) rickshaw driver. Largely based on a true story of an academic who committed suicide, the movie could not find a broad outlet in India; numerous groups tried to ban it from being seen on the campus where the professor been employed. Is academic freedom a cultural term that requires common understandings? Or does the locale of the university circumscribe its meaning?

India also has a relatively prescribed curriculum. Is the Indian historian and public intellectual, Romila Thapar, correct that centrally controlled, standardized syllabi are an infringement on academic freedom and an example of a "totalitarian society"? Committees create course syllabi in Delhi and other universities with specified readings, and professors are instructed to teach from the materials that have been created. If one wants to deviate from the curriculum, permission needs to be granted from a faculty committee and, ultimately, a governmental authority. The result is that an instructor who wishes to teach Rushdie's *Satanic Verses* is unable to use the book in class. Consequently, academic freedom is infringed.

Similarly, the Academic Council of Delhi University eliminated A. K. Ramanujan's "Three Hundred Ramayanas: Five Examples and Three Thoughts on Translation" from a B.A. Honors history course. The Hindutva student body, ABVP, had vandalized the history department of the university in protest against the teaching of this essay. The text was banned as a result, a decision that many individuals viewed as a capitulation to political pressure that violated academic freedom.

Communicating an idea in a classroom that others disagree with may lead to the termination of one's services and the elimination of a text. Rohinton Mistry's Booker Prize–short-listed novel, *Such a Long Journey*, for example, was eliminated from a syllabus when a student objected to certain passages. The novel tells the story of a bank clerk who belongs to the Parsee community. A few pages in the novel negatively portrays Indian politics and a specific political party. As an act of self-censorship, a university removed the book from its reading lists. Similarly, a professor at Banaras Hindu University was fired when he tried to screen in his Development Studies class the banned *India's Daughter*, a movie about a rape that occurred in New Delhi.

The challenge of what should be taught in the classroom also extends to the sorts of seminars, clubs, and activities that occur outside of the classroom. The limits of extramural speech are less clear—but the focus should be on the limits, rather than the assumption that an intellectual's speech should be curtailed. In theory, extramural speech affords the intellectual broad leeway outside of the classroom; at the moment, though, such activities are particularly dangerous.

In 2014, for example, Anand Patwardhan's 1992 documentary film *Ram Ke Naam* was supposed to be screened at the Indian Law Society College in Pune. The film explores the religious conflicts that led to the destruction of the Babri Masjid in Ayodhya and is considered one of India's most significant sociopolitical documentaries. After individuals received threats and concerns developed about potential damage to the campus, the college administration canceled the screening of the movie.

Sanjay Kak's 2007 film, *Jashn-e-Azadi* (*How We Celebrate Freedom*), which was critical of the Indian Army's role in Kashmir, met a similar fate. The screening of the film was canceled by Symbiosis University. In

2013, the screening of Anand Patwardhan's 2011 *Jai Bhim Comrade*, at the Film and Television Institute of India, was disrupted by a scuffle between two groups of students, one of which did not approve of the presence of an activist artists' group. The students claimed that the artists' group had members who were antistate. Some activists were injured in the skirmish, and the program was canceled.

Similarly, at the University of Allahabad, a seminar related to the theme of democracy, media, and freedom of expression was canceled when two groups of students threatened to clash over an outspoken journalist who was to be a chief guest. A keynote address at a seminar on Vedanta and Ayurveda at the Jawharlal Nehru University in Delhi organized by the university's Special Centre for Sanskrit Studies (in collaboration with the University of Massachusetts) was canceled. A group of students opposed the invitation to the speaker, a yoga guru, because of his political affiliation. The cancelation of films and activities of this sort is not uncommon on campuses, and many argue that the tendency to self-censor by canceling programs is only increasing.

The award-winning book *The Hindus: An Alternative History* by the former president of the American Academy of Religion, Wendy Doniger, is banned from Indian classrooms because conservatives view the text as an attack on Hinduism. Another Doniger book, *On Hinduism*, was also placed under review by experts before its reprinting. The practice of either banning a book or launching a severe backlash is increasingly common. Jeffrey Kripla's book *Kali's Child*; Paul Courtright's *Ganesha: Lord of Obstacles*; James Laine's *Shivaji: Hindu King in Islamic India*; Megha Kumar's *Communalism and Sexual Violence: Ahmadabad Since 1969*; and Sekhar Bandopadhyay's *From Plassey to Partition: A History of Modern India*—all have faced similar difficulties.

What one writes and studies can result in suspension of services, public controversy, withholding or suspension of publication, isolation, and even murder. In the 1970s, P. V. Ranade was suspended from the Marathwada University in Maharashtra because he wrote a critical article on Shivaji, a Maratha ruler who fought the Mughals. Around the same time, there was a national controversy pertaining to ancient history textbooks by eminent historian Romila Thapar that were accused of being anti-Hindu. In 2000, the Indian Council for Historical Research (ICHR) suspended the publication of Sumit Sarkar's and K. N. Panikker's volumes on *Towards Freedom*. The problems generally stem from either perceived critical reference to the Hindu Mahasabha and the RSS or failure to credit the RSS with any role in the anticolonial struggle. More recently, M. M.

Kalburgi, a Kannada literary scholar, asked sensitive questions related to the saint of his own community and the worship of religious idols. In what appeared to be retaliation, Kalburgi was shot dead in August 2015 outside his home in Karnataka.

The kind of events that transpired at JNU are what has provoked heated discussions about academic freedom. Some observers will suggest that to critique academic freedom in India today requires an understanding of academic freedom in India a generation ago. In essence, they are asking if today's concerns about academic freedom are simply a way to criticize the Modi government and portray them as conservative ideologues. History, to be sure, always helps us understand complex issues such as academic freedom. Just as understanding the roots of academic freedom in Hong Kong is helpful to understand the situation there today, we also benefit from understanding how academic freedom has been articulated in New Delhi. One also needs to ask, however, if a 28-year-old student should be put in prison for 21 days because he attended an event where controversial statements were made that some people define as seditious. Rightly framed, these sorts of discussions can be useful in helping academics to think through thorny issues that go to the heart of what a nation wants of its universities.

Two universities in India prohibited professors from addressing the media after academics made statements critical of antiterrorist policies. The Nobel Prize–winner Amartya Sen stepped down as vice chancellor of the newly (re)created Nalanda University and stated, "Governments must understand that winning a Lok Sabha election does not give you permission to undermine the autonomy of academic institutions" (Ghose, 2015). His comment had nothing to do with privatization; instead, it focused on what he perceived as governmental attacks on academic freedom. Scholars at Risk, a human rights organization concerned about the protection of academic freedom, has published numerous accounts of Indian academics who have been arrested, beaten, and in some instances imprisoned or killed because of what they have written or said in the classroom. The result of these and similar events is that in 2020, India dropped considerably in the Scholars at Risk global index on academic freedom. India remains above North Korea but is akin to Saudi Arabia and below neighboring Nepal and Sri Lanka.

All of these issues speak to governmental intrusion into the affairs of the university and the limits of academic freedom. At its worst, individuals are harassed, put in jail, or physically harmed. As in Hong Kong, a more common occurrence is a sense that one should not speak out. The result is a stifling of dialogue and a resultant self-censorship. India's academics may be less despondent than their counterparts in Hong Kong, but that is only the case because there are more of them. Metaconcerns, such as academic freedom, get worked out in local contexts, but they all highlight the challenges universities face in the search for truth.

Los Angeles: Make America Great Again (or Not)

A student walked into my class wearing a red "Make America Indigenous Again" cap and no one raised an eyebrow. Down the freeway, another student walked into a student meeting wearing the same cap except it said "Great" rather than "Indigenous." Another student snatched the cap off his head and marched down to a student affairs office. The offended student flipped on his cell phone so that everyone could watch the brouhaha as he demanded his hat back. The cap-snatcher said that on a multiracial campus wearing the "MAGA" hat of Donald Trump was racist and she was not going to be intimidated. The student responded that he was half-Latino and he could wear whatever he wanted. When they reached the student affairs office the two were shouting at one another and the surprised student affairs employees were unsure what to do, based on the video the student posted on YouTube.

A colleague with a disability and a wry sense of humor told me that students in one class had enquired how they might teach able-bodied people what it's like to be disabled. "I told them," my colleague laughed, "throw them down the stairs. Just throw them down the stairs." The individual also has many concerns about the many objectionable comments the philosopher Peter Singer has made about disabled people. "If he were here, I'd just want to shoot him," the person shrugged, "I'd tell someone with a gun to just kill him."

The former Israeli ambassador to the United States came to another campus in town to give a talk, and he was shouted down by students who oppose his views. The ambassador was unable to give his talk, and he was escorted off campus by armed security. Campus police arrived and arrested the students. Someone on my own campus commented that the ambassador is a thoughtful spokesperson with whom they have many disagreements. "He's very good at thinking on his feet and helping you think through positions," the person said. "He'd be good as a speaker for my students, but I'd never invite him. He'd be too controversial, even here. If BDS [a group that believes organizations such as universities should boycott Israel because of Palestinian injustices] got wind of it, there would be hell to pay."

A student informed me that an article assigned for my class was a triggering event for her and we should have forewarned her about the potential impact. I have used the article for the same class for a decade. The article is an analysis of different theoretical approaches to social science and their methodological implications. The article pertains to women who had been in abusive relationships. There are less than a half dozen quotes, and the article's focus is on interview techniques based on the theoretical framework the researchers are utilizing. The student explained to me that she has never been in an abusive relationship and knows no one in an abusive relationship, but nonetheless the article triggered her. No one has ever said that the article was triggering for them, but I agreed that I will no longer use the text.

I most likely would not have mentioned any of these events a generation ago. Baseball caps were not politically charged pieces of apparel, and what one wore to class was not thought of as a political statement. Statements about throwing people down the stairs, or shooting someone, by an individual known for an outlandish sense of humor would be taken, not as a threat, but as a frustrated aside. Speakers generally were not shouted down and almost never had to worry about personal violence to the point that they would need a security detail. I have never used sexually explicit material in my class and have never been told that an article was so upsetting that it should not be used.

We live in different times. These examples highlight not only the different times, but touch on issues of academic freedom in ways that are different, but related, to what I presented for Hong Kong and New Delhi. Academics in Hong Kong and New Delhi have challenges in part with a discussion about territory—independence in Hong Kong, and Kashmir in India—and certainly in Los Angeles we could have a peaceful, fulsome debate about California seceding from the United States. However, a discussion about various areas of the world on any campus in Los Angeles is likely to provoke reactions similar to what I reported about in Hong Kong and Delhi. Not only the government of Israel, but certainly also those of Armenia, Turkey, China, Taiwan, and Iran, among other countries, could easily provoke protests at any college or university in Los Angeles. And the inability to speak about these issues has ramifications for other issues, just as it did in Galileo's day. Ultimately, these are all examples of what can and cannot be said on a campus and who gets to determine what is a matter for deliberation and debate.

Clothing also has become a touchstone during the Trump era. We have long debated the appropriateness of personal attire. A male might have worn a t-shirt that was insulting to women, or perhaps a student came clothed in a skimpy outfit that someone critiqued as too informal. Many students might have worn a t-shirt or hat that advocated one or another position or candidate—legalize marijuana, U.S.A. out of . . . [any number of countries], or those ubiquitous screenshots of Obama. If a student wore a conservative piece of clothing, it might have provoked a comment by someone, but I never heard anyone call it hate speech—until Donald Trump and the MAGA hats arrived.

Donald Trump has succeeded in politicizing campuses in ways that I have never before seen in my lifetime. If a Muslim woman wore a djellaba and hajib, I never would have thought that her clothing could become controversial until 9/11, and especially after Trump was elected. I appreciate that different countries and cultures have different customs, and that in France such clothing is not to be worn outside. The same was true at universities when Turkey was a democracy. In the United States, however, and especially in Los Angeles, what one wore was never cause for comment. We might have commented if the clothing was unprofessional—someone's short shorts—but even that was not likely to provoke commentary in fashion-conscious LA, a city where it is possible to see someone wearing a tuxedo at a baseball game or jeans at a Michelin-starred restaurant.

Now, however, what was once apolitical becomes political. If a MAGA cap makes one student feel uncomfortable, then a woman's hijab makes another student nervous. If a Planned Parenthood t-shirt is acceptable attire, then so is one with a rifle and the logo of the National Rifle Association (NRA). In New Delhi, the sorts of movies that are shown in a classroom or by a club are subject to commentary; the cultural artifact may be different in Los Angeles, but the interpretation is just as heated. As in Hong Kong, professors in Los Angeles who make statements that get into social media come in for attack (usually from external groups), which then provokes commentary from the university administration. An African American professor who says that White people should be shot will first garner criticism from a right-wing group and then be rebuked by the college president until there is, usually, a begrudging acceptance that the individual has academic freedom. A right-wing professor who has a website that claims homosexuality is immoral and unnatural will encounter the same sorts of back and forth, but from the other side of the political spectrum.

Thus, Abby Ferber (2017) is partially correct when she writes the following: "Because of the growth of social media, it is now very easy to generate public outcry, or create a 'crisis' over things that would have been nonissues in the past. The Right is purposefully using social media to purposefully advance their political agenda and attacking faculty that use teaching methods or curriculum that challenges that teaching agenda" (p. 37). Because she has been attacked from the right, she fails to see that similar sorts of attacks also come at conservatives from the left. One difference, of course, is that the right is much better organized, with well-funded organizations, websites, and radio stations that are able to disseminate information that can overwhelm a professor and the campus.

The result, from both ends of the political spectrum, is what I heard in Hong Kong and Delhi: self-censorship. As Ferber (2018) explains, people employ "various forms of self-censorship as a safety measure, whether decreasing their use of social media, or even changing careers to end the harassment and constant fear" (p. 40). Once again, we see how the globalized world has changed our practices and policies on our campuses, regardless of whether we are in New Delhi, Los Angeles, or Hong Kong.

Perhaps most surprising in Los Angeles is the question of what sorts of texts one uses in class. In the Trump era, students arrive to campus perhaps more aware of their identity than at any time in the last generation. With regard to Donald Trump, there is no small amount of irony that, for someone who seeks to obscure issues of race, gender, and sexual orientation, he has only succeeded in accentuating them on college campuses, especially in multicultural metropolitan areas such as Los Angeles. One result of the literature on trigger warnings and microaggression is that students are aware of what they are reading and who the authors are. A Black student may claim that a syllabus that has all White authors is a form of a microaggression. Even though my student pointed out that she had never faced any of the problems that the women in the article faced, and that the article had few quotes from the women, nevertheless she felt the text needed a warning for women (and possibly men) where it might trigger emotions. Gandhi was a racist when he spoke about Blacks in South Africa (Desai & Vahed, 2016). Frederick Douglass was a racist when he wrote about Native Americans (Blight, 2018). Walt Whitman was a racist toward African Americans in his writings (Outka, 2002). David Starr Jordan was a eugenicist. Woodrow Wilson was a racist. What do we do with these figures who were formally revered?

We have long known that, even in science classes, which ostensibly have value-neutral curricular content, the form of teaching matters. Today, that observation is magnified. The instructor who only uses male examples in a math problem or the professor who uses a gay couple for a topic in a biology class run the risk of offending someone. Students will research on-line to find out the gender and backgrounds of authors to see if they meet the requirements of a woke classroom. In many respects, these sorts of inquiries can be useful. A reflective instructor is able to improve their teaching to more fully meet the needs of today's classroom.

Unfortunately, more often than not, what I have found is that the faculty mirror Ferber's observation. Rather than risk offending anyone, they try to offend no one. Administrators encourage the nonoffense so they do not have to deal with the inevitable backlash that is sure to ensue from someone who ruffles the feathers of the citizens, legislature, or an organized opposition.

We tend to think of academic freedom when it is violated. The infamous Ross case, regardless of whether he was a hero of the working class or the purveyor of hate speech, certainly pertains to academic freedom. We can have useful discussions about similar examples and whether they are infringements of academic freedom. The larger concern today, however, is that the absence of such examples ought not give us reason to celebrate. Instead, whether I have been in Hong Kong, New Delhi, or Los Angeles, what I continue to find is a reticence of the faculty to speak out and risk the confrontations that they are increasingly likely to face. Instead, they find ways to avoid controversy and those who court it. If the search for truth is to be aided by the protection of academic freedom and its structural guarantor, what we are currently experiencing is that the search is over.

What Academic Freedom Is Not

Autonomy Is Not Academic Freedom

Autonomy is a necessary condition for academic freedom, but a condition is not the sum of the ideas. Academics need autonomy to conduct their research and to teach in the classroom. When the government intrudes on academic work so that individuals do not have autonomy, academic freedom is at risk. However, in an environment in which higher education is undergoing rampant privatization, I am troubled by calls for institutional autonomy in the name of academic freedom. If by institutional autonomy we mean privatization, then it has very little to do with the abrogation of faculty rights and responsibilities. Those who wish to privatize higher education frequently bemoan governmental intrusion and suggest that a more efficient system would be deregulated. The case for deregulation is frequently made under the guise of academic freedom.

Arguments can certainly be put forward about the need to deregulate a public system and incentivize privatization. But such arguments have very little to do with academic freedom. Arguments that invoke academic freedom in their calls for institutional autonomy confuse the issue. The idea, for example, that private universities have greater autonomy and, therefore, greater academic freedom suggests that any governmental oversight is shortsighted and intrusive. And, of course, what one learns from recent experiences in the United States is that a lack of regulation of private, for-profit universities seriously compromises student welfare. No one would say that for-profit institutions have greater academic freedom than public universities such as the University of California. Thus, when leaders of private universities in the New Delhi area call for greater autonomy, one needs to consider the sorts of autonomy being suggested and judge whether they pertain, in any manner, to academic freedom.

Academic Freedom Does Not Afford the Academic to Speak on Any Topic in the Classroom

An individual ought to be free to investigate issues in his or her research area and in the classroom as he or she sees fit. In particular, a professor's domain expertise enables him or her to speak and teach on those issues on which he/she is most familiar. Further, as academics on a campus, the faculty members have the right and responsibility to speak out on a range of extramural issues. Tenure and shared governance are the obvious policies that protect faculty when they speak or write provocatively about their particular area of inquiry or on an issue that matters to the campus.

However, academic freedom does not extend to one's ability to speak out on every issue that arises in society in the classroom simply because the issue is of interest. For example, a professor of chemistry who offers several comments in the classroom on his personal experience of displacement in India, due to communal unrest between two countries, would be engaged in inappropriate behavior because of the setting—the classroom—and his subject area of expertise—chemistry. Likewise, it is inappropriate for a professor of music to argue in the classroom that Hong

Kong should claim independence. Such expressions stretch the idea of academic freedom when they are not about the individual's domain area of expertise. The question one might ask is why the individual's title of "professor" enables him or her to speak on a particular issue.

Academic Freedom Does Not Short-Circuit Peer Review and Full Disclosure

One ought not to be able to claim academic freedom if what one is saying is obviously incorrect. As absurd examples, if a math professor in an elementary math classroom teaches that $2 + 2 = 5$, then he or she cannot claim academic freedom and continue teaching incorrect information. A history professor cannot state that Lincoln fought at Valley Forge and Washington protected the Union during the Civil War. One of the strengths of academic life and a framework for academic freedom is peer review. If one's colleagues discover that such a professor is teaching math or history that does not add up, so to speak, then the professor presumably would have several options open to him or her—but one option would not be to continue teaching that $2 + 2 = 5$ or that Washington gave the Gettysburg Address.

To be sure, as with most issues pertaining to academic freedom, how one delineates "fact" from "opinion" can be finely argued and parsed. It is also subject to disciplinary conventions. In an age that some describe as postmodern, facts may be perceived as social constructs such that what one person sees as fiction, another sees as fact. At the same time, a particular rationale of the university is for scholars to search for "truth," however difficult and ambiguous that search may be. Thus, claims in India that thousands of years ago Hindus invented the airplane or performed open heart surgery obviously need to be rebutted by scholars, and rejected from even being accepted as juried papers at a scholarly scientific conference. If these papers are rejected, the scholar can make no claim that his or her academic freedom has been abridged. Academic freedom does not give the scholar the right to make statements or claims in the classroom, or in one's research arena, that have no factual basis in the relevant literature.

Academic freedom also does not enable the researcher to undertake research that favors the individual or company that funded them. Research funding is of increased concern because of its importance in furthering the work of researchers. The vast majority of funded research goes through peer review and is free of bias. However, there are examples of individuals who have been funded by the tobacco industry, for example, who found little evidence of tobacco causing cancer. Such research needs to go through peer review, and the funding for all research needs to be disclosed. Academic freedom is not a license for an individual to be paid to come up with a finding that supports the funder.

Academic Freedom Is Not (Necessarily) Free Speech

When an individual attends a rally in Los Angeles or Hong Kong to protest the policies of the current administration, they are practicing their right to free speech. If I protest at a religious conference because they believe homosexuality is a sin and that marriage equality should be eliminated, then I am practicing free speech. Both these acts have nothing to do with academic freedom. As Robert Post has posited, the First Amendment has three principles pertaining to speech in the public arena: (a) the state cannot regulate it; (b) there is no limit to the range of ideas that get presented; and (c) we cannot curtail speech except in dire circumstances—the yelling of "fire" in a crowded room is the most frequent example.

Private organizations do not exist as free speech arenas. I might be able to give a speech in front of City Hall, but I cannot necessarily do so within the walls of my organization. I might be able to protest abortion outside a health clinic, but not inside it. Public organizations are different. That's why a private university has greater leeway in the kind of speech it can restrict than a public university.

When I speak in my classroom, I am not exercising my free speech as a citizen. My job limits my free speech, just as my job enables my academic freedom. I am not allowed to simply blurt something out in my class and claim that I am exercising my academic freedom. I also am not allowed to utter any ideas I choose in my class and claim that I am exercising my free speech.

Academic freedom centers around shared conceptions of knowledge production; free speech does not. As Joan Scott (2019) notes: "These days the Right's reference to free speech sweeps away guarantees of academic freedom, dismissing as so many violations of the Constitution the thoughtful, critical articulation of ideas; the demonstration of proof based on rigorous examination of evidence; the distinction between true and false, between careful and sloppy work; the exercise of reasoned judgment" (p. 115). Academic freedom revolves around, in some fashion, the ability to utilize facts. Free speech can be fact-free. Free speech, then, enables people to speak in false ways. I noted earlier that academic freedom does not enable someone to say that $2 + 2 = 5$, or that Indians conducted successful heart surgery 2,000 years ago. Free speech allows individuals to say whatever they like outside of the classroom and off campus. I face no penalty if I stand on a street corner and talk about my new way of conceiving math or give a speech to a Hindutva gathering where I talk about the amazing accomplishments of Hindus 2,000 years ago. All opinions can be equal in the public square; all opinions are not equal in the classroom, or when I undertake research.

Post makes a useful distinction when he says, "We depend on doctors to create vaccines to immunize us against Zika; we rely upon engineers to build bridges. We do not crowdsource such questions or decide them by public opinion polls or my popular vote" (in Scott, 2019, p. 120). Free speech enables me to go on television and speak against vaccines. I can say that a magic carpet is an optimal way to get across the river and we do not need a bridge. Free speech is an individual's right as a citizen. Academic freedom is a professional and organizational right for a group—the faculty.

The Interplay of Academic Freedom and Free Speech on Campus

Although I have just explained how academic freedom and free speech are distinct, there is also a relationship between the two ideas that merits consideration. Sometimes, a professor may claim his or her right to academic freedom when actually the point has more to do with free speech, or vice versa. There are also corresponding issues that impact the campus in similar ways. Distinctions may not be so important to external audiences, but they matter for the campus culture. I turn here to four examples and elaborate how they are distinct or overlap, and the ramifications of each example.

External Speakers to the Campus

Assume a controversial speaker is going to offer a lecture at the institution and there is likely to be a protest. The context of the lecture matters, as much as, if not more than, the content. If the speaker is invited to give a talk in an individual's class, then this is a matter of academic freedom. The instructor has the academic freedom to invite whomever they want to class as long as the speaker and talk fall within the domain of the content of the course. By offering the class, they have been designated as academically qualified to develop a curriculum however they see fit.

From this perspective, one political science professor may invite Barack Obama to speak to her class, and another may invite Donald Trump to his class. The speakers clearly fall within the course frame and either should be invited. If two math professors, however, invite their friends in opposing parties to speak about homosexuality, then there is a problem. Speakers, however controversial, need to be allowed to speak. The only requirement is an intellectual one: is the speaker clearly within the domain of the knowledge that the professor has and is teaching to the students?

What if the instructor needs resources to enable the external speaker to come to class? The norms of the department, school, or sponsoring unit need to be followed. If the norm is that the unit simply provide resources, usually a set amount, to an instructor and the individual is able to spend it however they see fit, then again, the controversial speaker falls under the domain of academic freedom with regard to the professor's invitation to speak. A review of the speaker's credentials will not be done because the instructor is providing a lecture as part of the curriculum, as everyone else regularly does when they invite a speaker to their classrooms.

How about if the instructor needs additional resources, or the norm is that a decision needs to be made about whether the external speaker warrants the resources? Would this fall under academic freedom or free speech? Again, these are resources that an academic unit controls within the province of faculty governance. Rather than a singular decision made by an instructor in a classroom, if the tradition is a collective decision made by the faculty at some level (e.g., department, division, school), then we again are experiencing an issue of academic freedom. In effect, the sponsoring unit is making an academic decision, and the framework for the decision is academic freedom.

Invited lectures also can convey more than a speaker's comments to a class. An invited lecture may have an honor attached to it. At Commencement, an individual may be awarded an honorary degree. A program may award a fellowship to someone. All these sorts of decisions revolve around the idea of academic freedom. They require academic review and approval; the review and approval should have nothing to do with faculty agreement with the speaker's ideas. The question revolves around whether the professor or sponsoring unit has determined that the individual has the qualifications to speak.

When the president or a unit invites someone to campus without academic review, then either the decision was poorly made or it is a decision pertaining to free speech. A president may simply announce, for example, that a wealthy donor is to receive an honorary doctorate. A fraternity or religious center may decide to invite someone to give a talk without any academic review of the speakers, and no faculty are involved. These sorts of events do not involve academic freedom. They could be about free speech.

Regardless of the sponsoring unit, however, the potential exists that a protest will ensue, and the protesters will expect that the speaker be disinvited to campus. In all these examples, the institution needs to stand firm and allow the speaker to speak, whether the principle is free speech or academic freedom. The institution also does not, normally, have the right to require "balance," although a different unit is certainly able to offer their own speaker who offers a contradictory view.

Like free speech, however, academic freedom comes with the potential for dual costs. A real cost pertains to how much an institution may need to pay for security, and those costs may be significant. When the provocateur Milo Yiannopoulos spoke at UC Berkeley, the cost for security approached a million dollars. I do not blithely state that we need to find the resources to enable the speaker to give a lecture, but if the principles of academic freedom and free speech are core values, then we must spend the requisite resources to ensure that the speaker and community are safe.

The second cost pertains to those who might be harmed by the speaker. Obviously, a speaker might be controversial for any number of reasons. Someone may not support the idea of climate change whereas another speaker may be against gay marriage. Presumably, a speaker who does not support climate change would garner protest from individuals because the speaker's ideas are flawed or biased. The same might be true about the homophobic speaker, but the individual also has the potential to make members of the LGBTQ community uncomfortable. Again, I do not think we can casually state that the community's well-being supersedes that of an individual. We need to think through how we might best respond when we know that a member of our community will be harmed because of the invitation of a speaker, and I will do that later in this chapter. For now, however, the principle remains that the controversial speaker has to be allowed either on the basis of academic freedom or free speech.

One derivative of speakers being invited to campus pertains to the issue of balance. A controversial speaker in a professor's classroom only warrants a speaker with a different perspective if the professor wants that balance. There have been state initiatives, for example, that have said a discussion about climate change has to present both sides of the matter. In Hong Kong, prior to 2020, some people suggested that a discussion about independence for the island could only be done if the topic were presented as one among many possibilities (and even then, the likelihood of an independence-minded speaker would be low). Today, however, such a discussion would be impossible. Regardless, the sponsoring individual or unit should be under no obligation to provide balance when the decision pertains to academic freedom. Again, the overriding principle has to be that the academic has the knowledge and expertise to master what is being offered in the classroom. It is possible with regard to free speech that a speaker might present another viewpoint in some other forum.

Internal Speakers from the Campus

Criticism of faculty also may be made because of either current or previous comments they made in or out of class, on campus or off. A professor, for example, has a private website where he lists that he is a Christian and believes homosexuality is a form of deviance. Another individual who is African American lists on Facebook that White people are the cause of misery for Black people and we should appropriate White people's land. A third person states that Trump is America's greatest president, a fourth person swears consistently in class, a fifth individual uses derogatory words about immigrants, and a sixth person who is straight had a yearbook photo taken in college where he was dressed in drag and clearly was making fun of gay men and women.

I have put these various examples together because there is no clear-cut response to extramural comments. An academic freedom extremist might say that an individual is free to express whatever they believe is cogent and informed in any format, but most analysts of campuses today would not simply put out a statement advising everyone to "say whatever you want." There need to be limits on what one says and there is nothing wrong with investigating how one speaks. The challenge with reviews of speech on college campuses is that they frequently seem as if they are done off-the-cuff and helter-skelter rather than consistent and adhering to a particular protocol. In general, I think a case can be made that the extramural comments of individuals ought neither be sanctioned nor cause for penalty. The courts have consistently found that hate speech codes are in violation of the First Amendment. Similarly, what one says in the classroom or what one brings to the classroom ought not be grounds for removing someone from the classroom.

A campus should be one where conversations are rampant and ongoing. In a culture that is not spoiled, individuals should be speaking about their teaching as well as events that take place on campus. Everyone can improve their teaching. What we bring to a class, and how we interact in the class is going to be examined; unfortunately, though, we have not been trained to accept criticism, or modify our classes based on that commentary. Because we do not have these skills ought not suggest that we circumscribe speech. A case example will help elaborate the challenges we face on campus today.

A professor teaches a doctoral counseling class and has students break into small groups to discuss an issue that has been provided to them and provide possible interventions. One of the "problems" was that Black and Latina pregnant women do not access prenatal care often enough; a small group of students (all women) were asked to come up with some possible interventions. One solution was to sterilize these women.

The teacher nodded and asked for a report from the next group. Some students were upset and a discussion ensued during which the professor did not say very much. An African American woman was incensed at the comments, and equally upset that the instructor didn't say anything. The situation spiraled out of control over the next few weeks and ended up with a thousand students signing a petition demanding some sort of action for the instructor. The teacher's response was shock. She believed that she taught content, not students. Just as the student, and subsequently many other students, believed she had committed an egregious error, she was certain that she had committed no error. A committee found that she was within her rights to do as she pleased.

One never knows, of course, how one might act in a similar situation. My assumption, however, is that based on my previous experience I would never have countenanced a student group suggesting that someone of any race should be sterilized. The statement is absurd, pernicious, and ill-informed. I would have assumed that the students meant no harm, but they were putting forward an idea they had not fully considered. If the instructor had asked me between the week of the event and the subsequent week I would have encouraged her to undertake a conversation about the example, point out why the idea was weak and how it might be interpreted, and undertake a discussion about the topic and what to do in similar situations when a bad idea is put forward. These sorts of conversations can be extremely useful and the essence of what we like to define as a "teachable moment."

Neither the instructor nor her unit used the event as a teachable moment, and life went on as before, albeit with many students upset and some threatening to drop out. With regard to academic freedom, nothing should have been done. We frequently seem, however, to have a all-or-nothing approach to these problems when actually there is a great deal that could have been accomplished. That is, we either want the instructor removed from the classroom, and possibly fired, or we wash our hands of the matter. Clearly, this example was mishandled. We do not have to remove someone to get the right response that improves learning, ameliorates the problem that gave rise to the situation, and enables the teacher and students to participate in a learning community. Such a statement, however, seems almost whimsical on our campuses because relations are so fraught. One of the primary reasons for these challenges remaining unresolved and almost no one is pleased with the outcome has to do with how the academic community is defining what gets said.

Trigger Warnings and Microaggressions

One assumption about academic freedom within the classroom is that the professor is able to construct and teach a class however he or she sees fit. The instructor develops the curriculum, receives approval from a committee, and then teaches the class. Whether the professor decides to teach the class as a lecture, seminar, or in small groups is generally left up to the instructor's discretion. The curriculum committee largely plays an oversight role to ensure certain standards are maintained and offers suggestions about curricular content that are just that—recommendations for the instructor to consider. Once the class gains approval, there is frequently no oversight as a teacher, or a subsequent instructor, adapts the syllabus content and teaching style. A teaching center might offer suggestions about ways to improve one's teaching, and a miserable teacher might require help from someone, but in general, the assumption for a century has been that the classroom is sacrosanct. Such an assumption is at the center of the idea of academic freedom. The professor determines how to teach his or her course. By extension, we have an array of teaching activities that are also left up to professorial discretion; how office hours are determined, what takes place out of class, whom to invite to class, whether there are informal activities such as an end-of-term party, and the like are all professorial prerogative.

Over the last decade—and especially since the rise of Donald Trump and other populists who have fascist tendencies—we have nevertheless seen the autonomy of the professor in the classroom, as well as outside of it, challenged. Colleges and universities are not only arenas where we are able to wrestle with difficult ideas; they are also communities where these ideas get worked out every day. How we teach, what we do outside of class, what we might expect, or demand of one another, all speak to the tensions we face along the individual-communal spectrum. An individualist conception assumes that I should be able to say anything and have a free-wheeling discussion without limits. The communalist has a quite different interpretation: standards have to be imposed so that we all are safe. The challenge, of course, is not merely what those standards are, but who gets to determine the standards—and what to do when someone disagrees.

Microaggressions are commonly defined as "brief and common-place daily verbal, behavioral, or environmental indignities, whether intentional or unintentional, that communicate hostile, derogatory, or negative . . . slights and insults" (Sue et al., 2007, p. 271). We currently have the most fraught environment that I have seen in the last 35 years. Conversations are harder inside and outside of the classroom. Individuals are less willing to raise questions or disagree with someone, which seems to have less to do with an individual not trying to offend someone and more to do with the fear that a speaker's words will get the individual in trouble. The pity is that we are not thinking through these thorny issues; instead, we are just trying to avoid them.

Students of color, who have long felt unwelcome on campus due to both large and small slights, now wish to highlight which words and acts can and cannot be said without causing harm to the students. Women document a history of marginalization and abuse and will no longer sit still. The LGBTQ community demands visibility. People with disabilities are unwilling to put up with institutions that exclude them because of lack of accessibility. Intolerance will no longer be tolerated—but how we define intolerance is up for grabs. How might we live among one another without excluding some and silencing others? To answer such a question, we first have to consider what supporters and detractors make of the idea of "safe spaces."

In today's political discourse, conservatives have had a remarkable ability to use language that puts their opponents on the defensive. The tactic is largely to demean and belittle, but, in doing so, they also tend to win the argument. The use of the term "snowflake" is a perfect example. It is unclear when the term "snowflake" precisely entered daily discourse, but it was commonly used as far back as the early 1860s, when an individual opposed to the abolition of slavery in Missouri was called a "snowflake."[1] Obviously, the modern propagation of the term has a completely different meaning. The current usage is frequently credited to Chuck Palahniuk; in his popular 1996 novel, *Fight Club*, the primary antagonist, Tyler Durden, states, "Listen up maggots. You are not special. You are not a beautiful or unique snowflake" (quoted in Campuzano, 2017). Who wants to be labeled a snowflake, something fragile and able to melt away in the noonday sun? The language we employ helps frame the argument we are having. Unfortunately, when we employ terms like "snowflake," it is impossible to have a meaningful discussion that extends beyond name calling.

A decade ago, "microaggression" and "trigger warnings" were not terms that many faculty or administrators employed. Today, these terms are commonly discussed and debated and policies have been developed around them. Suddenly, the autonomy of what the professor says and does in the classroom, as well as what the professor might have done outside the classroom, have come under investigation.

While the terms are sometimes used in similar contexts, as I have pointed out, they actually have distinctive meanings. Microaggressions in higher education are a concern among those who worry about the unspoken comments and assumptions that students of color and other under-represented groups are compelled to endure. "Trigger warnings" are intended to "notify people of the distress that written, audiovisual, or other material may evoke" (Bellet et al., 2018, p. 134). Professors, in particular, feel increased pressure in recent years to include trigger warnings next to any material in a syllabus that might cause distress among students. The common thread between the concept of microaggressions and trigger warnings is an understandable concern about individuals who might not be able to participate in the classroom or campus life due to an environment that is perceived to be hostile or unwelcoming. A law professor at Harvard University, for example, served on the defense team for Harvey Weinstein, a powerful man accused of numerous acts of sexual harassment. Students then said they no longer felt comfortable having him as their dorm advisor. Some students asked, how could they feel comfortable discussing sexual harassment with someone who was defending a sexual harasser? The assumption, of course, touches on the idea of identity. Would a straight Christian be able to counsel a gay student? Is an able-bodied professor competent to understand the challenges faced by a student with a disability? Can a White professor understand why a Black student is upset with students' comments in class? In this case, the individual resigned from his post as dorm advisor, according to press reports.

If we contextualize each student's experience, we highlight the challenges of determining how to define microaggressions and trigger warnings. The life experiences of an undocumented student who fears deportation for himself and his family because of President Trump's policies are obviously different from those of a middle-class White student who is angry about the president's policies but faces no immediate threat. A student who believes that all Muslims are terrorists because of what she sees on Fox News is different from an individual whose parent died in the World Trade Center on 9/11.

Even those who call others "snowflakes" might acknowledge that some texts or some images may indeed be a trigger for some students. A survivor of rape may be uncomfortable with a graphic portrayal of rape in cinema or literature; at the least, one might want to alert this individual to what is in the text. What an instructor might think of as an even-handed discussion about the events surrounding 9/11 might also trigger memories and images of the building falling down for someone who was there.

Where do we draw the line? How do we draw the line? Those who call others "snowflakes" assume there is no line, or that only in the rarest of circumstances might a professor need to forewarn students about a discussion or text. The challenge, of course, is that because the idea of microaggression is a relatively new term, how one understands it and what one does once it is found are not yet clear. Some might argue that wearing a MAGA hat is a microaggression; others might suggest that even a discussion about the meaning of the hat could foster microaggressions if the conversation is not handled in an appropriate manner.

From a scientific standpoint, we do not yet have enough empirical evidence to ascertain exactly which speech or action would be considered a microaggression, and how it impacts learning (Lilienfeld, 2017). We have a great deal of narrative evidence, however, that microaggressions exist and impede learning when they occur (Pérez Huber & Solórzano, 2015; Solórzano et al., 2000; Sue et al., 2007). Individuals may learn how to adapt to such slights, but they are clearly placed at an educational disadvantage in ways that other students are not. We generally think of microaggression as any statement or occurrence that brings injury to an individual based on one's identity—race, ethnicity, gender, sexual orientation, gender, religion, disability, and the like. Sometimes these statements come as a back-of-the-hand compliment: "For someone like you, you've done great." "I have to hand it to you. I never thought you'd be able to do it." When we suggest that the recipient of the comment needs to learn how to respond to the comment, we are putting the onus on the victim of the comment. Why should those who are the recipients of hurtful comments have to be the ones who change? Those who look at microaggression ask why, in the name of free speech or academic freedom, we should force those who often have been at the margins yet again to the margins?

At other times, perhaps frequently, the slights are unintended. I used to work with a fellow who put in a lot of effort to appear comfortable working with a gay man. Every time he saw me, he'd comment on my clothes: "Nice shirt!" "Wow, I love those slacks." "That coat sure looks sharp on you!" Over time, I realized he made sartorial comments only to me—and alas, my clothes were frequently not so "sharp." In effect, he saw a gay man and reduced me to clothes because being concerned with fashion is a stereotype of gay men. By cordoning off conversations—speaking about budgeting to some people and clothes to another—we risk privileging some people and reducing opportunities for others. If a Monday morning meeting begins with a review of Sunday's football games, and at one point someone looks to the lone woman in the room and says, "A touchdown is when a player scores some points," that comment is more than a lame attempt at humor. The speaker has divided the group into individuals who are assumed to have knowledge about a topic (men), and others who do not (women), and the knowledgeable ones in the room have the advantage.

What we say and cannot say now revolves around these sorts of issues. When one raises the implications for academic freedom or free speech, the aggrieved are generally not so concerned. That is, in the abstract students tend to support academic freedom as well as free speech, although there has been a significant drop in support over the last decade (Lukianoff & Haidt, 2018). However, when pollsters offer examples that relate to microaggressions and ask whether academic freedom should be circumscribed, students largely support the creation of safe spaces. Indeed, safe spaces, in which what one says, whether one is a faculty member, student, or administrator, is increasingly viewed affirmatively by students and looked askance at by those who use the term "snowflake."

The arrival on campus of controversial speakers who deride microaggression and safe spaces accentuates the challenges we face in the twenty-first century. A speaker may have said or done something, inadvertently or purposefully, long ago or in the recent past; one's history no longer is immune for criticism. The result is that, however elegant an argument Peter Singer may have made about animal rights, because he has made hurtful comments about people with disabilities, his work ought not be used in a class. The right of the professor to determine what goes into the curriculum is no longer sacrosanct, and the absolutism of academic freedom has been reduced.

Of course, there are moments and actions that go too far. Sometimes, an individual's sole purpose is to disrupt, rather than engage in, learning. A member of the alt-right who walks onto campus dressed in a Nazi uniform and wearing a swastika is certainly not interested in learning algebra. There are some people whose only intention is to provoke and disrupt. We need to think through how to handle these sorts of actions and individuals. The challenge is always context and interpretation. We need to work our way around these meanings so that we improve the learning environment for all individuals but do not unnecessarily limit conversation and thoughtful dialogue on difficult topics.

The Holocaust and Pizza Parlors

The problem of academic freedom and free speech on our campuses is made that much more difficult because context and intent matter. I have drawn a distinction between what a professor gets to discuss in the classroom and extramural speech. An expert has broad leeway to discuss matters pertinent to one's specific area of expertise in the classroom. Thus, a scholar whose area is climate change determines the content in a course pertaining to climate change but would not be able to argue that he or she is able to speak about abortion in the class. That same scholar, however, could invite a member of Planned Parenthood to speak on campus during "Health Week" and the like. If that scholar were to protest to the state legislature about legislation pertaining to abortion, then the individual would be invoking their free speech rights as a citizen. If that same individual signed a letter on university stationary and used their academic title to criticize legislation about climate change, then the person would once again be calling upon their academic freedom.

Controversial speakers are similarly complex. I have made the differences based on if a speaker is speaking in my class, or at a larger event, if the speaker is to be compensated, and if the talk is attached in any way to an honor. Contexts matter. The intent of academic freedom is to enable as broad a discussion as is necessary to pursue truth. One assumption about a search for truth is that there are going to be competing ideas and interpretations and as fulsome a discussion as possible in order to reach consensus about a particular issue. How might we categorize contentious debates? My sense is that these sorts of topics fall under four broad categories that might be considered when speakers come to campus.

Settled Science, but Still Contentious

Enough data has been accumulated by respected scientists to affirm that climate change and global warming exist, and that vaccinations prevent illness. Nevertheless, academic institutions are well-armed to debate these issues. Some will argue that because climate change and the utility of vaccinations is settled science that we do a disservice to the academic community when we present alternative views. I disagree. We should be able to hear the issues that climate change deniers put forward and prove them false. There is value to presenting arguments in a manner that fosters dialogue on crucial topics. We assume when we pursue truth that ultimately, within a university, the logic of the idea ultimately succeeds. Accordingly, I do not think that every topic that comes before a post-secondary institution has to have two or three speakers as if every idea is up for debate. I do, however, think we need to allow people who have ideas that run contrary to the data and knowledge that academics have should at least be considered.

Not Settled Social Science and Contentious

Not all controversial ideas are settled matters of science, of course. Social science has an infinity of topics where scholars posit and debate ideas. The vast majority of these ideas are not controversial except among the academic community and are worthy of vigorous debate. In my own area, for example, the work of the French sociologist, Pierre Bourdieu, provokes multiple opinions that generate new ways of thinking about his work on social and cultural capital. Another matter pertains to federal plans to enact "college for all," and whether such a plan will help low-income students or benefit upper-income students.

More controversial topics are ideas pertaining to charter schools and teacher unions. We have individuals on both sides of the issues who feel strongly. Some believe that charter schools are anathema to public education, and others believe that unions should not exist in schools. Their opponents also hold strong opinions. The same could be said in the higher ed arena with regard to for-profit higher education. Again, I see no reason why we would not allow a speaker to present any view on these sorts of topics. I appreciate that the opponents of charter schools, unions, or for-profits will say that the arguments are weak, facetious, or ill-informed, but a university ought to be a place of fulsome debate. Simply because someone presents an idea with which I disagree ought not to suggest that the speaker's argument is pernicious or needs to be suppressed. The strength of a university in a democracy is that ideas with which we disagree are welcomed rather than suppressed. The assumption is that ultimately the right ideas will be put forward and that informed listeners benefit from hearing different viewpoints.

Not Settled Science or Social Science and Contentious

Still other ideas are not necessarily strict examples of science or social science, but they are critical topics of the moment. Gay rights have certainly been a controversial topic over the last generation. Gay people should or should not be allowed to marry, adopt children, be protected in the workplace, serve in the military, or donate blood. Those of us who have fought for gay rights have had to argue on all of these issues with our friends and neighbors and in our churches and communities. Although there is an increasing amount of helpful social science on these issues, many people also act from a position of religious belief. Although the science is clear about the quality of gay parenting, whether one believes homosexuals should be able to marry falls into the area of belief. Should these discussions not be held on our campuses? Or should only one side of the argument be countenanced?

Again, I think we benefit from thoughtful discussions of contentious issues in an academic setting. To say that only one side of an argument should be presented, or that we should avoid topics entirely, removes universities from playing a critical role in the twenty-first century and is an abnegation of our responsibility as centers for exploring truth.

I fully appreciate that contentious issues generate heated responses. President Trump's policy, for example, to exclude citizens of particular countries and frequent calls that equate Islam with terrorism are pernicious and wrong. These arguments, however, are going to be made in the public spheres beyond our campuses so why would we not allow them within the campus so that they might be defeated? Similarly, President George W. Bush's arguments to allow torture went against the Geneva Convention and the tradition of the U.S. military, but there were individuals who spoke on behalf of torture on television and on the floor of the Senate. Charles Murray has put forward numerous public-policy proposals based on questionable science that attack ideas such as affirmative action and have generated a great deal of controversy both on and off-campuses. Why would we not enable discussions about ideas with which we disagree? We run the risk of irrelevancy when we only air one side of a controversy or sidestep it.

By speaking for enabling ideas to be put forward with which I strenuously disagree, I need to offer two cautions. First, I am not interested in controversial ideas being debated by provocateurs who have no concern for the intellect. Obviously, there are numerous speakers who can blurt out whatever they like and take a particular stance merely to earn income or notoriety. I make a distinction between a biblical scholar who has (wrongheaded) views on gay marriage, and those members of Westboro Baptist Church who simply use profane language to scare and shame those with whom they disagree. An intellectual community gains nothing by enabling speakers whose modus operandi is simply to put forward issues by activities such as shouting obscenities at those with whom they disagree.

Second, these sorts of topics are likely to hurt some members of our community. The closeted gay student who attends a lecture where a well-informed speaker talks about why gay men should not be able to adopt a child may be drawn further into the closet. A person with a disability who listens to a speaker argue about the ethics of terminating the lives of those with serious disabilities could be similarly pained and/or outraged. A transgender person who hears people argue over bathrooms in public schools could feel discriminated against yet again. A Muslim or undocumented student who hears a speaker make a cogent argument against immigration could feel they have no place in the United States. All these points pertain to the previous discussion of the need for safe spaces, what microaggression is, and how speech acts and events can trigger unwelcome feelings or thoughts that will impede learning.

At the heart of this point is the observation that yet again, those who often find themselves on the margins are told, in effect, "Deal with it." We know, of course, that these potentially harmful ideas are stated in the larger society, but the argument can be made that we do not need to make them within our own community. Again, I believe that we must— and we must do so with care, concern, and a stated belief on where we, as an academic community, stand on the issues that are to be debated. By enabling a speaker to speak against gay marriage, we are not saying that we are against gay marriage. If anything, I would like to see our faculty and administrations be more outspoken, based on what we know as intellectuals, about these issues. Torture is wrong. Creating single-sex bathrooms is harmful to transgender students. Banning immigrants is against the national ethos. We are able to make any number of important points on where we, as a university, stand yet still allow a lecture and discussion to go forward. We are able to frame the talk by a controversial speaker so that faculty and administrators of prominence put forward questions and comments to the speaker that make clear the mistaken views of a speaker, and what we as a university community reject. But I do not think we—all of us—are well-served if we forbid contentious arguments to be aired on our campus. We have to be models for civility and community so that pernicious ideas are laid to rest. I know very few gay people who believed in 1980 that we would be able to marry and adopt children. The road, however contentious, occurred because we were able to make the case for equality, not because we stifled it.

Neither Science or Social Science, Nor Verifiable

Holocaust deniers have been a microscopic fringe element in society. Unfortunately, in the twenty-first century, the intellectual progeny of these individuals is able to generate a sizable following on numerous topics. Barack Obama was not born in the United States. He is a closeted Muslim aimed at overthrowing the government. The children at Sandy Hook and at Parkland were not shot dead; the events did not happen. Hillary Clinton ran a pedophile ring out of the basement of a pizza parlor in Washington, D.C. The pandemic is a hoax perpetrated by Anthony Fauci. As I suggested in chapter 2, these sorts of stories get at where I draw the line. Ideas that have no basis in fact do not warrant our attention as a matter of debate. Indeed, letting such individuals onto our campuses cheapens our discourse. I certainly could imagine a useful conversation about conspiracy theories. We should interrogate how individuals can be duped by individuals such as Alex Jones or websites that put forward all sorts of ideas that have no basis in truth. But the discussion of harebrained and malicious conspiracies ought never be debated in a way that I have suggested these other topics will be discussed.

Too often, we have inferred that free speech on our campuses in general and academic freedom by the faculty in particular suggests that all speech should be allowed. Such an inference is wrong. I have put forward why such an assertion is wrong in our classrooms, and why we need not allow these discussions happen in the broader academic community. There is no search for truth with a madman; we are simply enabling people to espouse lunatic ideas, as if they had a basis in fact.

I appreciate that I have made distinctions with which some people will disagree. Some will suggest that a belief that vaccines are harmful or that torture is permissible fall outside the boundaries of permitted speech. Such views fall into the same category as suggesting that 9/11 didn't happen and was a cover up by the U.S. government. I disagree for the reasons I have already elaborated, but I also believe that each campus should have a faculty-run committee that oversees these sorts of issues and topics. A central role of any institution of higher learning has to be in the search for, and articulation of, truth. Universities need to do more to enable conversation and dialogues about the multitude of issues that confront us. When we hide from these sorts of difficult dialogues or discourage debate, we diminish the exact kinds of conversations that we crucially need to reverse the current democratic recession.

Academic Responsibility: Creating Safe Spaces for Unsafe Dialogue

What might we do in a classroom or campus setting to enable our students to feel "comfortably unsafe"? What do we do when an unexpected statement or action in class is considered hurtful? A first step is to acknowledge that academic freedom and free speech are about power. Some have the power to make statements regardless of the ability to create harm. Most faculty are not particularly adept at recognizing what a microaggression is or how to handle classroom conflict; we need to begin by developing sensitivity not simply to the material being covered, but the learners being taught. There is no magic potion for teaching faculty to care about students, but an engaged classroom begins with the assumption that what we say and do in and out of the classroom impacts learning. A reflective professor not only plans for the upcoming class, but also thinks about the events of the class that just occurred and how students might have interpreted the messages they have heard.

Compacts need to be created with students at the outset of class about what they expect from one another. Some of these expectations may be simple requests about not eating in class or arriving to class on time. This is also an opportunity to clarify expectations that pertain to microaggressions, trigger warnings and difficult dialogues. Clearly, we have expectations that our students will not use vulgar language in class. What about the fellow wearing the MAGA hat? One might argue that someone should not wear a garment that makes another person uncomfortable. Fair enough, you might say. What do we then do with the student whose gay flag t-shirt makes a Christian student feel uncomfortable? Or that woman wearing a hijab? Or the fellow with a face mask that looks suspiciously like someone wearing blackface? There are no automatic answers, and these issues can be very different from one another based on the viewpoints of those who wear the clothes and those who see them. Some will think of a MAGA hat as a political statement whereas the hijab is an integral part of a religious practice. Others will be unable to differentiate politics from belief. We can sanitize a classroom and campus—no decorative caps, no t-shirts with messages, no religious clothing, no face masks other than single color, and such. But such actions stymie conversation rather than provoke learning. The cultural sanitization of a classroom and campus is precisely the wrong message to send, and it would probably not help us avoid controversy in any case.

We need to be able to deal with these issues on a careful, deliberative, case-by-case basis. We need to take seriously the concerns of students and others when they claim that a microaggression has occurred, or that a text or event has triggered the individual into feeling psychic or physical pain. The reflex response from critics when I make such statements is that the classroom ought not be one long therapy session. The rest of the class has material to master, observe many; we ought not sacrifice learning the material to help calm someone's nerves.

I disagree. I do not believe that a classroom or any positive learning experience will occur if we obsessively focus on the material at hand and ignore the larger contexts in which we work, and our students' concerns. We can chew pedagogical gum and walk intellectually at the same time if we recognize the concerns of those who are targeted, act with empathy, and create the conditions in the classroom and on campus that acknowledge the parameters of power at work under the framework of academic freedom and free speech. Indeed, an engaged classroom where students are able to confront one another openly, without fear of rejection or intimidation, is more likely to enhance rather than impede learning. Even if we do not yet have complete empirical evidence about the pervasiveness of micro-aggressions or their measurable impact on learning, we know that they exist and that they influence learning. Why don't we approach teaching and learning in a manner that seeks to affirm one's identity en route to learning the material at hand, rather than trying to make believe that what we say inside and outside of class does not matter, or that simply learning about one's own identity is an end itself?

The point of learning is not to avoid controversy, despite the conflict-averse attitude in many classrooms today. I do not want us to feel safe if safety means we avoid difficult conversations. In a linguistic sleight of hand, I want students to feel safe enough so that they might feel unsafe. We need classrooms where students are able to take risks and speak openly about difficult topics in a respectful manner, with the goal of achieving communion with one another through dialogue. To do that, we all need to feel vulnerable, not simply the gay student who is struggling with coming out or the only Black student in a class who feels out of place.

If a professor has a dialogical relationship with a class that is based on respect, then the culture in the classroom assumes understanding across intellectual borders. Individuals certainly can have strong opinions, but these comments need to be couched in a language of regard for each other. At the start of a semester, a professor might acknowledge that we come together out of respect for one another and with appreciation for one another's opinions. Our aim should be not to agree with everyone, but to make space for each person's standpoint and opinion.

In this framework, the professor is perhaps best considered, not as an authority who dispenses knowledge, but rather as a guide who is able to adapt the class based on the suggestions and comments of the students. Students feel free to point out when the professor has erred, and they are not afraid to voice sentiments that contradict the professor. In such a classroom, we need to acknowledge the legitimacy of individuals' identities, and we also need to be able to work out quite thorny issues. There are students today who come from a fundamentalist religious background and still believe homosexuality is a sin. Others believe abortion should be outlawed. Fundamentalist Christians and Muslims have views of women that are antithetical to my own ideas. I am concerned that religious students often feel marginalized. Should their viewpoints be respected as well? Yes. To respect someone's opinion does not imply I have to agree or that I should not make my own voice heard.

Too often, the discussion has turned on whether an individual has a right—does the professor have a right in his classroom to make a controversial point because he has academic freedom? Does another professor have a right to invite a speaker to campus because she has academic freedom? Do controversial speakers have a right to be heard at a public institution because of free speech even if their security will cost the institution a great deal of money for security? I have outlined my own answers pertaining to what we should think of as permissible. However, simply having a right to say something, either because of academic freedom or free speech, most certainly does not resolve our conflict. We only raise issues that are controversial. If they were not controversial, then they would not be debated as whether someone has a right to speak. Because we have determined that a talk can be given is a beginning step toward cultural engagement of the community. Indeed, if the discussion is not handled correctly, we may have made our point about the right to speech—but worsened the climate at the talk's conclusion.

Those who disagree with the speaker need to be able to approach the talk neither in fear nor in outrage. If we have a classroom and a campus that is a safe space, then individuals ought to be able to feel that their own selves are affirmed even when the speaker may be making points that are exactly opposite. The homophobic preacher who speaks against gay marriage, the Islamaphobe who calls for banning Muslims from the United States, or any number of similarly contentious speakers may be trying to make a serious point that nevertheless threatens members of the community. There are those who rightfully ask why we should give them a megaphone?

We do so not to signal that we agree with their views or that we want to further such ideas. However, we also approach such talks with a clear-eyed understanding that many people hold these sorts of opinions in the larger society. We are assuming that ultimately truth wins out. Justice Louis D. Brandeis's 1913 statement in *Harper's Weekly* that "sunlight is said to be the best of disinfectants" (p. 10) comes to mind here. If a university is to play a role in advancing democracy and aiding in overcoming the democratic recession, then surely, we have to engage speakers who put forward ideas that are inimical to the academic commons.

I do not think there is a recipe for success with regard to how controversial talks should be staged, but we do need multiple groups involved. There needs to be much more groundwork with our students to ensure that they understand the principles of academic freedom and free speech and why we court and respect controversy. Students are transitory; they attend an institution for a matter of years and then they depart. They are likely to feel passionate about why a particular speaker should or should not speak and we need to respect their ideas. The respect, however, needs to be put forward, not at the eleventh hour as the speaker sets foot on campus, but at the start of every school year and throughout a student's time at the institution.

Those students who feel most assaulted or insulted also deserve special recognition, acknowledgement, and respect. They are being asked to endure an assault, if it is perceived that way, in a manner that others are not. That preacher may annoy straight people, but he will give special animus for queer students. The religious bigot may make all people of religion ashamed but may give particular cause for concern to the Muslim family. The African American student who sits through a lecture by Charles Murray could interpret Murray's talk to say that Black students are inferior or do not deserve to be on campus because of affirmative action. Sometimes when such speakers arrive on campus the point is made that counseling will be made available—and of course that is fine and good and necessary. What we really need, however, is a robust discussion among those who are allies that is ongoing and comprehensive. The assault on democracy is not episodic; democracy's demise is an erosion that occurs not simply when a speech is given and the speaker leaves campus and moves onto the next event. The downfall occurs because we do not continue to speak about these sorts of assaults once the speaker has left. We fool ourselves, sometimes, by thinking that if we do not give a controversial speaker the right to express their ideas that we have made the right move. In our society, however, I am suggesting that a university must do the opposite.

One quality we have forsaken over the last generation is to think of the president as an intellectual leader of the institution rather than its chief fundraiser either with donors or the legislature and governor. At this point in time, however, we need presidents who are able to put forward robust comments that frame the sort of values that the institution holds that may be inimical to the controversial speaker who has been brought to campus. Frequently, presidents and their administrations seek to contain the controversy, almost wishing that it would go away. I am not suggesting that a president should be spoiling for an intellectual fight. In a globalized world, however, instantaneous communication occurs. At a talk, individuals will tweet in real time. We need leaders who are able to engage in constant, rather than episodic, communication about the values of the institution. We need individuals in student affairs who can provide ongoing support and enable clear lines of communication that is proactive rather than reactive.

Presidents are also temporary. A term of six or seven years is considered a long tenure for a college president today. But unlike students and the senior administration, the faculty are largely not transitory. Many will stay at the institution for a decade or longer. I have written about the import of tenure in all of this. Enabling these sorts of conversations and speeches requires a stable tenure-line faculty who understand the history of the organization and the ability to enable ongoing conversations of support that may be at odds or orthogonal to the controversial speakers who have been brought to campus. Ultimately the faculty controls the organization. If we have little regard for the nature of tenure, or we are too busy or uninformed to participate in enabling a climate for engaged communication, then we will fail. Obviously, not all faculty members need to speak in every class about how to deal with controversial speakers. They do, however, need to understand and support engagement. I have met many faculty members who remain wedded to their research and care little for involvement in the academic life I am suggesting here. Those individuals will not be useful for increasing democratic engagement.

The result is that we need to be a much more intentional community. We recognize that students still need jobs when they graduate from college, but just as critically we understand that students need to be engaged citizens. The way to be engaged is through involvement on multiple levels on their college campus. If we accept that academic freedom and free speech are the heartbeat of the institution, then we need to think more deeply about what precisely it is that most postsecondary institutions do, and to this I now turn.

CHAPTER FIVE

Understanding What Modern Universities Do

Goods and Services

Some services are relatively well-defined. When I go to the market with a list of groceries, I expect that the items will be on the shelves, afford-able, and in good condition. Presumably I go to this market frequently and know what to expect in terms of service, price, value, and quality. In many respects, the business is relatively easy to assess, both for the owner and for the customer. The owner wants to make a profit. The customer wants to buy what he or she wants and can afford. We all know that Whole Foods is going to be more expensive than Foodland, but customers pay the higher price because they can afford the money to get better service and, presumably, a better product. I may not buy paper towels at Whole Foods, but I will buy produce. Sometimes, I will go to the 7/11 down the street and pay the higher price for milk, simply for the convenience.

Radical libertarians will argue that the government has no role in overseeing my buying habits, but most of us believe that the government has some role to play. The libertarian's perspective is that the customer's comfort or discomfort will determine whether they return to the grocery store and whether the store stays in business. Most of us believe, however, that the customer is not simply engaged in a market-based transaction. The customer is also a consumer. The government plays a role in protecting consumers from dangerous or fraudulent practices. The fine points of how much protection a consumer should get from the government makes for a good argument. Nevertheless, the government regularly steps in when advertising is blatantly false or the product will make the consumer sick. We see announcements regularly about some type of produce or meat that is pulled from shelves because the government has determined it makes people ill. Those who sell products that are miracle cures for cancer, obesity, and any number of other illnesses are called to task for false advertising, and their products too are pulled from the shelves.

We also know that times change. Consumer preferences and expectations evolve. When I was a child, we simply bought "milk." On rare occasions, my mother let us drink chocolate milk. Today, milk comes in varieties, including almond, soy, and coconut. We will be disappointed if we cannot find milk that is 2 percent, 1 percent, nonfat, and skim. Some customers do not want the trouble to get vegetables that they must chop when they get home and instead want a bag of fresh-cut vegetables. We want strawberries throughout the year, not just when they are in season. We are willing to spend more money today on items that may not have existed or would have been thought of as extravagances a generation ago, such as avocados, and others of us will simply order online and have the food arrive at our doorstep.

This simplified way of looking at customers, their preferences, and the government becomes complicated when we look at different sorts of goods, especially nonprofit goods in regard to which the government has an explicit interest or role. This chapter considers what modern colleges and universities do—and how we should think about their role. Such an analysis is imperative if we want to ensure a more forceful role for postsecondary institutions in the public discourse about democracy. To discuss education, we need to consider the nature of a public good, as well as what the meaning of that public good entails. Even nonprofit higher education—private universities such as Stanford, Northwestern, and Vanderbilt—have a relationship uniquely different from a grocery store in terms of how they interact with the government and the citizenry. I appreciate that job preparation is one key role of academe; my concern is when we reduce all of higher education to vocational training. Accordingly, I first offer an overview of historical and traditional notions of the public good, and then I turn to how globalization and neoliberalism has refashioned how we think about what we might expect from higher education.

I then consider what the modern postsecondary institution does, and why. We typically think of university work in three domains—research, teaching/learning, and service. Just as our expectations of what consumers can find at the grocery stage have changed, so too has the desire for a different kind of education from what we once had. Students expect to see a syllabus online. They are not going to spend the day in the gymnasium at the start of the term registering for classes. They are going to use a variety of apps and tools to complete their assignments (and, in some cases, complete work on their smartphones), and they would find it odd to get hand-written notes from the professor.

What we want from higher education is less clear because of competing visions of the academy. Consider Toni Morrison's soaring words at Princeton University's 250th anniversary convocation in 1996:

> There are few places, very few places left, other than great universities, where both the wisdom of the dead coupled with the doubt of the living are vigorously encouraged, welcomed, become the very stuff of education, the pulse of teaching, the engine of research, the consequence of learning. No faculty member worth the profession has ever taken for granted as fixed truth or fiat all he or she has learned. The nature of our profession is to doubt, to expand, to enhance, to review, to interrogate.[1]

Although many of us might subscribe to such notions, there are also many who will not. Many others will object to even the assumption that there is no "fixed truth." Still others will say the college or university should have nothing to do with even the search for truth. Students need jobs; they do not need esoterica. In Hong Kong, there are many who claim that this search for truth has led to questioning authority, which has destabilized the government. To some in the Hong Kong establishment, universities are part of the problem.

In New Delhi, many students go to an IIT because—much like their engineering counterparts at USC or the University of California at Los Angeles (UCLA)—they want to be prepared for the workforce. They are not sure what workforce preparation entails, but they expect that the university is capable of giving them the necessary skills for gainful employment. What I shall point out is that these sorts of expectations are shaped in new ways given the environment we live in, and the students who take our classes. I then want to consider what the implications are for the modern university.

Traditional Notions of the Public Good

Public Goods

The definition of a public good has been typified by three concepts: non-rivalry, nonexcludability, and externalities (Kezar, 2004; Marginson, 2011). A *nonrivalrous* public good can be extended to others without significant effort or cost, and it is available to anyone who wishes to utilize it. In this sense, it is markedly different from a private good, such as a personal automobile where ridership is limited to the available seats in the car and the owner can decide where the vehicle goes. The subway, on the other hand, would be nonrivalrous in that everyone pays the same price to use the service, the costs of operation are subsidized, and theoretically there should be capacity for everyone.

Nonexcludability, as a concept, means that everyone participates in the cost of a public good and therefore cannot be excluded from using it. Since the citizenry pays for the construction of a subway, everyone can travel on it. Another nonexcludable public good is social security. Nonexcludability is an essential aspect because any excludability leaves a public good open to sharp political criticism. For example, Franklin Roosevelt knew that he needed to make social security available to everyone or it would not get broad acceptance. Conversely, affordable housing is not a public good because the government only provides direct subsidies to individuals who have a demonstrated need.

The creation and maintenance of a public good requires all individuals within a given society to share costs, but the full range of costs and benefits are difficult to determine from a market-based perspective. As stated by Sam Vaknin (2019), "Public goods impose costs and benefits on others—individuals or firms—outside the marketplace and their effects are only partially reflected in prices and market transactions" (p. 1). Hence, public goods are subject to *externalities* in that their social benefits, beyond the actual service that is provided, can be both impactful and expansive.

A lighthouse is a classic example of a public good. When a ship brings necessary materials to port due to the path outlined by the lighthouse, society benefits. Another example of a public good would be national defense. As new people are born or welcomed within a country's borders, the subsequent rise in population does not generally cause the expense of the public good—whether it is a lighthouse or a fighter plane—to increase. Citizens share the costs of a lighthouse and of defense when they pay taxes.

In general, a public good requires some form of shared expense because it would likely never be profitable in the market and would, therefore, be underproduced, or even neglected.

The views over which activities and products deserve to be designated as "public goods" is subject to context and time. For instance, fire protection was considered a personal responsibility in the nineteenth century, and private companies specializing in firefighting and rescue were hired by individuals who owned property. This arrangement was fine as long as the fire only affected individuals who had already secured the services of a private firefighting company. However, if a fire spread to a different person's home and that individual did not have fire insurance from the same company, the firefighters would simply let the house burn to the ground. Over time, the public decided that firefighting would be better supported through public funds so that everyone's property could be protected, no matter where a fire started. Through this view of firefighting as a public good, it did not matter if an individual was wealthy or not; everyone would benefit from the service because the entire community would be in less danger of a fire spreading to multiple properties.

On the other hand, the activity of policing is an example of a public good that is slowly entering the private sphere. In recent years, many people in urban, upper-class communities have bought property in gated communities and hired private security firms because they feel that their city's police department does not provide enough security. It is no coincidence, then, that many who believe strongly in lower taxes and a decrease in public services are also the same individuals who make extensive use of private services that were once considered necessary for the public good.

Other people argue that private companies can provide goods better and more efficiently than the government. For instance, many prisons today are run by private companies. Militias operate outside government oversight in some countries where citizens feel unsafe. As a result, public goods are being redefined, if not eliminated, both in functioning states where market forces are being favored, as well as in failed states where the political infrastructure is danger of falling apart.

Moreover, the theory of public goods is never as neat, nor as simple, as one might like. From a certain distance, national defense would appear to be a clear example of a public good, especially since the expenses of national defense would seemingly apply to all. Nevertheless, one could argue that the costs of protecting American citizens, for example, against a missile attack in Guam are much greater than protection in the continental 48 states. In a similar vein, rural counties often require more expensive investments of infrastructure for public goods such as water. In such circumstances, outlying areas may have to either pay more for the public good or go without it.

When one makes the assessment that a public good is either too expensive or not sufficient for the needs of society and turns to the market for a private solution, there are two policy-oriented implications. First, the public may evince decreasing support for other public goods, such as policing or education. Second, there may be an increased mandate to change tax structures around other activities that straddle the line between public and private goods. For decades, communities have increased taxes through municipal bonds so that much-needed highways or school buildings could be constructed. In an environment in which public monies are perceived to be wasteful and/or ineffective, though, citizens may expect the privatization of highway construction, special lanes for drivers willing to pay more so they can avoid traffic, and tax relief in lieu of a bond issuance.

Hence, the conception of a public good in the United States is diminishing. There was once consensus around the notion that national parks were public goods worthy of protection and universal enjoyment. However, budgets for national parks have shrunk precipitously; as a result, park fees are charged, and much-needed maintenance gets deferred from year to year. Rather than viewing national parks as a public good, today's politicians are likely to argue that only the individuals who use the park should pay for it.

Higher Education as a Public Good

Until the passage of the Morrill Land Grant Acts in 1862 and 1890, higher education was viewed as a private good that only elite and wealthy young white men could afford. Once land grant universities began offering admission to a broader economic range of young white men, however, the belief that the United States would benefit from a "massification" of higher education opportunity began to take hold. Initially, higher education at the Morrill Act land grant universities was focused on practical training in the agricultural and mechanical sciences. Those institutions began to expand their offerings as more and more people began to desire a postsecondary degree. Higher education was, of course, never completely nonrivalrous, as an influx of students raised the expenses of the public good. State systems eventually met much of the need by offering several different types of institutions—community colleges, technical colleges, teacher's colleges, and research universities, to name a few—thus ensuring access for many who would never be able to access higher education as a private good. Similar to how the federal government provides military defense for the nation, individual states subsidized access to higher education as a public good.

Although India and Hong Kong were British territories, their history is quite different. Indian higher education has a long and distinguished history, with Nalanda University, by many accounts, being the world's oldest university (Sen, 2015; Yeo, 2011). British colonialism, however, did not prioritize higher education and, even in the new capital of New Delhi, universities were reserved for very few. Of consequence, although Zakir Husain Delhi College opened in 1792, the first university did not open until 1922: the University of Delhi (DU). Today, DU has over 100,000 students and another 200,000 part-timers. Hong Kong has had higher education for over a century, with HKU and other institutions opening throughout the twentieth century. Although both cities think of higher education as a public good, there are more private than public institutions in New Delhi, and the entire system is grossly underfunded (National Institution for Transformation of India, 2018; Raman, 2019). Hong Kong's funding is the opposite. Students pay virtually no tuition and the government covers the costs. Private higher education in Hong Kong is minimal (Chiu, 2018).

The argument over public higher education as a public good has largely turned on two issues: form and function. As with their confreres in K–12 education, individuals have asked why public monies go to an institution rather than a person. Why not let the consumers choose how to spend their money rather than force them to choose public institutions? The call for expanded choices for the consumer has less to do with the quality of the content—curricular offerings—and more to do with the manner in which learning is conveyed. Public institutions, in general, have set geographic boundaries, and courses are offered at specific times. Some will point out that those times are arranged for the suitability of the faculty rather than the convenience of the consumer. The assumption here is that enabling the citizenry to receive a postsecondary degree is still in the public good and hence deserving of public monies; what is questionable is the organizational form that provides the education.

For-profit providers have built their course offerings in a way that any savvy entrepreneur would build a business—the courses are offered at convenient times and locations. Rather than the lockstep 15-week semester that begins around Labor Day, takes a break over the Christmas holidays, and starts again in January, only to end for the summer interregnum in

May, for-profits are more likely to offer classes around the year and not be wedded to any particular calendar. Classes might be offered in the evening or on weekends to suit the needs of working people, and a class is as likely to be held in a vacant room in a shopping mall as it is on a "campus." Thus, just as the K–12 discussion has morphed from a small constituency—Catholics—desirous of a specific kind of institution for their children, to a larger discussion of school choice, so too in higher education has the discussion moved toward wondering why public monies support institutions rather than people.

Such an argument is possible because the definition of higher education has been framed in a manner akin to K–12 education. The role of public schools is to educate children; the role of public higher education is to educate adolescents and adults. If the definition of public and for-profit institutions is equivalent, then naturally the criticisms of one become conjoined with criticisms of the other. Further, for-profit colleges and universities also are able to point to a diverse constituency with regard to race, class, and gender. That is, some might argue that public higher education increases access to a postsecondary education for previously disenfranchised groups. However, the percentage of African American students at four-year, for-profit institutions, for example, is 29 percent, while the percentage of African American students at four-year public institutions is 12 percent and the percentage at four-year private institutions is 13 percent. Indeed, when we speak of Black Lives Matter on college campuses a large part of the focus is not only on acts of discrimination, but also the underrepresentation of Black students and faculty on all campuses. Moreover, the percentage of Hispanics who attend two- and four-year for-profit institutions is virtually identical to the percentage attending public two-year and four-year public institutions (National Center for Education Statistics, 2018, p. 174). One can reasonably conclude that public postsecondary education is not doing a demonstrably better job at increasing access to higher education than the for-profit institutions.

Further, as I will elaborate, there are those who ask about "bad" public goods (Shaw, 2010). Hong Kong's parents will claim that K–12 education is a bad public good and will send their children to private schools, which in turn, prepares them for entry into public universities. The New Delhi government has poured revenue into its elementary schools to try to make them good public goods. Just as prisons have been criticized so that they were privatized and charter school advocates have bemoaned the state of local schools, there are those who have said that higher education may be a public good, but it is a "bad public good." The criticism largely turns on the perceived political bias that permeates public higher education and the lack of jobs available to students when they graduate. Such a perspective, as with prisons and charter schools, has tried to move the idea of a public good in a different direction. The good is still important, but the purveyor is not.

The responses by those who reject the idea of public funding of for-profit colleges and universities (FPCU) generally has focused on content: the curriculum of public higher education has a more noble purpose than merely training; hence, FPCUs should be looked on as suspect and certainly not as deserving of public monies. To be sure, certain classes in some traditional institutions have had the purpose of helping students think through thorny problems, and by doing so have made them more publicly engaged—even though the measurement of such engagement has proven to be difficult. The argument fails, however, when we look at the vast panoply of institutions and courses offered under the aegis of the public good. Surely an auto mechanics course at a community college or an accounting course at a state college have the potential of doing little more than training students for employment. The point is not that these courses fall short of expectations, but that not every course in every public institution is, or should be, geared toward liberal learning.

However, public higher education has never been about only schooling and learning for those who participate in higher education. A public good is intended to benefit more than just those who make use of it. Fire stations exist to protect everyone. The national defense protects all citizens. If a citizen's house is saved by the fire department or an individual saves time in getting to work because of the public subway, that's great for that individual. The philosophy behind a public good, however, has less to do with the private benefit that the individual accrues and more to do with the public benefit we all accrue by putting fires out and getting the workforce where they need to be.

Thus, the private benefits of a postsecondary education—if it is a public good—needs to help more than the individuals who receive that public education; in large part, that is why public institutions have been accorded the right to offer that service. The expectation has been that, in return for public support, colleges and universities will benefit all the citizenry, even if indirectly, irrespective of whether individuals actually attend the institution. If public universities are simply oriented to serving the private interests of individuals—of increasing the wealth of their graduates—then why shouldn't public monies be spread about all types of institutions that are able to do that in different forms and with different contents? Indeed, why should public monies be spent on a private good at all?

Stuart Tannock (2006) has a response that is worth quoting:

> Universities serve the public good, all else being equal, not when they contribute to "economic development" in some abstract and general sense, but when they help to increase the wealth and well-being of all individuals together; and more specifically, when they work to ensure that the college educated do not gain at the expense of the non-college educated. (p. 45)

Tannock's comment, while provocative, also points to the possibility that higher education should be privatized. On the one hand, Tannock usefully argues that the purpose of postsecondary institutions has to be more than merely as educational training centers for those who attend them. On the other hand, Tannock's suggestion brings into question, not merely the form that provides the public good—public colleges and universities—but also whether such a good is even worthy of public monies. In effect, Tannock makes the helpful point that universities are primarily oriented to serving the private interests of individuals and, if they are, then why have they any right to public funding more than other organizations that serve private interests? Such an observation, if followed to its logical conclusion, moves not merely toward defunding the form of the public good—public institutions—but also toward the definition itself of higher education.

Tannock and others actually believe that the idea of education and the market is anathema, and rather than ape market tendencies, public higher education has to be more focused on educational purpose. John McMurtry (1991), for example, has argued, "The overriding goal of corporate agents in the marketplace is to maximize private money profits. The overriding goal of educational agents in schools, college, and universities is to advance and disseminate shared knowledge" (p. 211). Such an opposition assumes that knowledge is to be shared openly rather than consumed privately. He also extends the idea of higher education as a public good by acknowledging that the advancement of knowledge—conceivably through research—is also a goal.

Those who argue for postsecondary institutions as a public good have never denied that an educational degree has private benefits for an individual. As Lazerson (1998) has noted:

> Higher education came to simultaneously embody both a public good—beneficial to the nation's economy, protective of its national defense, opening up new avenues of knowledge, and able to realize equality of educational opportunity—and a private benefit so that everyone who possessed it substantially improved their access to higher income, status and security (p. 65).

The point, then, is not that someone accrues personal benefit through a public good, but that the personal benefit cannot be the only, or even the primary, benefit. From this perspective, a public good has to entail more than the traditional components I outlined of nonrivalry, nonexcludability, and externalities. Perhaps commonsensical and tautological, but nevertheless, a public good has to demonstrate a good for the public. Such a claim assumes that the form of the public good is quite important—a public institution will undertake actions that a private company is likely not to do because of the profit motive.

To be sure, land grant institutions in the United States came about to develop a public good. In large part, however, their stated purpose was aimed at utilitarian content—training in the mechanical and agricultural sciences. Implicitly, the assumption was that a well-educated citizenry enables them to be that much more involved in the democratic public sphere. Such a purpose was critical in the nineteenth century because no one else offered such training on a widespread basis. Today, however, multiple providers are able to offer such classes. Some land grants once offered agricultural extension services to local farmers, but such services are less in need today than they were in the early twentieth century. Thus, to maintain the idea of a public good, just as with all concepts, higher education needs to be constantly in the business of redefining itself. As times change, the underlying ethos for a public good may not change, but the form and content may undergo reformulation.

Some who long for the idea of the public good of the past will look to the sweeping statements of college presidents such as Daniel Coit Gilman of Johns Hopkins University, William Rainey Harper of the University of Chicago, or Charles Eliot of Harvard University. They spoke about the obligation of academe to society. In Gilman's inspirational inaugural address, he said, for example, that universities should "make for less misery among the poor, less ignorance in the schools, less fraud in business, less folly in politics" (quoted in Benson et al., 2005, p. 193). These are noble sentiments, to be sure, but what is one to make of them? What do we do to turn such sentiments into public policy?

California's Master Plan of 1960 stands out as an exemplar of a public good. The state put forward the notion that all citizens of California deserved to attend a postsecondary institution if they desired, and the state was responsible for the costs of running the system. "Tuition" was not even charged; "fees" were for extras that an individual might desire. However, that public obligation has faded (Marginson, 2018). State and federal commitment to postsecondary institutions has dramatically lessened such that most students now have to pay some amount of revenue to enable the organization to provide the public good.

Globalization and Neoliberalism's Impact on the Public Good

If the meaning of the public good has been fluid in the larger arena in terms of how we think about fire companies and the like, then it also has changed with regard to higher education. In the United States, India, and elsewhere, we had an expansive notion of the public good throughout much of the twentieth century. As I noted, originally higher education was not part of the discourse of public goods. Colleges and universities either were the reserve of the wealthy or they were small religious colleges who largely trained people for the ministry. During the Civil War, however, Congress passed the Land Grant Act based on the stewardship of Senator Justin Morrill and the support of Abraham Lincoln in 1862. The assumption was that the federal and state governments should have a role in supporting higher education, not simply for the wealthy, but also for the working class. By the late nineteenth century, the second Morrill Act allocated monies for historically black colleges and universities (HBCUs) for African Americans, and eventually for Hispanic-serving institutions and tribally controlled colleges.

The result is that, in the twenty-first century, close to 40 percent of all U.S degree-granting colleges and universities are public four and two-year institutions. What is more important, these institutions enroll close to three-quarters of all undergraduate and graduate students (Weisbrod et al., 2008). Private nonprofit institutions are smaller; the for-profit sector had grown to about 12 percent of the total but has been shrinking because of the fallout from inquiries about their cost and quality (Sedmak, 2019).

Virtually all the postsecondary institutions in Hong Kong are public, and they are subsidized by the Hong Kong government. India's situation is more complex, but a fair estimate is that slightly less than two-thirds of postsecondary institutions are public, or related to public, colleges and universities.

The coronavirus has crippled postsecondary institutions, both public and private, small, medium, and large. Many students are unable to pay the cost for college, and governments have, to varying degrees, provided support, usually in the form of loans. What higher education will look like in a decade obviously is unclear, but I suspect that the revolution that so many have predicted will not occur. As I mentioned in chapter one, however much Clayton Christensen, and before him, Peter Drucker, have been academic Jeremiahs saying, "The end is near," it has not happened. Even today, when academe faces the worst crisis in a century, predictions are that about 5 percent of the 4,000 postsecondary institutions face closure. Two hundred institutional closures are certainly significant, but it does not represent total disruption and devastation for the postsecondary system. Certainly we need to be focused on the economic dilemmas that confront us when unexpected traumas and catastrophic events occur, but ultimately the issues I am raising here frame the way in which we respond.

Throughout much of the twentieth century, Congress, state governments, and the citizenry continued to think of higher education as a public good in a manner akin to K–12 education. We have to keep in mind, then, that a public good has been not simply something that benefits an individual, or a group of individuals. And, until recently, a public good was offered by the public. A commitment to clean drinking water did not mean that we could buy bottles of water from a company, but that the federal and state governments devised ways to bring, in theory, clean drinking water to everyone in their purview. The post office delivered mail to everyone, not just a select few. Nothing prevented me from buying bottled water or from using a privately owned mail delivery service, but the cost was borne by the user, not the government. The assumption of the use of private goods was that the beneficiary was the user, not the public.

Similarly, public two- and four-year colleges and universities were supposed to be subsidized by the government. There were costs to the student, but they did not reflect the actual cost of educating every user. There were also particular groups whom the government sought to support, or foci that were encouraged. The GI Bill was a way to enable access to higher education for veterans. Different initiatives encouraged individuals to study in the humanities or sciences. However, special initiatives aimed at people or ideas are not part of the public good. For a good to be public, we all have to benefit, or be capable of benefiting, in some fashion.

India has been no different; the only problem has been the shortage of funding to pay for public goods. The needs have been many, but the funding has not been available in a country that is soon to be the largest in the world. Hong Kong, however, has been different. Social expenditures for various social services have not been equivalent. Public goods were available, but the poorest people in Hong Kong could not avail themselves of these services. In *Poverty in the Midst of Affluence,* Leo Goodstadt (2014), a longtime student of the Hong Kong economy, points out how immigrants and the poor have been shortchanged and the business community has been promoted. "Hong Kong's social expenditure in 2001," he writes, "was at the same level as the average OECD [Organisation for Economic Co-operation and Development] members in 1960" (p. 13). The challenge in education was focused on the schools rather than the universities. The irony was that Hong Kong universities were fully funded, but to get into those universities, parents sent their children to private schools and after-school tutoring services[2] because public schools were considered "bad" public goods. What does it mean if something is a public good but many citizens do not avail themselves of the public good because they do not qualify? It's as if clean drinking water were a public good but the water came from fountains set too high for some people to reach.

Beginning in the 1980s, however, with the rise of globalization and the initiation of neoliberal policies, a critique of higher education began to take hold (Cantwell and Kauppinen, 2014; Olssen & Peters, 2005; Rhoades, 1998, 2011). The criticism of higher education was not orchestrated in any particular way—it came from various angles—and it has never faded. Unlike clean water or national defense, higher education is more diffuse. To be sure, we can debate the nature of defense—should we have this or that sort of weaponry—but no one has questioned the right of a country to defend itself against foreign invaders. No one questions that everyone should have access to clean drinking water. I support having a fire department for all of us so if my neighbor's house burns down, they can put the fire out and my house is not harmed. Whether I ever need to use the fire department myself is a moot question.

Higher education is different and particularly susceptible to a neoliberal/globalist critique. There are five linked criticisms that emphasize privatization of higher education. As Matthew T. Lambert (2014) has noted, "Privatization . . . is a result and a solution to the challenges that colleges and universities face across the country. . . . Higher education is increasingly viewed as a private good" (p. 77). These criticisms of higher education derive from neoliberal and globalization's way to view goods and are premised on five critiques:

First, not everyone participates in higher education, yet it is funded by public monies. The argument here is that a bachelor's degree, in particular, is much more a private good than a public one. Indeed, the credentialing of society does not benefit the individual without a bachelor's degree and conceivably even harms the individual by making them less competitive in the marketplace. Missile defense supports all the borders of a country; higher education benefits only those who attend a postsecondary institution.

Such a criticism is more persuasive today than a generation ago. When I graduated from university, there was no question about my finding a job; I knew that I had multiple options. By the twenty-first century, however, the working-class jobs that once employed millions and enabled them to climb into the middle class had been lost to globalization. A bachelor's degree became a marketing tool—go to college and make yourself more competitive than your neighbor with only a high school degree. While the argument may warrant merit, it certainly defeats the notion of a public good that I have been putting forward.

A second argument pertains to choice. The neoliberal position is that a sign of a vibrant society is the choices that individuals may make about their life. Such a point brings much, but not all, of a public good into question. Why restrict the choice a person makes with regard to attending a college? When I was a child, my parents sent me to a Catholic grammar school just the way every Tierney family member had been educated. There was no argument from my parents about the choice that they had made for their sons. They knew that public schools existed, and some of them were fine, but they wanted a special kind of education for their children and they acknowledged that they should pay for that education. In much the same vein, when my brothers and I applied to college, we only applied to private universities—they went to Notre Dame, and I attended Tufts. We received federal and institutional grants—again, different from a public good—but my parents were fine with the idea that they should pay extra for their boys to attend private universities.

The neoliberal emphasis on choice, however, emphasizes the potpourri of possibilities that exist and asks why all public monies need to go to one type of institution when many types exist. If the government were to be involved at all in education, why would we not fund the individual and leave it to them to decide how best to spend public dollars? This line of thinking extends to all of education. Charter schools have pushed this line of thinking. If parents want to send their child to a Catholic school, why should they be made to pay extra dollars as long as the school meets state standards? If an individual's primary choice for a postsecondary education is a for-profit college in a mall close to where the person lives and works, then why not subsidize the individual's education there and reduce the amount of money the public institution gets that will not be utilized? If choice is defined as an essential component of democracy and lack of choice is equated with "sameness" or "socialism," then such an argument gains currency.

A third criticism of higher education and the public good has to do with what I referred to earlier as a "bad" public good. The clearest example has to do with the post office. I do not know many individuals who enjoy going to a post office, but it is an essential public service; until recently, there were no private options.

We have come to equate public services with inferior quality. The Reagan (U.S.) and Thatcher (U.K.) administrations of the 1980s made such a critique an art form, and kept up a continual drumbeat about how poor public services and public administrative bureaucracies were, while emphasizing how superior the market was (Page, 2012; Pierson, 1994). The assertion from a neoliberal position is that the customer is always right: if a restaurant serves inferior food then the restaurant will go out of business. The post office served the equivalent of bad food, but never went out of business because they were a public good.

What we learned with the critique of "bad" public goods was that individuals were willing to pay extra for convenience. Individuals used Federal Express because they wanted to make sure their package did not get lost and arrived on time. Individuals went to a for-profit college because they didn't want to have to drive out of their way to attend a class or go through the hassle of parking, navigating a campus, and paying for services—such as the gym or the library—that they wouldn't use.

Public higher education also had completion problems. Less than 50 percent of young Americans complete a community college degree, much less a bachelor's (Cass, 2018). And when students graduate, they are either unable to find work or, at a rate higher than 40 percent, underemployed in jobs that do not necessitate a college credential (Kolko, 2019).[3] If there is such a thing as a "bad" public good and if we deem employment as the goal of higher education, then a fair critique can be made of the quality of higher education. Indeed, Aggarwal et al. (2012) make the case that there is a serious, significant, long-standing mismatch between what students in India say they want to study, what is actually offered, and what sorts of employment exist for them in India. There is also a discrepancy in terms of how students want to learn. The neoliberals will make the analogy that if a restaurant said it was only offering dinner from 5 to 6 on Mondays, Wednesdays, and Fridays, it would not stay open very long. And yet, that's exactly the sort of framework employed by postsecondary institutions who cater to the needs of the faculty rather than the consumer. This observation brings me to my fourth point.

Globalization's interface with social media and technology has added a fourth component that brought a commitment to public higher education into question. Just as email and its various iterations lessened the need for us to use the post office, so too did technology change the way we thought about higher education. Indeed, the pandemic interrupted academic life in a manner that was unprecedented.

Why take a set number of classes over a specific time period, if we can master the material online whenever we wanted? Consumers grew accustomed to watching shows when they wanted, not when the movie theaters decided they would show films. If a viewer wished to stream all of a particular show at once and watch 15 episodes over the course of a weekend, then so be it. Why did that same consumer have to sit still for a class for 15 weeks that the instructor delivered on Wednesday mornings because it was convenient for the professor? Why did that same consumer have to miss out on going on a trip because the exam was offered at a time that conflicted with the person's travel schedule?

Public higher education, from this perspective, was not simply a "bad" public good, but an irrelevant one. The assumption was once that education was the vehicle that propelled individuals into the middle class. In the early nineteenth century, Horace Mann created compulsory schooling because the assumption was that a better educated citizenry created the conditions for a better country (Tyack, 1976). Historically, Americans have responded affirmatively when there has been a question about increasing schooling for everyone—until now. By the turn of the twentieth century, elementary schooling was compulsory, and when a state was admitted to the union, it had to support public education. By the 1960s, dropping out of school was not allowed, and high school graduation became compulsory. The assumption was largely borne out—the more education a person received, the greater their earnings. Jobs were not scarce, and the labor force expanded as people became better educated

Globalization, however, moved manufacturing overseas. Unions declined. Jobs became automated. The match between what one learned in college and what one needed for the workforce became less clear. As Moretti (2012) has observed, "Middle-class salaries are declining. Good jobs are scarce. The typical middle-class worker with a high school education is making an hourly wage 8 percent lower that his father's was in 1980, adjusted for inflation" (p. 6). The labor market is going through seismic shifts because of a neoliberal agenda informed by globalization. One consequence of these shifts is that people question the value of a postsecondary degree. Economic growth over the last generation has come at the expense of the poor and to the benefit of the rich. As Cass (2018) notes about the United States, "While gross domestic product (GDP) tripled from 1975–2015, the median worker's wages have barely budged. Half of Americans born in 1980 were earning less at age thirty than their parents had made at that age" (p. 1). Whether one applauds this change or bemoans it, a result has been a lessening of support for public goods, in general, and public higher education, in particular.

There was no one reason that led people to question the education-to-prosperity assumption; nevertheless, by the turn of the twenty-first century, there was no consensus that we should increase mandatory education even for a community college degree, much less a four-year degree. The "College for All" movement has stalled because the mode, format, and content of a college education have been compared to specific skills one might learn online in a manner that was not simply different from, but unthought of and impossible to implement, a generation ago. Some people will also argue that the online version is not simply a substitute, but a superior version to the traditional format.

The final critique has to do with the polarization that occurs within countries. A post office, or drinking water, or national defense are not obvious intellectual outposts. We may disagree with nuclear weapons, for example, but the idea of defense is not automatically defined as a particular ideology or position. Colleges and universities, however, have become ideologically fraught. Rightly or wrongly, higher education is seen as a breeding ground for left-wing indoctrination. We see that in Hong Kong as the Chinese government criticizes the universities for supporting student strikes (E. Yu et al., 2019). Many observers see universities in Hong Kong as undergoing fundamental changes with the new law that China has passed. We see that from the governing BJP in India, which they have sent police onto campuses at Jawaharalal Nehru University (JNU) and the University of Delhi to stop protests or demonstrations in support of independence for Kashmir (Agrawal & Salam, 2020; Prasad, 2020). And we have seen it in Los Angeles when a speaker at a campus was shouted down because of a particular ideological stance. The result is that higher education has undergone withering criticism as left-wing and supporting a particular view of society that is inherently ideological. The assumption is that public monies should not go for such tasks.

What the modern university does is no longer as clear as it has been. Throughout the twentieth century, higher education had been widely admired. As a country climbed into the middle class, one critical component was the expansion of colleges and universities. Countries such as China and India sent their students abroad, frequently to the United States, because they saw a well-educated citizenry as key to economic development (Altbach, 2009). Research was not questioned because it served multiple roles in augmenting the well-being of society. What, then, is it that the university has done? And, perhaps more importantly for our purposes here, what should it be doing in the twenty-first century?

Tomlinson and Lipsitz (2013) are worth quoting at length to help answer this question because their statement fleshes out the parameters of neoliberalism and globalization:

> Neoliberalism is not just an economic system. Unimpeded capital accumulation requires extensive ideological legitimation. Neoliberal practices seek to produce neoliberal subjects through a social pedagogy that aims to naturalize hierarchy and exploitation by promoting internalized preferences for profits over the needs of people, relentless individuation of collective social processes, cultivation of hostile privatism and defensive localism based on exaggerated fears of difference, and mobilization of anger and resentment against vulnerable populations to render them disposable, displaceable, deportable, and docile. The grandiose aspirations of neoliberal pedagogy, however, are often undermined by the system's ruinous effects. Neoliberalism promises prosperity but delivers austerity. (p. 3)

I have offered their assessment of neoliberalism, and, by inference, globalization, because they help summarize the underlying framework of a rationalist structure. The critiques I have put forward all have a degree of logic to them—of course there are inefficiencies, for example, in the system—but the solutions that have been put forward rationalize inequities rather than overcome them. What we need to think through, then, is what is it that we expect of the modern university? And how do we evaluate what the modern university is accomplishing?

Explaining (and Ranking) What the Modern University Does (and Why)

The normal way to think of a postsecondary institution is to divide it into tripartite roles of research, teaching, and service. Teaching institutions largely have only a teaching and service function, and community colleges have no expectation of research. At public and private research universities, the divide is typically 40-40-20 for the percentages of research, teaching, and service. Research is more robust in Los Angeles than in Hong Kong and New Delhi, and graduate education in the hard sciences is more fulsome in LA than either Delhi or Hong Kong. However, Delhi's IITs are well-respected for their focus on engineering.

We tend to historicize practices and assume that what we currently have not only is the way the organization was structured in the past, but also is the way it must be in the future. We know, however, that our structures are always in flux, that what we have today differs significantly from yesterday, and, hence, can be different tomorrow. The assumption that structures are unbendable creates a brittleness in our work lives so that we assume we have few alternatives; either we fit within the overarching structure or we fail. Further, neoliberalism and globalization also have smothered diversity at the expense of a simplified analysis about what counts as knowledge, and, by inference, how we judge the success or failure of an institution.

When we point out that the structure has privileged particular groups and marginalized others, there is generally a bifurcated analysis. On the one hand, the response is to acknowledge the high standards of a structure and either explain that people need to meet the standards or we will create ways to help them do so. The point here is that there is nothing wrong with the structure itself, and it is the people who have to change. A neoliberal response then builds in ways for the marginalized to catch up. The problem is that the marginalized stay marginalized. And those who are marginalized—whether by race, gender, disability, class or sexual orientation—are the ones who have to own the problem. The adequacy of the structure is not questioned; the people are.

Again, recognize the intuitive logic of neoliberalism. We set arbitrary standards, but they are not seen as arbitrary. We develop standards that assume a meritocratic world. If individuals merit promotion or tenure, then their work will demonstrate that they have met the standard. Objectivity is key.

I understand the rationale behind the framework and, as always, understand many good-faith attempts to help people who cannot meet the standards. Some people do not know how the system works and they need advice; others need to work on their argumentative skills in writing and such, and, in order to meet the standards, they need to be supported. The problem is that such attempts inevitably reinscribe the status quo. In this light, the structure is unchanging; individuals need to change, not the way we go about doing our work.

On the other hand, the choice is to create alternative criteria for those who are different. We have the standard way and an alternative path. The problem, of course, is those who choose the alternative path are inevitably regarded as second-class citizens who in some fashion do not deserve to be at the university. The assumption is that the structure is fine, but the individuals are flawed. In the United States and India, discussions about affirmative action have devolved into this sort of neoliberal critique. Those who have benefited from affirmative action do not really merit admission. Really, this framework is a variation on the first one in the sense that the structure is not the problem, but the people are.

Who can argue with a framework that appears neutral, is based on merit, and—when inequities are found toward a particular group—resources are provided so that marginalized individuals can improve? Here we have the argument that neoliberals make, even more so in a globalized world. We look at the modern institution and assume that criteria are transportable, that they simply move from country to country. The example par excellence of the globalization of this sort of framework has to do with institutional rankings.

Only in the last 30 years have rankings taken on prominence. Now, the ranking of the world's top 200 universities is met with fanfare, jubilation, or shame. I was in Malaysia when two of its universities dropped out of the top 200, and the tragic assessment was front-page news for a week. The prime minister held a news conference saying that such a national disgrace would not happen again. China has consciously aimed to enter the academic "arms race" and improve its standing; India has stood by and belatedly come up with a version of the second response I just outlined: it will create their own rankings because none of their institutions rank in the top 400. Hong Kong has some of the world's best universities, and HKUST is the one of the newest of the world's universities in the top 100 (Postiglione, 2011). One way Hong Kong was able to hold off China was to point to the superiority of its universities. With the rise of universities in Beijing and Shanghai, the primacy of Hong Kong has come in for criticism, and many observers believe that the new National Security law that China passed will particularly impact Hong Kong's universities, which in turn, will impact their rankings.

Rankings are simply an organizational response to neoliberalism in a global framework (Amsler & Bolsmann, 2012; Lynch, 2015; Olssen, 2016; Tierney & Lanford, 2017). The entire world subscribes to the same standards. If we have one definition of "good," then surely a university that aspires to be "good" needs to meet those standards, regardless of location. The framework for rankings and how to improve them has become a cottage industry. The *Times Higher Education (THE),* in particular, has extended the gospel of uniform rankings largely to boost its own revenue at a time when print copies of newspapers are shrinking. It has also recognized ways to increase interest (and revenue) by analyzing the rankings. In addition to global rankings, for example, there are also regional rankings and rankings done by type of institution. Conferences abound where people can learn how the rankings are done and how to improve their own institution's rank, and they will pay hundreds of dollars for registration fees to do so.[4] In true democratic fashion, *THE* even countenances criticism and will invite individuals who hold contrarian views. All this, however, fits nicely into a neoliberal framework about how we think about academic quality.

In the hard sciences, should we not want a 'one-size-fits-all' framework that judges quality similarly irrespective of location or institutional type? Wouldn't anyone want the "best" surgeon to operate on their child? It is difficult to argue with a leveling logic that quality can be transported, irrespective of nation or area of inquiry, if we subscribe to a notion of science where scientific objectivity is the sole criteria on which we base the worth of a postsecondary institution. The problem is that not all knowledge, nor our response to intellectual inquiry, can be reduced to provable mathematical equations.

I once had a Fulbright Grant to go to Central America, where I studied perceptions of academic quality in the developing world. My initial question to all interviewees was, "Is this a good institution?" They invariably responded by asking me what my definition of quality was, and I parried in return that I wanted them to give me their interpretation of quality. Most, but not all, the faculty and administrators I interviewed held doctorates from the United States or Europe. Their internalized definitions of quality were largely threefold—one had to do with international rankings, a second had to do with the region (Central and Latin America), and the third had to do with their own country (In this case, Costa Rica, Panama, or Guatemala). Recognize that if we are to hold all institutions in all countries to the same criteria, then developing countries either need to commit enormous resources from meager national budgets to compete, or they are deemed substandard. Should a nation such as Guatemala commit the resources necessary to compete with Harvard University? If it does not, then are we to conclude that its institutions are second-rate?

Rankings epitomize the environment in which we currently live. Neoliberalism thrives on a competitive environment of winners and losers and a false logic of rationality. Because graduate training has largely been in the industrialized nations of the United States and Europe, Western notions of science have been the marker for excellence. Globalization has exacerbated the intellectual arms race.

The rankings are predicated on two assumptions. First, postsecondary education is an important product. Although there have been worrying signs that some observers, especially in the United States, feel that a postsecondary education is no longer useful or necessary to succeed in the marketplace (see Bennett & Wilezol, 2013; Caplan, 2018), the overwhelming view from around the world is that postsecondary education remains critically important for individuals to succeed, and, by inference, for the nation to succeed. India, which has long lagged behind China in investing in higher education, has caught up because it recognizes the need for individuals with a bachelor's degree. Hong Kong also has remained convinced that higher education is an important commodity for its youth, albeit not necessarily for the poor or immigrants. The curious logic of these ideas, however, is that jobs are increasingly difficult to find in ever-tightening markets. Whereas a bachelor's degree was once a certain ticket to the middle class, a house, and a stable income in most of the world, globalization has made that promise much less certain. Further, one might assume that if rankings represent the importance of higher education on a global scale to countries, then its cementing as a public good should be certain. But that has not been the case. If anything, the opposite is true. Rather than being assured of a certain share of public funding, universities in Delhi, Hong Kong, and Los Angeles continually scramble for funds to help support themselves and rise in the global rankings.

The second assumption is that the criteria employed to judge institutions for global rankings are largely correct, regardless of country. Again, if we are playing baseball, the rules do not change from country to country, so surely rankings should not change either. The neoliberal assumption is also that we should welcome tinkering with changes as long as the basic premises are stable. The criteria that are employed largely mirror what large research-intensive universities do. One wonders about the standardization of criteria. If a vice chancellor, faculty, and board of trustees are at a university in Hong Kong, wouldn't they all want to be part of the global rankings? And yet, does Hong Kong need every university to be listed as globally ranked? Delhi, a city of 16.8 million people, has 27 universities, 176 colleges, and 98 other standalone institutions (Ministry of Human Resource Development, 2018). Do they all need to be listed? Is that the goal? And if some are not, then how are we to judge them? All rankings, but especially global ones, have winners and losers.

There is a certain rationality to rankings such that if one is listed in the top 30 one year, then the goal is to get into the top 20 the next year, and so on. Again, I fully appreciate the desire for improvement and that we are to judge improvement by an institution's rankings. The challenge, however, is that a one-size-fits-all approach is neither logical—not everyone can be number 1—nor useful for a country or city. We need a synthetic approach that tries to wed the needs of the times and the city/region with the particular strengths of an institution. Such an observation is particularly difficult to implement within the parameters of a neoliberal/global logic that rationalizes how we approach education, academic work, and the values of democracy.

How might we think about research, teaching, and service within the confines of a neoliberal logic commented on by Tomlinson and Lipsitz? The straitjacket of rankings falls by the wayside. Cities focus more on the needs of the citizenry and provide resources to enable faculties to address different issues in different ways. The privilege of the "best," as defined by global rankings, is changed so that different needs are addressed and honored, as opposed to the homogenization of quality, whereby everyone chases after the same criteria.

I appreciate, as an abstraction, the challenge of developing criteria first in terms of what we might do, and then determining how to judge an individual, department, school, and university's work. However, until we reject the overarching premises of neoliberalism and globalization, we will be wedded to that framework. I am not, obviously, simply trying to ignore our present reality or delve into a fantasy world where the scientific paradigm is rejected and something of lesser value is put in its place. What I want to avoid, however, is the fatalism of neoliberalism, which nicely makes the argument against alternatives. If we accept this argument, we will conclude, logically, that there are no alternatives. Only when we strip away a fatalist mentality to organizational work that subsumes the values of democracy and social engagement to efficiency will we envision an alternative way to configure tertiary institutions.

I am not calling for a utopian ideal that suggests pie-in-the-sky goals. Such goals may be nice thoughts, but they are irrelevant to the harsh realities in which we currently live, given constricted budgets because of the pandemic. If anything, I am trying to envision a different framework precisely because of those realities. Neoliberalism divides the world into a few winners and many losers. Globalization has reduced a workforce where jobs were plentiful as the economy expanded to one in which one feels lucky to get a job and not much else. Health benefits, a pension, or learning opportunities during work are thought of as unaffordable luxuries. Such an assumption only has increased with the economic consequences of the pandemic. One should simply be gratified at having a job in a difficult global economy. When we think with such assumptions, then we have very few alternatives from those the rationalist framework provides. Our job is to envision an alternative environment so that we might implement what we wish to put forward as a democratic university in the twenty-first century. To do that, I turn to a consideration of research, teaching, and service.

Rethinking Research

Modern research has transformed from infancy, just over a century ago, to a formalized process that is governed by common norms, structures, and processes. The scientific research enterprise assumes a disinterested stance, and for good reason. Following Max Weber's directive, the researcher concentrates on their work and assumes objectivity as paramount. We have built research, however, from that largely unilinear framework. Consider the researcher in the laboratory trying to find a cure for cancer. They have a disinterested stance and try to test various hypotheses to find the correct response. The laboratory is sterile; the individual who conducts the research should be, on one level, irrelevant. Indeed, one key component of academic work is the reproducibility of one's findings. Whether I conduct research in my lab in Los Angeles or a younger colleague in New Delhi conducts the same experiment in her lab should not matter. We should be able to come to the same conclusions. I appreciate such research and, unlike some postmodernists, who will critique all of knowledge production as inherently biased and socially constructed, I have less concern about biases than the scientific box in which we are all placed.

Donald Stokes's (1997) *Pasteur's Quadrant: Basic Science and Technological Innovation* is a different way to think about research. Stokes rejected Vannevar Bush's (1945) dichotomy between basic and applied research, which tended to privilege the basic scientist. Instead, Stokes posited research as lying in four quadrants—all viable, all important, and, critically for my commentary here, all relying on different criteria to conduct and evaluate research. The first quadrant pertains to basic researchers who are trying to understand phenomena without concern or focus on external influences or the application of their work. Niehls Bohr, who spent much of his career mapping the structure of atoms, is a useful example of the scholar doing research in this quadrant. The second quadrant is where applied research gets conducted. Thomas Edison, who was more concerned with practical applied discovery than Bohr, is the example here. These are the sorts of researchers who are concerned with innovation, and to a certain degree, entrepreneurial action. The third quadrant is unnamed but largely has to do with taxonomic research, whereby the researcher is trying to classify particular phenomena. Audubon's work in classifying birds is the typical example here. Those who have created encyclopedias and have tried to systemize knowledge from a neutral perspective are another example.

The fourth quadrant, known as Pasteur's quadrant, is the one that has generated the most discussion and what I want to concentrate on here. Louis Pasteur's research in microbiology is neither applied nor basic, and it is certainly not taxonomic. As Stokes (1997) notes, Pasteur's focus "was a commitment to *understand* the microbiological processes he discovered and a commitment to *control* the effects of these processes on humans" (p. 72). Stokes defines this sort of research as "use-inspired basic research" (p. 84). This form of research utilizes basic research and social existence and is in constant motion back and forth between the two. Knowledge is not linear from theory to application but instead it is bidirectional and dynamic, calling into question the long-held Enlightenment ideal that only pure research produces understanding that furthers the human condition (Tierney & Holley, 2008).

Such research enables us to think about a university that has a diverse view of knowledge, rather than as a singular concept that adheres to a singular framework. The analysis not only enables the academy to move away from the dichotomy of basic/applied, but also creates one that makes a distinction between hard and soft research, or high status and low status fields. What I am suggesting is that research based on neoliberal standards of rankings inevitably is going to privilege those of us who do work in one quadrant. We need a more robust, protean framework that abolishes unitary views of knowledge production and instead enables research to function in multiple domains. If we are able to accommodate diverse streams of knowledge production, then we also can decenter the Western concept of knowledge. Such a movement obviously has significant consequences for urban centers, such as Hong Kong, Delhi, and Los Angeles. With Narendra University, India has, arguably, the oldest university in the world, but its universities today try to ape Western universities, as does Hong Kong. Indeed, India has made hiring foreign superstar faculty a priority, presumably in order to rise in the global rankings.

The concentrating logic of rankings and neoliberalism on the global stage tries to homogenize academic work in a way that inevitably creates categories of winners and losers. As Lynch (2015) notes, "What Hacking (1990, p. 10) termed 'the avalanche of numbers' has profoundly transformed what we choose to do, who we try to be, and what we think of ourselves in higher education. Assessment measures permit the easy conflation of what is with what ought to be, of what normal is in the statistical and moral sense." (p. 201).

A variety of changes occur when we reorient the university from a research model in an intellectual straitjacket and instead move toward multiple ways to understand and advance knowledge. Translational research gains credence. For those who choose to work within Pasteur's quadrant, "Translational research involves the application of basic scientific discoveries into clinically germane findings and simultaneously, the generation of scientific questions based on clinical observations" (Rustgi, 1999, p. 1285). Translational research calls for greater involvement with the field, and a redefinition, or an expansion, of one's audience. One's peers remain critical in the evaluation of work, but the potential users of the findings of research, and those implicated by it, also become involved. Indeed, at a time of a global pandemic Pasteur's Quadrant has become a logical place to conduct one's work. Further, issues of race are not necessarily useful to be undertaken without cross-cutting research that is also translational.

Use-inspired research will be more interdisciplinary and team-oriented. A range of methodological approaches will be employed, and the metaphor of science and the laboratory will be dropped as the only way to undertake research. Disciplinary structures are expanded in some cases and dismantled in others. In essence, this quadrant calls upon multiple avenues to travel down theoretically and methodologically.

In suggesting this form of work, I am consciously calling into question the traditional structures of knowledge that have defined the twentieth-century academy. The reward structure, how we decide what is useful, interesting, important, and iterative all gets rethought. The model is not substitutive but expansive. It calls for defining the reward structure and lessening our fascination with rankings and easy comparisons. Such a framework goes a long way to enabling the university to be more involved in a manner required during a time of social transformation and when the fabric of democracy society is under attack.

Rethinking Teaching

Academic learning is more than the vocational skills required for employment. Obviously, individuals need to find jobs once they leave the institution. We have reached a point, largely because of a neoliberal ideology, where an individual does one or another task; developing simultaneous ways of thinking about teaching and learning is as difficult as in the research paradigm. And yet, as with the discussion of research, I am suggesting that we want to develop a more protean model that equips learners not simply with the skills needed for the job market, but also offers ways to think about what it means to be a citizen and how to engage one another in the twenty-first century in meaningful interactions. Such an observation is particularly germane given the challenges that have erupted over policing and the murder of Black people.

Tomlinson and Lipsitz (2013) point out, "Whereas the neoliberal university values some of the knowledge considered to contribute directly to employment, all other forms of knowledge are seen as hurdles requiring minimal rote learning rather than the skill building necessary to become a critical thinker, creative problem solver, and life-long learner" (p. 16). What we need to do then, from the perspective advocated here, is enable students to enter into multiple conversations where they learn how to articulate the sorts of citizens they want to be and how work is involved in that vision, rather than simply learning the skills for a particular type of employment upon graduation.

We also need to recognize how different today's students are from yesterday's. The university is more diverse, more gender differentiated, and more open to individuals from multiple classes, than ever before—whether we are speaking of Los Angeles, New Delhi, or Hong Kong. For instance, Los Angeles is a highly diverse area where Latinx people constitute the highest proportion of residents. at 44.9 percent. White non-Hispanic residents are 39 percent of the population, while Asians are 12.3 percent, African Americans are 7.0 percent, and 20.2 percent of residents fall under an umbrella category of "other races." Due to the diversity in Los Angeles, many people resist identification with a single race or ethnicity, much less binary notions of sexuality or gender. Instead, intersectionality plays an increasingly important role in how people both express and understand themselves.

Although diversity certainly has made a significant difference about the way we teach and the content of many courses, we also need to acknowledge the differences between this generation and those with whom I studied. An argument can be made that students of the 1960s socially may have been quite different from their parents' generation, but in terms of their daily lives there were many commonalities in how individuals accumulated information and communicated with one another. To be sure, common advances took place so that television sets and other technologies were improved and became more widespread, but in many ways, these were typical advances to modernity rather than a paradigm shift.

Today's students, however, do not know what the past was like, other than as an artifact to be studied. Television and newspapers were how we got the news, and, when we think back to high school, we are likely to conjure up shared memories with our fellow students. The "good old days" were days that may not have been good, but, when we think about them, they are memories of people involved in various forms of group activities. Contrast that with the students of today.

The average teenager checks their iPhone 80 times a day. Twelfth graders in 2015 went out less often than eighth graders in 2009; there are fewer 18-year-olds getting their driver's license today than a decade ago; iGen teens, a phrase coined by Jean Twenge (2017), "are less likely to experience the freedom of being out of the house without their parents" (p. 20). Fewer teens work during the summer, not because there are fewer jobs, but because they do not want to work and prefer to stay at home in their room with their iPhone (p. 31). Teenagers spend at a minimum of three hours a day on their iPhones, even though less time on iPhones is linked to more happiness and less social isolation (p. 78). Their identification of a good time has less to do with shared group experiences and more with being alone in one's room, chatting, watching Netflix, or texting one's friends.

One interesting finding of the pandemic, however, has to do with online classes. The academy has been billed as static and unchanging, but within a matter of weeks, tertiary institutions throughout the world canceled in-person campuses and faculty took to Zoom and other modalities to teach online. Even more interesting is that although most students adapted to online classes, there was no great rush to keep teaching online. Students actually preferred in-person classes with other students and a professor.

Schooling, of course, is identified with getting a job. Even though students are less prepared for the world of work when they arrive to college because of their social isolation, they also see schooling as a way to learn skills. If schooling is a consumable good, then clearly what the customer wants is what the customer should get.

Students are more depressed and less religious these days. The percentage of students who say they are not members of a church but have spiritual beliefs continues to rise. They are less socially connected via clubs or group activities, and more prone to suicidal tendencies. They spend more time communicating with their friends on social networks than they do in-person. Work is looked on as a way to pay the bills, rather than to find any intrinsic enjoyment. The less time at work, the more time being able to play video games or be in chat rooms (Twenge, 2017).

My point here is that if a teacher is involved in teaching the content of a subject and those who are to learn the content, then, for the first time in our lives, the learner may have changed more than the subject. The instructor's role in any college course must be to stay current in the literature, whether it is an introductory general education course or an advanced graduate seminar. For the last half-century, we also have spoken about teaching to the student rather than the content, but we now have evidence that, for the first time, these students are dramatically different from learners in the past. Teaching to the student is not merely recognizing that who we teach changes the content of our classes, it also changes the modalities we employ.

I am not interested in bemoaning the fate of today's students or suggesting that we reverse the inevitable and try to be more socially, rather than digitally, focused. However, I do not think it does us much good to construct pedagogies aimed at students of the twentieth century when the iGen are so radically different. In some respects, their desires, regardless of location, are the typical neoliberal response: give them skills to get a job that will enable them to spend more time alone in their rooms on their social networks. When jobs are not found for those who concentrate on skills, then the obvious critique is that they did not learn the correct skills; if they learn a certain amount more, they will find employment. The possibility that it is not their lack of rudimentary skills that is the culprit, but an economy where there is less work is not considered.

How do we then respond? The answer is particularly difficult insofar as universities rely on students to attend their institutions. The points I mentioned in chapters 1 and 2, about how postsecondary institutions have lost their legitimacy, means that students are consumers who can look elsewhere for what they ostensibly need. In turn, the university will suffer with a downturn in enrollment and the concomitant fees from its consumers. I offer this observation because, again, there is no easy response. Unless we move away from a rationalist pedagogy that makes it appear that college-level classes are little more than vocational training, we will never get ourselves out of the environment in which we find ourselves. Mission drives action, and we need to be clear about our goals.

Pedagogical engagement from what I am suggesting here is more than good tips for teaching or a simplified list of instrumental skills that students might learn that will make them highly employable. Of course, students have to learn how to write, how to present arguments, and how to think about the world of work so that they are competitive in a restricted market. What particularly matters, however, is that students are also versed in the art of critique, the ability to seek out community, and the willingness to engage in reflection, and, subsequently, social action.

We tend to cordon off individuals—he does history, she does chemistry. And yet, in an increasingly interrelated world, we need to infuse in people the ability intellectually to cross borders so that they are not merely prepared for the world of work, but also the world in which we live. Students rely on education to provide them with skills because they mistakenly believe that a college education levels the market. What they are missing is that the current framework of society marginalizes all but the wealthy. No amount of skills or acquisition of social or cultural capital is going to enable groups of people to break through to the vaunted 1 percent. Because of neoliberalism, however, students are like lottery contestants. The odds may be only a million to one that they win the lottery, but they play under the mistaken belief that they stand a chance. The system is rigged, however, and everyone else loses. A college degree should equip students with the skills to analyze the strengths and weaknesses of the societies in which we live and how to make the playing field more level.

Ultimately, we want students to graduate from a college or university, not only well versed and prepared for the world of work, but also ready to critique that world and come forward with innovative solutions to the challenges we face. To do so, we need different kinds of learning opportunities and different structures that acknowledge the current connected worlds students inhabit, the obstacles posed by those worlds, and how to better attune students to this new environment. Recognize I am not suggesting that we try to re-create a lost world. Even without neoliberalism and globalization, students are still going to have cell phones and seek connections with friends over the internet. The leisurely, some would say lethargic, pace of coursework has to be an artifact of the past. If how students spend their time is key, then we need to focus on the temporal aspect of teaching, as well as the structure of the curriculum.

Moretti (2012) has noted, "Universities are most effective at shaping a local economy when they are part of a larger ecosystem of innovative activity, one that includes a thick market for specialized labor and intermediate services" (p. 197). The same can be said about any number of ways to be involved in the larger community. Success for universities today points much more toward active engagement than walling their students off in an ivory tower. I appreciate why we have removed ourselves from society, and, to a certain extent, academic contemplation is always a plus— it's good for the research we do and the teaching we undertake. Students benefit from the contemplative life just as much as we all did when I was in college, but today is also different. We have to have a better sense of engagement with the larger community, and this arrangement benefits the faculty and students as well. How these engagements are handled will vary based on institutional type, region, and community. What students do in New Delhi obviously will be different from Los Angeles or Hong Kong. What I am suggesting, however, is that, irrespective of location, we need a relationship to pedagogy—one that is more engaged, involved, and focused on building community within the class and outside of it.

I recognize, along with Hacker and Dreifus (2010), that over half of all undergraduates enroll in vocational training programs (e.g., nursing), and such training is decidedly different from what I am suggesting here. As they argue, "College should be a cultural journey, an intellectual expedition, a voyage confronting new ideas and information, together expanding and deepening our understanding of ourselves and the world" (p. 3). I agree, but I am more optimistic that if we can first settle on what we want to do, and concur with some version of the assessment that they offer here, then we can implement a new way of teaching and interfacing with the larger communities, regardless of curricular focus. Such a hope extends, irrespective of geography. Too often, we assume that one or another group needs skills and nothing more; such an assumption, particularly today, is wrong-headed, whether we are trying to educate the poor in New Delhi, those who want middle-class jobs in Hong Kong, or the potpourri of students in California attending either a private university, such as my own, or the public university across the freeway, the UCLA.

Rethinking Service

Service is the weak link in academic life. One's service is often not counted for promotion and tenure, and it is not something that gets counted for an organization's purported quality. When we define service, we generally mean what an individual has done either in service to the institution or to their profession. I have served as chair of my institution's Academic Senate, and I have reviewed too many articles to count for academic journals. Both activities are examples of what gets thought of as service. The result is that most academics try to eschew service, and when individuals look back on their careers they typically overlook what they did for their institution or profession and instead focus on major events in their teaching and research.

The twenty-first-century university cannot have service as a weak link. I appreciate that the typical activities we associate with service are most likely not going away. We still need to write letters of reference, serve on committees, and make voluntary contributions to the academy and profession. In the next chapter, I elaborate more on the specifics about what I am calling *cultural citizenship*. For now, however, I am simply making the argument that service has to be raised to the level of research and teaching. Service is not something one does for others within the academic community, but instead, or in addition, scholars need to be much more engaged with our various communities and organizations.

Communities could be our local community that surrounds the institution, or it could be any number of virtual communities that will benefit from academic involvement. The idea of cultural citizenship extends beyond geographic boundaries so that we acknowledge we are not solely citizens in a nation-state. Globalization has reframed the dialogue and reemphasizes our obligations to one another, irrespective of border. The pandemic has forced us to reconsider our relationships to one another and to our community, and my expectation is that the sorts of relationships we have developed will not evaporate over time. Similarly, issues of race remain at the forefront of national dialogues about how society can privilege some and disadvantage others.

Cultural citizenship is an act whereby college and university faculties engage in meaningful dialogues with communities as part of our core identity. The work involves transcending the borders of the university and trying to understand difference. We invite people to the university with whom we may fiercely disagree, and we welcome respectful dialogue and debate, rather than run and try to avoid it. I have previously pointed out that "academe as a community revolves around interactional meanings and redefinitions of what it means to be a citizen" (Tierney, 1993, p. 143). To reach out, communicate, and translate our research becomes a central service. The activity is not of a missionary engaging in a one-way conversation with a heathen population in need of knowledge. Rather, service is a dialogue of mutuality and respect that enables the academic to bring some kinds of expertise as those in the community have the opportunity to demonstrate other sorts of skills. Bourdieu (2000) called this a "scholarship with commitment" that enables intellectuals to intervene in the public sphere. At a time of global crisis, then, service becomes a key component of academic life rather than the weak link of a triad.

I have continued my analysis of neoliberalism and globalization by first focusing on how we think about a public good, and then thinking through what we want a university to do. The challenge is to pave a new way for institutions to act with their various communities. To forge this path, we must reject a form of historicism that frames action today as if what we have always done is what we must do today and tomorrow.

What I have been trying to comprehend is how we might, at one and the same time, think across horizons so that we are not constrained by narrow assumptions of what accounts for academic life, but also engage with our various local communities. In effect, I am suggesting we have created organizations that no longer meet the needs of the larger communities. However, why would we expect organizations framed in one way to act in another? If we want change to occur, then we need to delve into and understand the structural and cultural constraints that exist, and with that understanding create a more engaged institution for the twenty-first century. To construct such a vision, it will be helpful if we think about the competencies we want for the twenty-first century and how we might go about gaining them.

CHAPTER SIX

Academic Competencies for the Twenty-First Century

Higher education faces four competing pressures, and each has a degree of validity. Taken together, they are hard to reconcile, but this is necessary if we want higher education to advance democracy. First, as I discussed in the previous chapter, there are problems stemming from our current obsession with rankings. Second, it's generally understood that students and their families as customers want employment upon graduation. Third, alternative providers—particularly for-profit higher education and on-line learning programs—have forced traditional public and private nonprofit institutions to rethink their traditional model, especially in light of declining enrollments, and the consequences of the pandemic. Fourth, the ascendance of Donald Trump and other leaders, such as Narendra Modi in India, has provoked concern among many about the rise of populism, the implications for higher education, and how, if at all, academe should respond.

Rankings can be deceptively simple. Those of us who are faculty all have opinions about our colleagues. If our son or daughter asked us whether they should take a class with Professor "X" at our institution, we would answer based on a variety of internalized criteria. We know our kid. We know the instructor. The teacher may be great for some students and not others for one reason or another. The teacher also may be a total waste of time. I know no parent who is a faculty member who would shrug their shoulders and say, "I have no idea." When we are proffering advice, we are, in some fashion, contributing to the idea of rankings. Ranking is the extreme version of your child asking for advice. If we have internalized criteria about what might be a good class, or stream of courses, for our children, then why wouldn't we want to be explicit about our criteria and let other students know as well? Essentially, this is what rankings are about, at least from a benign perspective.

I have discussed how unimportant it was for my friends and I to know we were being trained for jobs. We assumed good jobs awaited us, and they did. Today we live in a different world, and the job market is much more difficult to navigate for a college graduate (although much easier than for a high school graduate). We know that the role of colleges and universities has never really been to have a 1:1 correspondence between college and the world of work. Nevertheless, students expect to get something when they graduate, and simply shrugging our shoulders and saying "That's not our job" is not a viable plan of action if we want to stay in business.

We also have different types of organizations and learning formats that have entered the scene, such as for-profit higher education, online courseware, and related developments in social networking. I appreciate the baggage that the for-profits bring to any conversation. We also need to acknowledge that online courses have not done what they promised, which was to bring down the cost of learning, much less improve learning (Newton, 2018). When the pandemic required all institutions to switch to online instruction one outcome was that many students appeared to prefer in-class learning. Although faculty are much more adept today about teaching online because of the pandemic, I know very few who say that their online courses are better than what they do in person.

Many of the for-profits have participated in corrupt practices that have sullied their reputation, and those who provide online courses frequently charge significant prices because the related infrastructure costs for the delivery systems remain high (Angulo, 2016). Nevertheless, the critiques of traditional higher education have hit their mark. People wonder why they can read newspapers and journals online whenever they desire, but our courses are in particular places at specific times. Why can I watch 15 weeks of a television show's season in one weekend, but the same format is not available for a college course? The temporal aspects of higher education and the format of learning is clearly an issue, and many of our "customers" do not believe we are dealing with their concerns very well, if at all.

Finally, the rise of Donald Trump has energized some in the news media to up their game. The media has fought the various lies and misinformation that have come forth from the White House, even while they were reviled by the president. Colleges and universities are still trying to figure out how to react. In large part, this book has been an attempt to think through what that response should be. Although a protest or a teach-in may be a useful tactic and make individuals feel good, I am arguing here that a deeper, more structural response pertaining to the nature and culture of the university is necessary. We need to reconfigure what we do to be a more vocal participant in advancing the democratic public sphere regardless of who is in office.

The goal of this chapter is to discuss the academic competencies we require for the twenty-first century for those who attend colleges and universities, for those of us who work in them, and for the educational system itself as an organic unit. My own sense is that we cannot discount any of these pressures. Sometimes I feel as if I am traveling in entirely different intellectual lands when I hear one group talk about the need for students to have jobs when they graduate from college and another speak about the intellectual goals of academe irrespective of job prospects. Some long for the sort of education I experienced as a traditional student on a traditional campus, and others think of those experiences as irrelevant and want to create a curriculum pertinent for the twenty-first century. Some want to know what it will take for their institution to rise in the rankings, and others worry about the citizenship skills of their students.

Are these competing, contradictory, or overlapping issues? In order to answer this question, I first expand on my discussion about the external world of work and what that suggests for students. I then consider the work of the citizen and its implications for our students. Subsequently, I turn to what this suggests for those of us in academe and the organization as the structure that holds all of this together. In the next chapter, I conclude with a sketch of what that suggests for a competent university.

The World of Work

The California State University (CSU) system is the largest state university system in the United States, with 484,300 students.[1] In a recent analysis, only 60 percent are college-ready when they enter the system (LAO, 2017; Mangan, 2017), and only 25.5 percent will graduate from a Cal State university within four years; 61.2 percent will graduate from the university within six years (Gordon, 2019). The estimate is that COVID-19 also has made it harder for poorer students to attend college and less likely to graduate on time. At the same time, we know that in California there will be a need for 4-year college–educated graduates; the Public Policy Institute of California (PPIC) estimates that by 2030, the state will have 1.1 million more jobs that require a bachelor's degree than the California higher education system is currently educating (Johnson et al., 2017). Hence, although the PPIC predicts that, by 2030, the state will require approximately 70 percent of high school graduates to go on to some form of postsecondary education (a certificate, AA/AS or BA/BS degrees), around 20 percent of high school graduates should be able to find employment with their diploma.

Such findings highlight the challenges we face, and they speak not only to global challenges for developed economies, such as Los Angeles and Hong Kong, but also to developing economies, such as we find in New Delhi. Job creation, obviously, does not speak about remuneration and benefits, only the skills that are needed for the workplace. In today's global economic climate, individuals want a postsecondary degree because they believe that (a) a job is more likely with a degree and (b) the job they get will pay a living wage. However, the jobs that exist increasingly do not provide the wages, benefits, retirement plans, or health insurance that past generations received (Kalleberg, 2011; Mishel et al., 2015; Rutledge et al., 2019). Herein lies the misalignment: jobs will exist, but they are not the kind of jobs that college graduates want.

Nevertheless, there is a degree of truth to the assumption about the importance of a college education; in the United States, for example, we know that over a lifetime of employment an individual with a bachelor's degree is likely to earn 84 percent more than a worker with a high school degree, according to the Georgetown Center for Work and the Economy (Carnevale et al., 2011). Similarly, the Hamilton Project at the Brookings Institute estimates that a "typical college graduate will earn $1.19 million . . . more than twice as much as the lifetime earnings of a typical high school graduate ($580,000)" (Hershbein & Kearney, 2014 p. 1). There is some truth to the adage that "the more you learn, the more you earn," although the belief entirely stalls with those of us who get advanced degrees where earnings vary by field. An individual with a PhD in a humanities discipline is not projected to earn more than the student with a bachelor's degree in engineering, although the medical doctor will certainly earn a good deal more than most college graduates. Moreover, college graduates who major in areas associated with low earning potential (e.g., elementary education or drama) tend to have a much wider range of lifetime earnings between the 25th and 75th percentile than college graduates with degrees in high earning areas, such as engineering or finance (Hershbein & Kearney, 2014).

The challenge, however, pertains to the recompense one gets for all work. As Cass (2018) has pointed out, gross domestic product has tripled over the last 40 years, but salaries for workers have barely budged. The result is that a majority of Americans born in 1980 earned less at the age of 30 than their parents, irrespective of job type (p. 21), and they are likely to end up less wealthy than their parents. Further, over the same time horizon, the proportion of men between the ages of 25 and 34 earning less than $30,000 rose from 25 to 41 percent. Benefits are also curtailed. When I took my first job after my PhD, I knew next to nothing about the retirement and health benefits of the place where I worked; my lack of knowledge is typical of young wage earners entering the market. We do not think we will fall ill, and retirement is for old people, not for someone in their 20s. Fortunately, I always have had good health care and a fairly generous retirement package; such is no longer the case for the vast number of workers, regardless if they are in New Delhi, Hong Kong, or Los Angeles.

We cannot blame those sorts of outcomes on colleges and universities, and we also cannot expect that what one does in college is going to remediate a structural problem created by neoliberalism and globalization. Optimally, of course, we would like to see these numbers moving in the opposite direction—people are earning more than their parents, salaries are rising, and expectations for the future are bright. Such is not the case, especially in the immediate aftermath of the pandemic, and we have mistakenly blamed academe. Yet those who never reach higher education or who arrive unprepared for college-level work ought not be looked on as failures in higher education. If the job market has jobs that are available but their recompense is meager, then the fault lies largely with the structure, not within the walls of higher education.

It is worth noting that in 1975, when I graduated from college, a college graduate earned more than a high school graduate. Nevertheless, significant differences are twofold. First, jobs existed for high school graduates; second, those jobs were an entry to the middle class, and they paid enough to raise a family, buy a home, and send a child to college. We are expecting of postsecondary institutions something that we have not expected in the past. A college education leads to jobs when there are jobs that exist and those jobs pay a livable wage. The problem, then, turns on the structure of the job itself, rather than an abundance of employment that individuals are not being trained to assume. Uber, Lyft, and multiple other companies are ubiquitous because customers like the new idea, whether it be transit or meals on wheels, but the employees get a job that does not cover expenses, much less help them save money for future needs. Amazon may deliver the book I ordered in record time at the click of my cursor. What we fail to acknowledge, however, is that the employees at the local bookstore are now out of work. Furthermore, the workers in the Amazon warehouse not only make less in total compensation than workers in other warehouses (Long, 2018), they are under constant surveillance and expected to meet quotas at a rate that places their physical health in serious peril. According to one investigative report, workers in Amazon warehouses suffered serious injuries at a rate double the national average in other warehouses (Evans, 2019).

In India, Aggarwal et al. (2012) observed that students want to study for the sorts of jobs that do not exist or there is a low supply and Indian universities are not training students for high-need areas, such as veterinarians. The larger environment in India, as elsewhere, however, is also not creating enough structured, full-time jobs that provide benefits, especially in manufacturing. The result is that we have a mismatch for scarce jobs, students are unaware of what they should study, and universities are unsure of what they should teach. We also have a neoliberal environment that rewards only the top 1 percent of earners and defunds jobs that were once the route to the middle class. In part, the protests in Hong Kong have to do with an economic environment that makes it impossible for young people to think they will ever own a home or live a middle-class life like their parents (Augustin-Jean & Cheung, 2018). My point here is not to absolve tertiary education of its role in helping prepare students for employment, but to point out the obvious: colleges and universities do not create jobs—the larger environment does—and as long as we define that environment entirely by way of the market, then we are not going to provide any social safety net, fewer jobs will exist, and those jobs will provide inadequate wages and benefits.

The weight of improvement in making students college-ready has to rest with secondary education. High schools in general do not adequately prepare students for postsecondary work, and yet they graduate students because they have met the basic requirement for a high school education. Ironically, around 64 percent of high school teachers believe they are turning out college-ready students (Killion, 2011). When college and university faculty who teach first-year students are asked the same question, around 78 percent of them say their students are not ready (Hart Research, 2015). The point is not simply that postsecondary institutions need to give guidelines about what they expect, but that a greater synthesis is necessary between what happens in high school and what will occur in college. Without this synthesis, students suffer from a lack of information about their own college readiness and a lack of clarity concerning their undergraduate instructors' expectations (Lanford, 2019; Tierney & Duncheon, 2015; Tierney & Sablan, 2014; Venezia & Jaeger, 2013). We have been making such recommendations for a generation and significant discrepancies still exist, as evidenced by CSU's college-ready rates.

We also have an intellectual hurdle to get over and that pertains to vocational education. We have a "college for all" mentality when the numbers from the Public Policy Institute of California that I outlined previously clearly point out that we do not need everyone to go to college (Johnson et al., 2017). About 40 percent of high school graduates will have an adequate array of jobs with the skills they have. The rationale for a "college for all framework" is in large part a concern for a democracy, whether we are speaking of Los Angeles or New Delhi. When we track students to vocational education, we are dooming them to even lower-wage employment, goes the thinking. What we have discovered when we look at those who are "tracked" is that they are the poorest and least advantaged—people of color in the United States, students from lower castes and Dalits in India, and the poorest immigrants in Hong Kong (Oakes, 1986). Gender discrimination means we train women for nursing but not medicine. The result is that we tried to detrack schools and enable everyone to go to college. And yet, some students are less academically talented students than others, and some would prefer a vocational track to a college preparatory track. The problem, again, with tracking is not that there is anything less honorable to the work of a beautician or truck driver than that of a financial analyst or business executive; it is that all jobs are not financially rewarded in a manner that makes the vocational work honored.

I do not want to excuse higher education, but I find the assumption that either we can train everyone for employment or and they will find employment when they graduate from our institutions, foolhardy. Not everyone should go to college because the economy does not need everyone with a college degree, and not every high school student wants to go to college. Surely we can find fair and honorable ways that do not discriminate against individuals based on race, gender, or disability, and we can collapse the wage discrepancy between high school and college-educated workers.

We also need to recognize that, in general, the vast majority of universities are not job creators. Sure, the institution hires individuals, but most postsecondary institutions do not create businesses. A handful, but certainly not all, postsecondary institutions can help stimulate the economy of a city. Moretti (2012) nicely summarizes by saying that "the rise of innovation matters to all of us [because it] has to do with the almost magical economies of job creation. Innovative industries bring good jobs and high salaries to the communities around where they cluster, and their impact on the local economy is much deeper than their direct effect" (p. 13). His point is that when we create a job for a software engineer, for example in New Delhi, there is a ripple effect. The engineer may need different people working with them today than a generation ago—someone in information technology (IT) rather than a secretary—but there is also a spillover effect for those in skilled occupations (teachers, lawyers) and less skilled occupations (waiters, plumbers).

The problem is that in actuality, very few universities can have that sort of impact. We like to think of the example of Stanford and Silicon Valley and the symbiotic relationship they have had in generating the technology revolution, but I point to Stanford so often because there are so few other examples that exist. To be sure, some universities have had modest success—those around the research triangle in North Carolina, or some postsecondary institutions in Bangalore, India. However, in the vast majority of cases and, in particular, for the cities I'm working with here, the impact of the university on job creation through innovation has been modest. The University of Hong Kong (HKU) is perhaps the best university on the island, but HKU's impact on the city is largely in employment, not in creating new jobs or technologies. New Delhi does not look to its universities or IITs as the primary source of job creation, and they are too underfunded to do much more than the basic functions of an institution—which includes severe shortages in deferred maintenance. Although my own institution of USC is the largest private employer in the county, it has not been known as a source for job creation beyond the university.

Such observations are important because we tend to criticize universities for tasks that I do not think most of them are well-suited to do, or for tasks that are outside their control. We expect all our institutions to have outreach in their community, but because of a neoliberal mentality, we now define outreach as creating a profit for the community and the institution. That's not going to happen, and it is a waste of human and financial resources to assume that all postsecondary institutions are going to turn into incubators for companies that generate millions of dollars. Less than 5 percent of venture capital companies ever turn a profit (Dean, 2017). That's why we call it "venture" capital. So why would we believe that such activities are a good use of a college or university's time unless they are explicitly oriented toward that goal? Perhaps one institution might be encouraged to pursue innovation, but when an institution has a focus on innovation, it does not have the opportunity to focus on other activities.

Just as we are not going to create a potpourri of revenue-generating companies, we also cannot create jobs or assume that students are able to work in jobs that do not exist. Sure, modest efficiencies can be developed. We could work with high schools to create better prepared students. We could work with the state and high schools to create a career track in high school that prepares students for the workplace in a way that does not track one group of students into low-paying employment, and, at the same time, provides skills that move them more smoothly into a work environment. We could create greater awareness of students while in college about the sorts of job opportunities that exist and create a greater synthesis between what students learn and the skills that they will need. We have been talking about these sorts of improvements for over a generation, and we have shown modest improvement. At the same time, however, the larger economic picture has worsened for both those who have a college degree and those who do not.

Unfortunately, all these proposed changes will not reach the outcomes we want to achieve. Yes, we can create greater synthesis between high school and college, lesser time to a degree while in college, and a greater synthesis between college and the world of work. I don't mean to give these changes short shrift, but we also need to be aware that really these are changes that will improve the system as it currently functions rather than the way we want it to function. What we need to reckon with is that, in a neoliberal environment framed by globalization, wage discrepancies between the wealthy and the poor will remain. The quality of life will not improve because we are unable to break out of the framework that rewards the richest and penalizes those at risk. The haves and have nots will remain such that those in vocational education may be better trained for the world of work but not necessarily more engaged as citizens who can critique the material changes in which they live.

The Work of the Citizen

My suggestions thus far intentionally move away from what many call "responsibilization." In recent years, much discussion about student outcomes has revolved around this idea of responsibilization and a consequential emphasis on students' self-discipline, determination, and grit. Grit, as initially proposed by Angela Duckworth and embraced by many in education, is a character trait that represents an individual's "perseverance and passion for long-term goals" (Duckworth et al., 2007, p. 1087). The reforms of education that have been inspired by concepts like grit and responsibilization move away from the notion of education as a public good. Instead, they are deeply influenced by neoliberal beliefs that all individuals can succeed, no matter what sociocultural or financial barriers they face (Almedia, 2016; Stokas, 2015). If those individuals do not succeed, then their failure is entirely an individual shortcoming, and it is not the concern of the state. As a result, the psychology literature generally discusses grit with little regard for individual differences in race, class, gender, or other factors (Schechtman et al., 2013).

What I wish to suggest here is that the role of the academic is not simply to acquiesce, but instead to engage in an analysis of the overall cultural politics that define the era and proffer ways for social engagement. Democracy is always a process, and consequently, we have to enable citizens with the power to assess the processes employed. One of the very successful strategies of those who work from neoliberal and globalist positions is to force everyone else to work from those premises as well. The linguistic trick is to create a framework that is hard to refute based on the notion put forward. If one calls for effective organizations, for example, the appearance is that one is either for effective organizations or ineffective ones. One is for a fair admissions system based on the merit of an individual, or one is not. The result is a linguistic trap that is hard to escape. And when we buy into neoliberal notions of education, then obviously there are very clear winners and losers. Those who are not responsible will fail. Students who do not get jobs upon graduation face one of two explanations—either they did not work hard enough, or their institutions let them down. Sklair (2006), as well as other scholars (e.g., Rizvi & Lingard, 2009), have noted that such neoliberal and globalization discourse is "suffused with a good deal of fatalism, popularly known as the TINA (there is no alternative) philosophy" (p. 101).

What I turn to here is a different formulation that does not discard the idea of human agency, but it also argues that globalization compels individuals to behave and consider their lives in a different manner from previous generations. Individuals are connected in much more immediate and sustained ways due to technological advances and the emergence of social media. Not just daily interactions are transformed. The nature of major crises and protest movements is radically different, as exemplified by the activists and organizers behind the Arab Spring. What students should know both in the larger marketplace, but also as a citizen in the public sphere, has also inexorably changed.

My uneasiness with responsibilization is that it frames the world in a hypercompetitive manner such that if one does not get the sort of employment that he or she wants, then it is clear who is to blame. We focus only on outcomes, and the outcomes themselves have nothing to do with personal happiness or intellectual engagement, much less enabling an understanding and critique of our situations. The individual is paramount, and the community is little more than a loosely affiliated holding company. Such an analysis helps explain the culture of assessment I discussed earlier. When there is a "bottom line," then all human action can be quantified and evaluated. Rankings are simply the result of our obsession with responsibilization, rather than a cause of it.

Under responsibilization, we end up with a society of winners and losers, or, as Gulson and Fataar (2011) contend, "neoliberalism constructs policies and practices that enable and embody the entrepreneurial educational and urban self as the ideal citizen" (p. 277). States have changed their focus on the welfare of the citizenry as a whole to a more consumerist viewpoint where individual success gets emphasized. The pervasive nature of governmentality was accurately predicted by Foucault (1991), while the theoretical lenses of cultural and social capital proposed by Bourdieu (1994) have illuminated how marginalized individuals struggle to move beyond the margins of society due to their lack of capital. And yet, Bourdieu and Foucault could not have predicted the atomization of the individual in contemporary society. Globalization has enabled markets to reign in the absence of effective state policies and meaningful regulation. The twin forces of globalization and responsibilization have had multiple impacts in education. Curricula are reduced to instrumentalities that students must simply replicate. Teachers, in turn, repeat the pedagogy of external agents without any deviation or interpretation. The construction and expansion of knowledge is no longer a concern of schools and universities. Instead, the transmission of unquestioned knowledge is tested by qualitative methodologies that sort out which students have "won" and "lost."

My concern here is that the enormous force of the neoliberal agenda has not been consistently met with counternarratives pointing out how educational institutions are cultural sites where knowledge not merely gets transmitted, but also defined. Advocates of assessment, grit, and responsibilization, however, assume knowledge as static and preordained. Public goods are not useful, and, when they exist, they are usually "bad" public goods.

Especially at a time of an increasing danger of fascism, we need universities to do more than comply with a very real concern about helping its charges find employment. The pandemic has only accentuated our responsibilities. Jacques Derrida highlights the way I am thinking about the danger the university faces:

> Because it is absolutely independent, the university is also an exposed, tendered citadel, to be taken, often destined to capitulate, without condition, to surrender unconditionally. It gives itself up, it sometimes puts itself up for sale, it risks being simply something to occupy, take over, buy; it risks becoming a branch office of conglomerates and corporations. This is today, in the United States and throughout the world, a major political stake: to what extent does the organization of research and teaching have to be supported, that is directly or indirectly controlled, let us say euphemistically sponsored by commercial and industry interests. (p. 900)

Derrida is making the point here, however murkily, that has motivated this book and I discussed in chapter one: there is a moral role of the university, and we have to teach more than vocational skills to students, regardless if they are white-collar or blue-collar jobs. We need them to be able to understand and critique the subject positions they inhabit and to equip them with critical skills, not merely to assume a position in the market economy, but to understand the limitations and strengths that the market provides. We need citizens who not only have the hard skills they might carry into the workplace, but also soft skills that some might think of as secondary or irrelevant, such as an understanding of art, a passion for introspection, a reverence for the spiritual, and an ability to reflect. I do not think the skills of citizenship are simple measures to place on a multiple-choice test, as if being an active participant in a democracy is a quiz filled with right and wrong answers. Instead, students need to think about the diverse ways that they might come to understand their place, and other people's places, in the world. I want them to consider how to reach across boundaries and within themselves to achieve what I have called earlier a community of difference.

We, of course, run risks when I call for a sort of learning that is more than simple facts and figures that will strengthen one's vitae for an ever-tightening job market. Some will mistakenly assume that I am saying nothing more than to teach the identity politics I discussed in chapter three. Some will go so far as to suggest that I am calling for indoctrination. Others will assume that to focus on one's identity is shortsighted. Andrew Sullivan (2018) has pointed out these risks:

> When elite universities shift their entire worldview away from liberal education as we have long known it toward the imperatives of an identity-based "social justice" movement, the broader culture is in danger of drifting away from liberal democracy as well. If elites believe that the core truth of our society is a system of interlocking and oppressive power structures based around immutable characteristics like race or sex or sexual orientation, then sooner rather than later, this will be reflected in our culture at large. (para. 2)

His worry is that teaching in this fashion will move us all in lockstep with one version of reality. I appreciate his concern. I pointed out in chapter three how identity politics runs the risk of enabling individuals who do not want to move outside their comfort zone. It also allows them to simply be told truths that they already know to be truths, rather than to be questioned about what they believe. What I actually want, however, is robust discussion and disagreement, because it is our best way to find, perhaps not truth, but at least understanding. I appreciate the challenges. As noted in chapter four, we shouldn't have to debate everything. There was a Holocaust. We did land on the moon. The earth is not flat. There are, however, a multitude of ideas and concepts that we all may talk about, but not have perfect information on in order to reach a conclusion. Some of these ideas will make some of us uncomfortable. Sullivan's concern about identity politics is that if we solely teach about oppression across identities, then there can be no group cohesion. However, we ought to be able to use difference as the organizing concept that unites us. It's not so much that you and I are different, and therefore there is nothing to talk about because we cannot understand or respect one another. Rather, you and I are different, and therefore there is nothing more important than to talk and to listen. Unless we understand and respect one another, we all will fail.

How might such ideas work? In higher education systems with 5,000 postsecondary institutions in the United States, almost 41,000 in India, and 20 in Hong Kong, there clearly is not one imprint that will fit all institutions in the same manner. There are, however, six axes that we need to consider if we wish our colleges and universities to reclaim an historical legitimacy as institutions concerned about the greater welfare of community and its citizens, rather than focused on the narrow interests of the individual:

Recognize the Intellectual Role of Limiting Human Suffering

The public sphere, as highlighted by colleges and universities, has long been focused not simply on vocational skills but also, by way of pedagogy and research, to help advance the democratic public sphere, rather than restrict or ignore it. As Giroux (2015) has noted, "[the university] is infused with the promise of cultivating intellectual insight, the imagination, inquisitiveness, risk-taking, social responsibility and the struggle for justice" (p. 110). Such a view asks how we can create the conditions for learning that disrupt, disturb, and inspire young people as agents to create a better world, rather than as singular individuals in search of job security.

Move Toward Access and Away From Merit

If we learned one thing from the "Varsity Blues" admission scandal in the United States and the ongoing higher education corruption scandals in India, it is that people will go to great lengths to get into a college or university, and the result is that the wealthy are always steps ahead of the rest of us. In the United States, wealthy parents have paid hundreds of thousands of dollars to get their children into an elite institution. In India, there are examples of enormous cheating on various exams such as those for medical school, as well as instances of corruption within universities. When one can buy one's way into college, then those who have no resources to provide are always the ones who will be shortchanged. During Harvard University's lawsuit about affirmative action we discovered that 43 percent of White admitted students were legacies, recruited athletes, applicants on the "dean's interest list," or the children of faculty and staff (Arcidiacono et al., 2019).

At the same time, all these methods of entree exist in a system purportedly focused on merit—does one merit entrance to the institution? Again, rankings consider the selectivity of an institution that holds up the idea of merit. If we shifted from a concern for rankings to one concerned about access, then we do not necessarily move simply to open admissions, but we do have closer relationships across schools, colleges, and universities. Rather than a high-stakes admissions test that actually reflects the wealth of the applicant rather than one's knowledge, we have a more synthetic process across educational institutions.

Emphasize Translational Learning

All knowledge is transmitted from teacher to student, but the intent of learning has significant variation. "What do I need to know for the test?" is the sort of question students ask who have little interest or understanding of why the information is useful to them in some fashion. Not far removed from such a question is the assumption that learning is instrumental—"Do I need to know this for my job?" If we take seriously the democratic function of higher education, we are more concerned with students being able to translate what they learn into ideas that transcend boundaries and enable them to work across barriers.

I appreciate that the math instructor might scratch their head with regard to how a beginning calculus course can achieve "translation." Indeed, it is much easier to think about answering what one needs to know for the test or explaining how what is taught in class can be applied to one's job. Let's also recognize that, by emphasizing translation, I am not rejecting the idea that students need to know what's on a test, and that the information presumably will help them in their work. However, the way one constructs a classroom, the way one teaches content, and how one constructs learning activities also teach us how to transcend learning differences rather than simply learn the bare minimum necessary, rendering everything else irrelevant.

Acknowledge the Structural Constraints of Race, Class, Gender, and Caste

Translational learning suggests that we are not all alike. It is essential to go beyond surface-level understandings of critical components of our lives and interrogate the structural constraints that have enabled racism, casteism, and sexism. One need not be a Marxist to delineate the economic constraints of capitalism, neoliberalism, and globalization.

I am troubled that sometimes we focus intensely on one aspect of our identity and ignore other parts. I am equally troubled that we swing between two poles—one saying that any problems an individual has was brought on by the individual, and a second saying that because I am different from you, I have no ability to understand your struggles and hopes. When we discount or ignore the history of slavery and racism in the United States or the arbitrary hierarchy of caste, we shortchange everyone. Our challenge is consistently to consider differences and how structures have constrained some people and enabled others. Lasting change occurs when we go to root causes rather than look at surface-level symptoms. The way forward is through communion with the Other through understanding difference rather than ignoring it or assuming that we are all alike.

Foster an Ecology of Knowledge

We have yet to move into Pasteur's quadrant and instead try to operate in one or another quadrant where our differences are cordoned off rather than transcended. Humanities is for humanists; science is for scientists. If we have general education or distribution requirements, they are more political compromises across warring departments for funding rather than intellectual attempts to cross intellectual borders. De Sousa Santos (2010) calls for a more integrated attempt at learning where "the ecology of knowledges is a kind of counter-extension or extension in reverse, that is from outside the university to inside the university. It consists of the promotion of dialogues between scientific and humanistic knowledge produced by the university on the one side and the lay or popular knowledge that circulate in society" (p. 7).

Such a framework enables a more holistic intellectual approach whereby the goal is to cross boundaries rather than reinforce them, to question received knowledge instead of simply accepting it, and to see how what we learn fits or does not fit with the knowledge that we all bring to learning. Rather than epistemological absolutism, we place the university where it traditionally has been strongest—in questioning what is being brought forward and trying to make sense of what we are saying for ourselves and the broader society.

Acknowledge Moral Responsibility

Derrida's plea was to position the university in a way that asserts that knowledge, and, by inference, learning is not neutral. Consequently, we have to consider the position and identity of the learner, not as sacramental or sacrosanct, but as part of the learning process. No one has the right to assert, "Because I am X, I have this to say about the topic and I must be correct." However, we also have to acknowledge that because a person is "X," their identity counts for something in terms of their contribution and their learning.

We have, then, a moral responsibility toward learning that is not value neutral. Yes, a topic may be presented neutrally, but, by definition, learning is a process imbued with moral significance that requires an ethical commitment to ourselves and one another. The responsibility extends beyond any laboratory or any classroom. Of course, one has ethical standards to uphold in the kind of research that is done and how one acts in the classroom with students. For the student, however, knowledge is a responsibility to recognize that they are involved in something bigger than simply a task that will enable them to move into the marketplace and improve their social position. Responsibility calls, not for incorporation into the existing order, but for investigation and the disruption of norms so that we move toward democracy.

Affirm the University's Central Role in Advancing Democracy

Because of the rise of fascism in countries around the world, there is no more critical role for universities concerned about learning than to place themselves in the center of current controversies that attack democracy, such as what has taken place in Hong Kong. We are currently in a democratic recession in which countries long thought to be securely democratic have moved toward fascism—and none more so than the United States. A culture of democracy is one that affirms the centrality of knowledge production in decision making and rejects authoritarian calls to crown an individual with all decision-making authority. An understanding of civic life and our responsibilities for all higher education's participants is crucial. Democracy functions best when people with strong beliefs are able to argue with one another and ultimately come to some kind of accommodation.

The conditions that make democracy are manifold. As the prolific democratic student of democracy Larry Diamond (2019) has stated, "Education is particularly key here" (p. 31). I will extend his assertion by pointing out the central role of postsecondary institutions in democracy's defense. When we educate students merely for jobs, we are doing little to defend democracy. Students need to be thought of more than simply as receptacles for canned knowledge that will land them employment, and instead brought into the discourse as engaged citizens with the ability to participate in democratic public life.

With these six points I am saying something more than that the main objective of a student is to become a valuable economic agent. Recognize, again, the linguistic box I am in when I say that one does not need to be a "valuable economic agent." Any student will care about being able to provide for themselves and their families. I am not dismissing as irrelevant the notion that individuals want a life in which they are not worried about the next meal, or providing for their family, or being able to care for themselves in old age, and the like. We all want to live lives without fear of economic displacement. However, we need new conceptualizations of what it means to be human, and once we have these ideas, we can then put them into practice. Without a framework, we have no ability to argue with a different portrait of what education in a democracy is about and what we can do to construct it.

The Work of the Academic

Education, like any other human endeavor, is affected by neoliberal agendas and globalization's transfiguration of the marketplace. Thus, it is important to critically examine how academic labor has been impacted by these forces, even if existing power relationships and ideologies make such an examination difficult to conceptualize (Braverman, 1974). As Giroux (1988) has observed, "Ideology becomes useful for understanding not only how schools sustain and produce meanings, but also how individuals and groups produce, negotiate, modify or resist them" (p. 5). Hence, I argue that a transformative academic acts in certain ways as a teacher and as a scholar. As a teacher, the transformative academic eschews the simple transmission of knowledge and instead embraces dialogues that enable and foment new ideas and concepts. As a scholar, a transformative academic rejects dogma that is inherited from neoliberalism and instead interrogates beliefs and interpretations that globalization's adherents seem to have made self-evident and indispensable. Certainly the pandemic and the subsequent protests over the murder of a Black man in the United States required that the transformative academic not assume that the classroom is a neutral site walled off from larger events.

Previously, I have argued that the transformative academic can then "[focus] dialogue on the reconstruction of the social imagination in order to advance a cultural politics of democracy that honors diverse voices":

> Such a stance stands in contradistinction to . . . governmentality where the state's power becomes vast and invisible and the individual's voice mute and homogenous. Hence, I am concerned with how those of us in educational organizations might be more engaged in promoting democracy and empowering those who are most at risk of being responsibilized for failures that are not of their own making. Concentrating on the cultures, ideologies, and discourses that enable them provides the potential not for submission or adherence to norms, but instead disrupts them and, in doing so, advances democratic organizations. . . . My assumption is that when an educational organization's discursive strategies are about common goals to enable diverse voices, rather than homogenize them, by way of standardized assessments that students, faculty and staff will move closer to creating bonds of reciprocal obligation. (pp. 105–106)

This position may seem utopian, but I follow Giroux's (1983) argument that "human beings not only make history, but also make the constraints; and needless to say, they also unmake them. It needs to be remembered that power is both an enabling as well as a constraining force" (p. 38). An issue like university rankings is created by human beings and can be subject to change whenever human beings feel compelled to act. The challenge for a transformative academic is in reshaping processes so that they can foster diversity, dismantle structural conditions that thwart individual achievement, and promote democratic values. Through the promotion of democratic values, we can also assist the voices of those who might be powerless in the current milieu.

Academics have long played a critical role for societies, especially democratic nations. In a thoughtful book, *Organizing Enlightenment,* Chad Wellmon (2015) tracks how the research university has helped organize knowledge. He usefully points out how radical changes, such as the printing press, expanded our ability on a mass scale to think about knowledge production. Technology always changes what gets transmitted and who is able to get hold of information. We sometimes forget that, just as social media is transforming society today, so too the printing press changed our way of life when it came into existence. The technology advanced, and mass production of newspapers and books became possible.

Wellmon, analyzing Kant, pointed out that "Kant eventually embraced the university as the only institution that could sustain and form people in accord with science. Kant represented not only a shift to technologies of the self but a direct effort to tie them to the university and its epistemic authority" (p. 123). Such an assertion points to the faculty as the arbiter of knowledge. We have long held this position, but attacks on the idea of knowledge and science have brought into question not only how we think about knowledge—an abstraction—but also how we live our lives in the world.

Such a viewpoint creates a portrait of an academic that is important to consider. The academic is not simply the transmitter of knowledge to the student—another technology—but rather the interpreter of knowledge. Although I may be making an obvious point, the argument goes to the heart of the challenge that the university and faculty face today. If students learn, and indeed if society learns, from the neutral presentation of a researcher's data—as if there is such a thing—then really the obligation of the intellectual is to simply present information and let the receiver of the information decide what they will do with the information. From this perspective, the argument of the teacher-researcher is irrelevant. The teacher simply presents facts for the student and reader to ingest.

Kant and others, however, recognize that, with the explosion of knowledge, the professor has to be much more than simply another technology that is transmitting information. The professor makes sense of all this information and coordinates it in a way that makes an argument. Based on the persuasiveness of the argument, the students and public are likely to accept or reject it. The professor is not simply someone who accumulates knowledge, but interprets it—whether by lectures to students or by text via research. A vulgar interpretation of what I am saying is that the professor is thus trying to indoctrinate students/readers. Indoctrination, however, assumes that there are no other alternatives acceptable to the professor and what is being said must be believed simply because the speaker has made the comment. In the academy, what we are after is the opposite of indoctrination; we are trying to persuade individuals based on the evidence we have accumulated. If the data and ideas are not persuasive, then the participant (whether listener or reader) will not be convinced.

Obviously, there is a delicate balance between the view of someone simply cataloguing information—one of Pasteur's quadrants—and then presenting it and someone who tries to make sense of knowledge by way of argumentation. Nevertheless, the view of a university as a large neutral library, and faculty as librarians, is very different from one that came of age in the Enlightenment, when the university and its faculties were trying to shape individuals, produce citizens, and create knowledge that informs society about how to think, what to believe, and how to function.

I have pointed out how simply listing information, as if what we are discussing is a neutral topic, is impossible. All knowledge, all information is mediated. And yet, the point that the intellectual's job is to make sense of information and develop a coherent argument stands in contradistinction from the fascist's goal to use their own facts in making an argument, or putting forward an alternative agenda, absent factual evidence. The modern academic is making an argument based on facts, built on the assumption that the university's research, whether modern, postmodern, scientific, or critical, is framed around the elegance of an individual's framework. Such an assertion is one with which many of us agree, even though we are working from different perspectives and paradigms. Specialization points out that most individuals cannot be polymaths and understand everything. Instead, we adhere to disciplinary/community-based guidelines about knowledge; from those guidelines, we develop an argument that can be debated, accepted, modified, or rejected by one's peers.

The rise of fascism in society puts higher education in a difficult, and critical, position. Jason Stanley (2018) has pointed out how "fascist politicians justify their ideas by breaking down a common sense of history in creating a mythic past to support their vision for the present" (p. 9). Myth, and the romantic view of the past, play a critical role in the advancement of the fascist agenda and is the opposite of what we are trying to do in the academy. We have seen the fictionalization of events happening, or trying to happen, in Los Angeles, New Delhi, and Hong

Kong. In each location, we have leaders who are rewriting the population's shared understanding of reality, whether it be Trump's calls to build a wall to keep out murderers and rapists who will make up a significant percentage of LA's population, or Modi's demonization of Muslims, or Xi's rejection of "one country, two systems" for Hong Kong. Los Angeles used to be the epitome of the democratic ideal because it is a melting pot of cultures; Trump has turned this history on its head by saying the country is stronger if it is monocultural. Consequently, Los Angeles is a "disgrace," to use Trump's favorite attack. Gandhi died trying to promote a pan-secular state that celebrated all religions. Members of the Bharatiya Janata Party (BJP), Modi's governing party, now reject what Gandhi advocated and instead call for a religious Hindu state. Islam has become the focal point of many of the major problems that India faces. The protests in Hong Kong have largely focused on democratic reforms; the protesters want to have a voice in the governance of their city, and China vociferously rejects such demands.

What China is putting forward instead are false beliefs based on invented facts to fit a narrative. By naturalizing group difference, fascist ideology normalizes outliers and prioritizes one group over another. There are "good people," stated President Trump, who marched with the Nazis, and by inference, Black Lives do not really matter. Muslim accomplishments in India were negligible, according to state members of Modi's party; what has made India great was what Hindus have done—in spite of Muslims. The Hong Kong government installed by Beijing insists that "real Hong Kongers" respect the law; the disturbances are the provocations of outsiders. The result is that the law enacted by China in 2020 only sought to uphold law against hooligans. Consequently, those on campuses who speak out against the law ought to be penalized and lose their jobs.

What we are learning about "deepfakes" (Schick, 2020) only adds to our concern. When technology gets so good that not merely the consumer but also those versed in deducing truth cannot detect a falsehood, then we run into problems we have never before experienced. Schick has labeled this sort of activity the "Infocalypse" (p. 168) and describe it as a coming challenge for which we are unequipped. During the COVID-19 pandemic, for example, Russia was able to exploit the bitter relationship between China and the United States by putting forward the false idea that the virus was a Chinese bioweapon. Although we still are able to ascertain which information is true and which is not, the efforts to ascertain truth are time-consuming. And soon, we will no longer be able to ascertain falsehoods at all because of the growing ability to develop deepfakes.

Although there are several traditional organs of power and information that might be utilized to work against fascism—the press, the judiciary, the legislature—universities have the potential to play a critical role. The falsification of the past and the development of pernicious arguments based on a lack of legitimate data are best refuted by those in the academy. "Make America Great Again" evokes a nostalgia for a past that never existed. I understand the point in terms of a rallying slogan, but certainly for LGBTQ individuals who were persecuted, African Americans who were enslaved, and women who were relegated to being homemakers, among many others, the nostalgia for the past is wrong-headed. Fascist politics invokes a mythic past destroyed by those who are not friends, but enemies. The demonization of those who disagree with the fascist narrative is also important. People do not simply agree or disagree. One group is right and good, and the other is wrong and demonized for their beliefs.

The articulation of "what is truth" in multiple areas, and how to argue with one another and not demonize the other into submission, is precisely the sort of work that universities should be doing. The "facts" of the pandemic, for example, were frequently obscured by a president who used his own facts to obscure his administration's failures. Stanley rightly points out that "history in a liberal democracy must be fateful to the norm of truth, yielding an accurate vision of the past" (p. 19). I will take his point even further, because fascist ideology is not only content with rewriting the past. There are legitimate areas of science, social science, and the humanities that can be attacked because they do not fit the fascist agenda. Faculty should work against these attacks in as vigorous a fashion as possible. The Trump administration argues that climate change is not real. Members of the Modi administration have attended gatherings that make statements about Hinduism having invented heart surgery thousands of years ago. China has reneged on basic agreements about Hong Kong's governance. These are the sorts of issues that academics need to reveal and refute.

We also have to argue about these issues vigorously and persuasively. Those of us in academe have not done as good a job as we should have done in being in the vanguard of fighting against lies and malfeasant information. Communication is an art, and the act of communicating with large audiences is different from writing for one's peers when that is the only register one knows. We also have to be comfortable in having fulsome conversations and debates. Campuses are so fraught right now that people prefer not to talk about difficult topics when these types of conversations are exactly the sorts of activities we should be having. I appreciate that deciding what to debate, and arguing over who gets to decide, is difficult in itself—but that is precisely the sort of conversational framework that universities have facilitated for centuries.

We also know that democracy is not simply a natural process, as if individuals would simply gravitate toward it. As long ago as Socrates in *The Republic*, the point has been made that self-governance is hard; people tend to gravitate toward a strong leader to follow. Consequently, the classroom has to be a setting where students learn about democracy, learn how to argue and respect one another, and learn how to think through issues so that they are able to sift through fallacious arguments and reject them. If we simply feed students comfortable ways to engage with those with whom they agree, then the sorts of fascist propaganda and arguments that are currently put forward will be tolerated, even if they are not accepted. The voices of the fascists will drown out the more sobering voices of the academic.

I am suggesting that the work of the intellectual, which is always important, is even more so at a time when populism is on the rise and a commitment to truth becomes secondary to the needs of the fascist leader. Truth is the victim, and that's in part because the citizenry is ill-prepared to battle against ideas that are made out of whole cloth but have little basis in fact. For much of the twentieth century, academics had good and useful arguments about objectivity, science, fact, and truth. We reached a point, however, where we seemingly went off in our own intellectual corners and believed what we wanted within our epistemological standpoint and let the others believe what they wanted to believe. We mistakenly thought our beliefs were incompatible. One useful point about the rise of fascism is to clarify to those of us in academe that we have basic agreements about many ideological ideas, but we do not know how to articulate them.

Stanley has usefully observed the following:

> Fascist politics seeks to undermine public discourse by attacking and devaluing education, expertise and language. Intelligent debate is impossible without an education with access to different perspectives, a respect for expertise when one's own knowledge gives out, and a rich enough language to precisely describe reality. When education, expertise, and linguistic distinctions are undermined, there remains only power and tribal identity. (p. 29)

Academics in universities are frequently intellectual punching bags that make for easy targets to fascists. The claim to "truth," the cornerstone of academic life, suggests that because a fascist leader makes a statement, individuals should not simply agree with it. If fascism cannot defeat this claim, then they will have problems in mounting an effective campaign to assume power. The result is that fascist politics seek to undermine the credibility of colleges and universities, not merely to discredit those who will disagree, but to put forward an equally credible and more compelling version of truth.

What has concerned me with faculty and the universities is that we are more frequently observers to the rise of fascism rather than active opponents to it in any strategic sense. Our inability to engage successfully with fascists come from three positions. If truth is the sine qua non of academic life, then fascists simply need to point out the discrepancies in our positions. To external observers who go about their lives and do not spend time parsing academic discourse, academic life seems at odds with itself. Although climate change is a fact to the overwhelming majority of scientists such that scientists believe the matter settled, we can find those who disagree. Sure, some of them are crackpots, but some are not. When we have respected scientists who disagree that the earth is warming, then there is an opening that fascists have been quick to exploit. For those who are unsure how to gauge academic arguments, it seems that one side is claiming consensus when there is not. It is not an effective strategy to then go into the arcana of how academics come to the decisions we make. The only message the consumer takes away is that not everyone agrees about a warming trend.

In part, the lack of consensus on scientific issues baffles those of us in academe. There is no push to hire people who think the earth is flat or that the moon landing was staged. No one who believes in free speech and the aggressive debate of controversial issues is interested in having arguments about whether 9-11 was a government conspiracy or if the Sandy Hook massacre of children actually happened or was a hoax. Adding flat earthers and their ilk impedes objective inquiry—but not to the fascist. The fascist is less interested in the logic of the academic viewpoint and more concerned about how to get the point across to the broad populace that academic institutions are biased.

A second, related, strategy is to argue that postsecondary institutions are hypocritical, that we believe one thing, but do another. Stanley points out, "a contemporary right-wing campaign is charging universities with deceit on the issue of free speech. Universities, they say, claim to hold free speech in the highest regard but suppress any voices that do not lean left by allowing protests against them on campus" (p. 30). As I noted earlier, academics feel conflicted about free speech.

There are right-wing protagonists whose interest is really only in provoking those with whom they disagree to demonstrate that universities are not really interested in free speech. Milo Yiannopoulos is a useful example of someone who financially profited by giving controversial talks and sought little more than to provoke people into a frenzy of outrage. When he tried to speak at the University of California Berkeley, and protestors successfully shut down his talk. He not only made money off the speaking engagement, but he became a media sensation and thus generated even more revenue for himself. His talk really was of little intellectual value, but fascists could point to his inability to speak at Berkeley as yet another example of the liberal bias of academic institutions. The message was stated like a drumbeat that universities are not really interested in free speech; they are only interested in speech that furthers the liberal cause and demeans the conservative one.

The third point pertaining to our inability to defeat fascists has to do with how we respond to the charges that we are biased and unwilling to accept alternative views; this point has to do with our communicative skills. When fascism succeeds, fascist speakers and orators are able to convince the populace of the rightness of their position. As Stanley notes, "A core tenet of fascist politics [is] that the goal of oratory should not be to convince the intellect, but to sway the will" (p. 380). Such a statement is antithetical to academic life. My goal for this book is to convince the reader's intellect of the soundness of my position; I am not making a claim for one's emotions or sentiments because of their backgrounds or biases. I am acting as an academic who makes an argument, proffers evidence, and, through the piecing together of the evidence, hopefully convinces the reader of the rightness of my position.

The scaffolding of academic life is founded on this principle. Peer review of journals and conference proceedings occurs with the assumption that reviewers can render a judgment about the quality of one's argument. When a candidate's dossier for tenure is put up for review, the reviewer is trying to make a decision about the individual's intellectual worth over time. The background of the author or candidate is irrelevant. To be sure, I am well aware of the flaws in the system; we know that people of color and women, for example, have a more difficult time, not because of the weakness of their ideas, but because of the biases of the reviewers. However, those of us involved in academic decision making have been trying to overcome the flaws in the system. The fascist is bent on showing the corruption of that system.

The problem is that when fascists undermine the principles of the university, they cast into doubt the nature of reality. I do not think that academics have been quick enough to realize how fundamental the attack on truth has been connected to the nature of academic life. When we, as a society, can no longer agree on truth, then we have absurd arguments about how many people attended Donald Trump's inauguration because "we use alternative facts," as his advisor said. What then happens is that the hallmark of democratic engagement—reasoned debate—is replaced by fear and anger. Anger gets funneled into the fascist who can state with resolve that the fascist and his or her group can solve the problem—that only he has the answer.

Hannah Arendt and others have spoken at length about how this sort of argument arises and succeeds, but I am more interested in what is the best response of the university with regard to defeating the fascist. Arendt (1951/1973) nicely summarized how the fascist functions:

> The effectiveness of this kind of propaganda demonstrates one the chief characteristics of modern masses. They do not believe in anything visible, in the reality of their own experience; they do not trust their eyes and ears but only their imaginations. . . . What convinces masses are not facts, but only the consistency of the system of which they are presumably a part. (p. 351)

By undermining trust in academe, as well as the press and other neutral observers of life, fascism replaces the democratic ideal of truth being the arbiter for decision making with an appeal to the leader who will tell us what to believe and how to act. Spreading suspicion and distrust erodes the bonds of fellowship on which a democracy must exist; it subverts critique of one or another group, and it focuses critique on whoever the "other" is that the fascist has named—in India this would be Muslims, in the United States immigrants, in Hong Kong it is "outsiders" who are provoking Hong Kongers. The fascist overlooks structural inequality in favor of a framework that points the finger at a group. Hong Kong's version of strongman mentality is to heap abuse on those who support democracy and try to shut down communicative vehicles—such as bookstores—that offer a different version of truth from that of the Communist Party of China.

The focus of the fascist is on the threat to the individual and the group to which they belong. Internationalism is inevitably frowned on. Once again, the university and the academics who run the institution come in for criticism. Why would we try to understand the "other" when they are the threat we face, whether the "other" is terrorists trying to destroy the country, or foreigners invading the country to take our jobs? A call to nationalism is at the core of the fascist identity, whereas universities are among the most cosmopolitan of organizations. Those who call for social justice and speak as, or allies of, people of color, the LGBTQ community, or religious groups who are marginalized are often found on college campuses. They are markers for fascists about the problems that exist. Group identity as an American in Los Angeles or Indian in New Delhi or a Hong Konger in China and group identity for a fascist are two different identities. One is multicultural and based on pluralism and the idea of democracy; the other appeals to nativist tendencies that includes some and explicitly excludes others. One is inclusive and the other is exclusive.

"Fascist ideology" writes Stanley (2018), "rejects pluralism and tolerance. Everyone in the chosen nation shares a religion and a way of life, a set of customs" (p. 88). Where, more than universities, is the search for multiculturalism greater? To be sure, universities often fail, and they have a history of exclusion and unwillingness to move toward pluralism. But like democracy itself, universities have tried to provoke dialogues of understanding. All within the institution, and, by inference, the wider society need to try to understand difference, and one needs to respect individual liberty while struggling to define the greater good. The result is that the university is at the epicenter of the fascist attack. Defeat the academic and provide victory to the fascist.

Because the university is also home to multiple disciplines with different foundational epistemologies, all knowledge is vulnerable to attack. When the fascist attacks affirmative action, for example, because it is giving special privileges to a group that purportedly should not be given any special privilege, we are, by inference, also saying that all knowledge is suspect. The fascist does not try to parse difference, but instead creates a univocal critique: "The university is biased on this point; therefore, the university is biased on all points." If a university supports gay marriage, then climate change is suspect as well.

We know that universities are easy targets. We have enabled the fascist to level critiques at an institution that remains elite insofar as not everyone participates, and what the institution does presumably helps some and harms others. Although the logic is faulty, politicians rhetorically deride tax dollars being spent on public institutions that promote ideologies that are at odds with what the dominant group says the country is about. Their arguments fit nicely into the perception of elite privilege that matches the demagogic narrative of the fascist.

Our response to these attacks has been muted and largely ineffectual. We certainly should not respond to false arguments with our own false arguments. I also pointed out earlier the challenge of playing to a narrative that is "against"—against effectiveness, against merit, and the like. How then might we begin to think through how to respond to the fascist narrative by developing our own framework? Answering such a question is hard in an organization that historically has fought against a singular narrative of its core. Nevertheless, at this moment in academe's history, it is essential that we do so. There are six areas, in particular, where academics and universities need to think through how to respond to fascism.

Clarify Authoritative Knowledge

Those of us who have written about postmodernism have pointed out that knowledge can be provisional, constructed, and change over time. Critical theorists have argued persuasively that knowledge is to be fought over—and that knowledge production is not something merely consisting of facts and figures. All these sustained critiques are well and good, and they come out from a particular moment in time when we came to understand how those of us on the margins came to be there.

A simple truism is that history goes to the winners who get to write that history. Carlyle's (1841) invocation of the "great men theory" in terms of leadership is not merely a historical inaccuracy, but it fits mistaken assumptions that men were leaders and the "fairer sex" were not, or that the primary players in the American Civil War were all White men. The critique about how people view the world has been good and necessary. And yet, to point out inaccuracies or identify how epistemological standpoints aid in understanding particular phenomena does not by necessity reduce the critical role of the university in adjudicating knowledge.

Certainly, one of the outcomes in the United States after the murder of George Floyd was the rejection of statues and memorials of individuals who had been portrayed as heroes even when they were seriously flawed. Until the United States reckons with its racist past, there will be those who point out how the country has made claims to authority that were inherently racist. Thomas Jefferson may have been a great founding father, but he also was racist. Statues of Confederate generals ascribe to them virtues such as courage even though they fought to destroy the country and enslave a people.

When we reject the idea of authoritative knowledge, we run the risk of reestablishing norms that have been proven false. However, the claim that all knowledge is provisional opens up society to any claims a fascist state wishes to put forward as possible. I do not think that we must have intellectually an "either-or" environment where either all knowledge is up for grabs or we have the reinsertion of norms that lead to the privileging to those in power—whether of gender, race, ability, or other characteristics. Indeed, a critical role for the university is to be able to foster these discussions that broaden understanding, rather than disabling it.

Embrace Knowledge Diffusion

I run the risk of trying to reinsert the university as a citadel on a hill that determines what is knowledge and what is not. Such a portrait enables professors to be removed from society and contemplate questions about which they will ultimately decide and let society know what to think. Such a portrait, if drawn, would be outdated and wrong. Knowledge always derives from a variety of sources, and today such a point is even more important. As de Sousa Santos (2010) has pointed out, "The idea of a knowledge society implies that knowledge is everywhere" (p. 9). In the twenty-first century, there are many other centers of knowledge production, and that is all to the good. We need broader definitions of knowledge that are neither monocultural nor ideologically narrow.

In some respects, what I am recommending always has occurred. Academics have always incorporated information that they found outside the university, but they did not often acknowledge it. What we need to maintain, however, is an understanding of how to reject what passes for knowledge that is incomplete or positioned in a way to ensure that the fascist acquires power by way of a particular point that is intellectually groundless and based on false information.

Interrogate Racial and Gender Identities

I have pointed out the critical role that identity plays in Los Angeles, Hong Kong and New Delhi. Identities vary, of course, but even our understanding of what we mean by identity changes over time and location. A

Hong Konger's identity is different from that of someone in Los Angeles or New Delhi. Isabel Wilkerson, in *Caste: The Lies That Divide Us (2020)*, points out how rigid, arbitrary boundaries divide and damage us today, regardless of location. In 2020 the United States had to struggle not only with the pandemic but also with more violence against African Americans, men in particular, largely in the form of assassinations by the police. India enacted legislation aimed at Muslims that generated violence, and legislation further discriminated against those from a low caste.

I appreciate the often fraught dialogues that occur on college campuses pertaining to race and gender. The hesitation of many individuals to engage in conversations where they might be censured because of the discussion highlights how difficult these dialogues are. Nevertheless, universities must center on issues of race, gender, and identity. We need to seek ways to make the citizenry's concerns cross-cutting, rather than individual and isolated. Ian Haney Lopez has pointed out how antidemocratic forces have successfully employed "dog-whistle politics" (2020, p. 19) to isolate groups. A dog-whistle is one that only dogs can hear. Racist dog-whistles are those that speak of "those" people but do not speak specifically about race. As an antidote to strategic racism we need to seek arenas where we might put forward discussions that lead to cross-racial solidarity. If we do not confront and interrogate our history of racism and gender bias, then we will be unable to lay claim to fighting fascism and promoting democracy.

Reaffirm the Import of Global Knowledge

I have long pointed out that all knowledge is local. How we come to understand ourselves and others is played out in local contexts. Fascism is national in context and assumes, however, that knowledge is specific to the nation. Those who put forward other pieces of information or proffer different viewpoints at a minimum are irrelevant, but more important, are harmful and pernicious to those from the fascist's country. Global knowledge—knowledge that transcends borders—is critical to defeating the fascist's desire to define reality.

Universities stand for the opposite point from the fascist. One merely need glance at Nobel Prize winners every year to find a collection of individuals who worked on a particular intellectual puzzle with colleagues from other universities in other countries. Universities need to be leaders in the discourses pertaining to national borders and the import of educating people, irrespective of the nation-state. When the historian, biologist, or social worker is studying particular phenomena, the point is not simply to improve the nation but to add to the knowledge base for individuals throughout the world. Slogans such as "Make America Great Again" have a rhetorical ring, but they are antithetical to what the scientist tries to do. Objective knowledge, with all the intellectual warning signs attached to it, still enables the academic to step back and try to prove what they are studying, rather than simply appeal to fascist rhetoric.

Establish Critical Reflexivity

All of what I am arguing for here creates an intellectual schizophrenia for the intellectual. We must acknowledge the historical importance of disinterestedness and truth; never forsake one's role as an intellectual in search of truth wherever it may take us; reject claims to emotion that overlook evidence and accept that findings can be real, genuine, and confirmable.

At the same time, the intellectual of the twenty-first century cannot sit on the sidelines and act simply as a referee about knowledge by writing articles in journals that only other academics read and get published at the leisurely pace of academic publications. The university as a monastery, however important for upholding the virtue of disinterestedness, is no longer viable. The fascist cordons off the academy and argues that its claims to truth are irrelevant.

Intellectuals need to engage with the surrounding communities. We need to critique claims to knowledge that are wrong, but we need to do so in a reflexive manner that acknowledges and critiques our stance, position, and claims to authority. The leaders of the Umbrella movement in Hong Kong were initially academics who then gave way to a broad-based student movement; the protests in 2019–2020 were led by students. What troubles me about the United States is that academics and their universities are almost irrelevant in the attacks that Trump and his supporters' machine have put forward. The same can be said about India and New Delhi. Occasionally, individuals are singled out and step to the stage, but more often than not, rather than stepping forward, we are retreating behind the confines of the ivory tower.

Accept the University as a Locus of Informed Debate That Stimulates Action

Academic institutions, in multifaceted ways, are involved in the definition, creation, and refinement of a better future for the local and global community. We do so through philosophical treatises, as well as laboratory experiments that seek cures for disease. The poet aims to give to their poem something that will enrich the reader's life, just as the engineer works on a problem that, in some fashion, will advance our understanding of different phenomena. We are cartographers of the mind.

A strength of academic life always has been the debate that informs our intellectual selves. Whenever possible, we have to reinsert our postsecondary institutions into the public debate. Rather than exist as a preserve of individuals divorced from society, we should serve as the town square, which actively solicits informed dialogue and debate. We should welcome all those who offer thoughtful arguments on all issues that confront us, and we have to create the conditions so that these arguments are seen as scholarly interchange, rather than as attacks on one group or another.

These debates, however, are not simply academic exercises, as if the university were a scholarly debating society and little more. Debates need to lead to action. I have put forward six axes of purpose and five areas for reform with the intent of summarizing the ideas I have discussed in the preceding chapters. Those walls that isolate the university from the larger community need to come down and enable academics to generate ideas and actions that stand against the fascist onslaught of misinformation. We cannot stand idly by while democracy falls from a recession into a depression. Larry Diamond (2019) has pointed out that "Democracy requires trust in the decency and benevolence of other citizens, toleration for different points of view, and thus a bit of modesty and doubt about one's own political stances" (p. 27). The university needs to accentuate this trust, but it must also be a forceful advocate for the knowledge that gets disseminated. How we go about this is the focus of the final chapter.

CHAPTER SEVEN

Academic Responsibility

Toward a Cultural Politics of Integrity

I have written this book with an overriding concern about the future of democracy as the world has experienced the rise of fascism yet again. I suspect I would have written a different book on a different topic if Donald Trump had not been elected president of the United States, if Narendra Modi had not been reelected in India, and Hong Kong had not erupted into violence and ended up a vassal of China. As I studied and wrote in New Delhi, Los Angeles, and Hong Kong, I began to see that the circumstances in general, and the actions on the campuses in particular, were not isolated incidents. A trend had surfaced, and I do not believe we can ignore it. True, Trump (and perhaps Modi) will have left office by the time you read this book, but the stance of the university, regardless of the individual leader, needs to be rethought, and that is what I have tried to do here. Since I began this book, a pandemic spread across the world. Explosive protests have rocked the United States after yet another Black man was killed at the hands of the police. Trump's refusal to accept the results of a free and fair election, and the attack on the Capitol by traitors, was one of the greatest attacks on American democracy since its founding. In a moment of crisis, it is too easy to say, however, that the world will never be the same and everything will be different. My assumption is that after the pandemic has subsided and Trump and Modi leave office, the world will return to a semblance of what once existed—but universities and colleges must do a better job at advancing democracy. Hong Kong universities will have become a simulacrum of themselves. Even there, however, a framework is necessary to think through how the university might best respond to assaults on truth.

I have not wanted to be overly dramatic, but many other observers pointed out a twofold danger: democracy is in recession and fascism is experiencing a resurgence (Albright, 2018; Diamond, 2019; Eisen et al., 2019; Gessen, 2020; Levitsky & Ziblatt, 2018; Snyder, 2017, 2019). The data are clear. We tend to have historical amnesia when we think about democracy, as if it's a system that has been firmly established and implemented throughout the world for a long period of time. We think the world is moving, perhaps inexorably, toward greater freedoms and more democracies. By democracy I mean a system in which all citizens are able to choose and replace their leaders in regular, fair, free, and meaningful elections. This liberal idea has been constructed around representative democracy, human rights, and a belief in human capital complemented by a strong social safety net. In 1974, only 29 countries with a population above 1 million were democracies (Diamond, 2019). Democracy then had an incredible 30-year growth spurt, which may account for our amnesia. Now we have the opposite trend, which in large part has been the impetus for writing this book.

We are experiencing a populist surge around the world. Democracies are seen as failing individuals. Jobs are harder to come by, and having financial security into one's old age is difficult for all but the wealthy. Interest-based politics minimize communitarian notions of the public good. Populist politicians win elections by attacking representative democracy. They argue that the government is too weak to protect hard-working, native-born people. The borders of a country have become rallying cries to keep immigrants out and to suggest that foreign lands are dangerous areas marked by terrorism.

Established democracies are giving way to illiberal forces driven by popular passions. The economic forces resulting from globalization and neoliberalism are the stimulants for populism. Rather than a respect for democratic organs such as the judiciary and the press, the "strongman" has come into play. Democracy is always a process rather than a singular event; citizens argue, disagree, and hopefully reach common goals.

Populist leaders from the left and the right develop a cult of personality. Think of Huey Long, Father Coughlin, or George Wallace. Trump's statement at the Republican convention when describing a crisis that the United States faces—"I alone can fix it"—(Applebaum, 2016) fits this version of populism. The populist leader can solve problems—no one else can. Modern democracy, however, functions by way of liberal institutions—the legislature, the judiciary, a free press—and academe. These institutions serve as a check on those in power. The populist sees these sorts of institutions as roadblocks, as impediments to enacting their agenda. Consequently, the populist seeks to ignore the impediments, discredit them, or do away with them. Along with others, I have claimed that we are experiencing, not simply a populist surge, but one that falls within the scope of traditional definitions of fascism. In this closing chapter I wish to elaborate on what I think of as fascist tendencies that are on the rise.

Fascism sets aside democracy and due process in public life, and instead it promotes what the fascist sees as traditional society before invaders threatened the fabric of society. When fascism advances, we see mass enthusiasm for the despot and the curtailment of traditionally independent institutions such as the press, the legislature, and the judiciary. Robert Paxton, in *The Anatomy of Fascism* (2004), stated:

> Fascism may be defined as a form of political behavior marked by obsessive preoccupation with community decline, humiliation, or victimhood and by compensatory cults of unity, energy, and purity, in which a mass-based party of committed nationalist militants, working in uneasy but effective collaboration with traditional elites, abandons democratic liberties and pursues with redemptive violence and without ethical or legal restraints goals of internal cleansing and external expansion. (p. 291)

The contours of fascism strike at the heart of democracy; feelings, rather than reason, reign. The fascist narrative is inevitably that a crisis exists, which was not caused by the populace, and that the demagogue can fix it and return society to what it once was. To resolve the perceived problems, whether real or imagined, business as usual needs to be supplanted by executive authority. The fascist argues that individual and minority rights have corroded what made the country great and the majority must retake their country in order to save it. Those who have enabled the problems to arise are not simply wrong, but evil, and they must be defeated and possibly jailed or eliminated. The country, as defined by the majority, has a destiny that must be met. If traditional facts do not conform to the necessary narrative, then "alternative" facts will be used. The utilization of alternative facts by the leader, as well as their repetition, leads to the facts becoming truth. The fascist leader embodies precisely the values that the group wants to put forward and restore. Naturally, the leader's instincts and intelligence are dominant; abstract, universal reason is less important. Violence may be unfortunate, but it is a necessary tool to overcome the state's decline.

When one looks at the actions of President Trump in coming to power during his term in office and his behavior after he lost the election, we see the classic actions of a fascist. Encouraging chants of "lock her up" about his opponent and his repeated declarations that any news he didn't like was "fake" derive from the fascist playbook. Trump famously claimed he could shoot someone in the middle of New York City's Fifth Avenue and his supporters wouldn't care; this statement underscores the blind support he inspires (Dwyer, 2016). These supporters saw in Trump someone who could build a wall on the border, stop the "invasion" of dark-skinned people, and return America to greatness again. Instead, the country experienced a pandemic that he mismanaged, the rise of racism, and the disdain of democratic countries around the world.

A half a world away, Modi's Hindu supporters had the same feelings: India was once a great Hindu nation that had been subjected to Muslim domination. Secularism led to India's downfall and continued their humiliation on the global stage; the way to greatness was to reinscribe Hinduism throughout all the country's cultural and social institutions. Hindus deserved Modi because he spoke to their economic, social, and cultural needs. Just as in the United States Mexican immigrants were to be cast out and defined as the root of the country's problems, if not simply evil, so too were Muslims in India (Chopra, 2018; Filkins, 2019; Gettleman et al., 2019). A direct line can be drawn from Modi's ideology to the violence in New Delhi that began in early 2020 that killed scores of Muslims.

Hong Kong is a tougher example because of the insidious nature of its domination. When China was forced to hand over Hong Kong to the British, the islands were largely uninhabited, but the people who were there were either indigenous or Chinese. Over time, as the island grew, so too did a Hong Kong identity. By the time the British returned the islands to China, there was a neat bifurcation, which was defined as "one country, two systems." Part of that system, which has only accelerated over the last quarter-century, is a Hong Kong identity whereby a concern for democracy has been at the heart of people's conception of self.

China, of course, is not a democratic system, and part of the traditional definition of fascism is that it is a movement away from democratic structures and traditions. Fascism also claims there is an external threat and preys on economic failures as a rationale for the authoritarian leader to take power. In this light, what we have seen in Hong Kong is not a classic case of fascism. However, consider the situation Hong Kongers face. They are being told that they are the threat—that their identity is the problem—and their hopes and aspirations for their families and one another are at risk. Just as fascist countries seek to absorb different lands and groups, China seeks to absorb Hong Kong culturally, economically, and politically. For example, it seeks to replace the Cantonese language and traditional Chinese characters, which approximately 80 percent of the Hong Kong population uses as their primary form of communication, with Mandarin and simplified Chinese characters (Liu, 2017). Property values have soared way beyond the range of the Hong Kong middle class as wealthy mainland Chinese have been granted an endless stream of residential permits to buy property on the 425 square mile island, which is inhabited by 7.4 million people (Jayantha & Oladinrin, 2019). In the middle of the 2020 coronavirus crisis, Hong Kong police surprisingly arrested two pro-democracy politicians for participating in an unauthorized assembly held months previously. Moreover, a media scion who was critical of Hong Kong and Beijing's leadership, Jimmy Lai Chee-ying, was arrested under dubious allegations of intimidating a journalist from a competing news outlet that is much more complimentary of Beijing and the policies of Xi Jinping. In both instances, the charges were widely condemned by international rights groups and journalists, and the timing of the arrests—while public attention was focused on quarantines, mask shortages, and school closings related to a public health emergency—was viewed with widespread suspicion (M. Chan, 2020; Kwok & Yiu, 2020). Then the Chinese legislature passed the National Security Law, which all but eliminated any good-faith attempt to promote "one country, two systems," and the universities overwhelmingly fell in line with their leaders in vocal support of the changes.

The assumption is that democracy and self-determination are not simply a luxury that cannot be afforded; they are culturally, socially, and economically flawed. Fascism, like any ideology that gets analyzed and theorized, is never static and never neatly tied into a formula that defines how one acts and thinks, along with the eventual outcome that is expected. The determinants of fascism, however, help us identify where there are similarities and differences across situations, what accounts for these differences, and most important, what might be done.

In each situation, we see that one particular social organization is problematic—postsecondary institutions. In times of crisis, the very heart of academic life—reasoned analysis and argument—is either seen as a nicety that is not useful in a climate of crisis, or worse, as hostile to reforms envisioned by fascists. The result is that universities have either been sidelined or are anathema to the current crisis that confronts the country, as seen by fascists and their confreres.

Unfortunately, my sense is that in the United States as well, universities also are not points of resistance. To a certain extent, universities have played key roles in protests in New Delhi, and students are leaders of the reform movement in Hong Kong, although faculty and administrators are not. As I noted in Chapter 3, we need universities to develop a language of community that celebrates commonalities and honors differences. We need a respect for democratic agencies that put forward opinions that force us to question authority but maintain respect for the integrity of the process. A language of public life that starts with the recognition of deep differences among us and builds faith in meaningful communication across lines of difference is essential to combat fascism. We need the ability to comment on flaws in our political, economic, and sociocultural systems without assuming that everyone must agree—or that if we disagree, the end is near—or even that those with whom we disagree are evil. We need to build what I am calling communities of difference. In the previous chapter I put forward axes of purpose and then areas for reform with the intent of distilling my arguments about the need for universities to claim a greater voice in the protection of democracy and the advancement of communities of difference.

The creation of communities based on difference is not simply something someone announces, after which the project is over. Rather, a community of difference is a way of being, of structuring academic life in a larger framework that enables us to speak out where we are currently muffled. Our hesitancy has largely been because of the economic structures in which we currently find ourselves, which I have defined as globalization and neoliberalism. If we understand these frameworks, we will be well situated to craft a response.

I first revisit what I have outlined as globalization and neoliberalism. Based on the axes of purpose and areas for reform that I discussed in Chapter 6, I put forward steps to action for students and faculty. I then summarize the ideas by offering a framework for action for those of us who are concerned about reinvigorating democracy. My intent is to help create the conditions that enable us to involve ourselves in a politics of possibility and hope.

Globalization and Neoliberalism Revisited

Because globalization is tied to changes in technology, it is hard to envision a future that is not predicated on the present use of social media. We are not going to give up our iPhone or ban other forms of technology in search of a better world unless some better technology comes along. When fascists speak of a return to the past, they imagine themselves armed with their smartphones and free to tweet about the good old days. We might bemoan the strength of companies such as Amazon and the power they have to determine a great deal over our lives, but we still expect our packages to be delivered to our doorstep in 48 hours. No one likes a bookstore more than I. However, I sometimes feel like a fool ordering a book from a bookstore simply to keep it in business when I know I could get the book cheaper, faster, and more conveniently if I simply went home and ordered it online. Likewise, I once had cabinets full of articles neatly filed under subject headings that I might peruse when I wrote; I've written this book with all my articles stored on my laptop in the cloud.

We also ought not to elegize the past. We are prone to romanticize those days when, in reality, they weren't all that good. Academics cut down a redwood forest in printing their articles. The ability I have today to coauthor my work quickly and efficiently with scholars around the world was impossible when I entered academe. The support structures that I think of naturally today when I write a book—whether it's the autocorrect function when I make a typo or the bibliographic mechanisms that are at my disposal to find and correctly organize citations—make my life as a writer much more pleasant than when I was a graduate student and rummaged through the piles of my books and articles to find a correct citation.

I know very few people, and no academics, who suggest that by criticizing the consequences of globalization, we swear off the advances we have made because of it. When people frame the discussion in terms of the importance of an organization being effective or accountable, it places those of us who are critics as seemingly desirous of ineffectiveness or a lack of accountability. Thus, we have challenges in effectively critiquing globalization. I raise this point because many critics of globalization tend to overlook the advances we have made and our relative comfort with the changes that have been put in place.

To wit, my discomfort with the more nefarious consequences of globalization does not mean that I need to reject all the changes that have occurred or that I end up wishing for a return to a premodern age. What, then, are the most far-reaching challenges of globalization that we need to think of reframing? I am assuming, of course, that one does not need to change everything to change something. I refuse to be put into the intellectual straightjacket that makes me an antiglobalist because some of what has come about has been harmful. Consequently, then, there are eight primary outgrowths of globalization that we need to deal with in general, and in particular with regard to higher education.

Assumptions Deriving from Globalization

Globalization as Destiny

When I was in college, I did not think much about what I was going to do after graduation, but when I left Tufts University, I knew that I could find some sort of job that made sense. Through the postwar period to the 1970s, capitalism assured children of the middle and upper classes that they would get a good enough paying job that they would be able to pay the bills, buy a house, and raise a family. The comfort of the populace does not automatically lead people to question the underlying principles and structure that have enabled them to live the way they live. We felt we could do anything because the structure of the economy enabled this feeling as a frame for middle-class White life.

It turns out that the same is true with discomfort. Students who go to college today assume that they may not get a job when they graduate, and, consequently, they may not be able to pay basic expenses, raise a family, or buy a house. Today, we feel that if we do not find employment, then either the university did not do a good enough job in preparing us for the workforce or we failed. What we do not question is the underlying structure of globalization, which frames how we think and act.

Marxists might rightly claim that I am speaking of false consciousness (Augoustinos, 1999; Eyerman, 1981). Globalization as ideology serves to promote the interests and maintain relations of power and domination. Language and discourse, pace Foucault, make the environment appear as a structuring structure (Bourdieu, 1984) that we fit into or fail, rather than a structure that we might try to change so that it more justly meets our needs. The result is that we divide society into winners and losers, and everyone deserves what they have got.

We Are Observers of Our Lives

A curious dichotomy exists where individualism is prized so that we divide society between winners and losers. At the same time, we do what we have to do to exist even though we may not want to conduct our lives in the way that we are forced to do. Those who struggle against the overarching ideology of globalization are misfits or dreamers, but they are most certainly not winners. Critiquing the manner in which the world functions has little utility in a competitive economy where markets function across borders and competition is key. We prize speed, utility, outcomes, and growth. Very little else matters.

Jacques Brel, the French composer and lyricist, once wrote a song titled "Carousel," which tells how we all got on the merry-go-round and it went "round and round" faster and faster and we could not get off. Globalization is the twenty-first century carousel. We can jump on or stay off of it—the choice is ours. If we do not get on, we will fail. If we get on, it will go faster and faster and we may well get thrown off, but what choice do we really have? Therein lies the inherent contradiction of globalization. A radical form of individualism exists that enables us to think that we ourselves determine our success or failure. Within the larger picture that is globalization, we stand outside ourselves and observe our actions, but we cannot determine how to alter the structure in ways that are more equitable, fair, and compassionate.

Universities Are Enablers

Although there is some movement, especially in the United States, to claim that a college degree is unimportant, the vast majority of the industrialized world still assumes that sending children to university is critical. Indeed, that belief is invested with even more importance today because the assumption is that students will learn skills that equip them for employment in a very difficult job market. We obsess, through an array of "real" facts, that college pays off. "The more you learn, the more you earn" is a commonsensical statement pointing out that holders of college degrees make more than their high school counterparts. Indeed, there is enough evidence to conclude that an individual with a bachelor's degree will earn 84 percent more than an individual with a high school degree (Carnevale et al., 2011).

Because of an increasingly nervous clientele and a less secure funding base, universities have increasingly focused on their students' employability.

In the parlance of strategic decision making, universities today focus on "adaptive strategies" (Chaffee & Tierney, 1988), whereby the environment is viewed as an ecological system. The job of the university is to adapt—or die. Again, the point is not to critique that environment and try to alter the more nefarious aspects of it because that is little more than a fool's errand. The point of adaptation is survival. In a competitive environment, one must figure out what is going on out there, see the students as consumer and customer, determine what they need, and provide it to them. Those that do not do so, or do so less well than their competitors, will go the way of the dinosaur.

What was once seen as a compliment is now made to be a death knell for the organization: universities are among the world's oldest organizations. Such a statement used to be said with pride because everyone understood the import of the university. The result was that there was a direct link between places like the University of Bologna, Oxford University, and Nalanda University (in India), as well as today's postsecondary institutions. The past in a globalized world, however, is an artifact not worthy of replication. Adaptation is critical. You must drop what doesn't work and figure out what is needed. In fact, you must reinvent yourself.

In such a world, any critical function of the university is seen as superfluous and harmful. Globalization opens up universities to cross-border comparisons to determine whether they are competitive, and, of course, competition is key. Just as we choose items in the market largely based on cost and quality, so too must we do the same with regard to higher education. Cost is to be borne by the consumer, and quality is determined by the ability to enable students to get through the system efficiently and effectively—as defined by the acquisition of a job.

Neoliberalism Is the Only Viable Interpretive Framework

Globalization's relationship to neoliberalism is clear and compelling. If globalization is the environment in which we find ourselves, neoliberalism is the interpretation we have chosen to make sense of the surroundings. Or we have not so much chosen neoliberalism as the interpretive framework but have had it imposed on us as the one logic of how things work. Success is measured through economic growth and a consumerist mentality that more is better. Competition is valued, and outcomes are relatively clear—winners succeed and losers lose. The market logic is that capitalism is the one best system, and, if anything, globalization has only exacerbated the tension between the individual and society.

The government's role is not to protect or advance well-being or social goods. Whereas the government once sought to protect individuals as a communal right, today the assumption is that the best government is a minimal one that gets out of the way and destroys the red tape that reduces competition and individual rights. A new Gilded Age enables the market to define our relations to one another, and the government's role is to be one of oversight, if at all, in ensuring consumer protection, rather than to provide a framework for communal goods. The neoliberal framework retranslates the citizen and community into shareholders in a market. Efficiency is prized, so to the extent that the government can reduce regulations is all to the good. The market is more efficient. Shareholders have a better chance at generating increased revenue.

The most successful shareholders are entrepreneurs, because they are willing to take risks. The assumption is that, in a competitive environment, all individuals are going to work hard, but many will not wish to compete in a way whereby they can lose. However, the market is framed in a manner that provides significant rewards for the entrepreneur. Less understood are the significant disadvantages for those who lose or who do not wish to compete in such a manner. We no longer look at the rights of individuals; instead, we focus on the ability for individuals to compete against one another. The result is job insecurity in a world where organizational flexibility is essential. Recall my point about the importance of adaptation. Organizations adapt and evolve when they create new units and shed old ones. Workers come and go, and if they do not fit the plans for the new units, then they need to be let go. When we speak of a gig economy, we are simply acknowledging the market logic of workers as interrelated components of a market-based mechanism that can be discarded and shed if their utility does not meet the demands of the market.

Globalization's introduction of technology and social media has helped neoliberalism redefine higher education in three primary ways. The clientele for a college or university used to be straightforward. A state public university in Los Angeles drew students largely from Los Angeles, just at universities in Hong Kong looked for students within the region. But online learning makes the market much more expansive.

First, on the one hand, bigger is better, and to increase one's market share is of obvious benefit. On the other hand, as support from state governments has decreased, institutions have needed to pinpoint other ways to generate revenue, and the expansion of the clientele has become one obvious possibility. Second, the faculty, who were once the center of the institution, have become expendable. Others can do their work as far less cost. If a university is simply defined by teaching information in a preformed manner, then the market to hire such individuals is vast. And third, privacy has been redefined. What was once private is now public. Monitoring of individual activity leads to the importance of assessment. We are all in competition with one another so we all have targets to reach or surpass, and how we do that is by way of the processes we take to reach a goal.

Critiques of neoliberalism and the market are usually focused on inefficiencies. Inefficiencies inevitably require increased oversight, efficiency, and control. The goal is to make the system more efficient, and other goals, such as human liberation or happiness, are forgotten, overlooked, or even mistakenly assumed to be directly aligned with market efficiency. Management has grown because oversight is paramount; those who support such a stance are simply pointing out the obvious. There is nothing nefarious about claiming that we need greater speed; the world has speeded up. The inherent logic, again, is hard to refute. Time becomes a commodity, as with everything else. The adage that "time is money" has never been truer than in a world framed by globalization. Autonomy, privacy, and collaboration are eschewed in a competitive environment that privileges the ability to get ahead on one's own terms.

Colleges and universities have followed the script provided to them because they also either subscribe to the overall framework or, more likely, see no alternative. When the state cuts our budget, then no amount of hand-wringing will suffice. We can say that we need to make a better case to increase funding at the state and federal levels, but these are long-term strategies, and new budgets start in July. In June 2019, the U.S. state of Alaska's higher education system was faced with a 41 percent budget cut of $135 million from its normal $327 million operating budget (Axelrod, 2019). The cuts were devastating, and they not only caused Moody's Investors Service to precipitously downgrade the credit rating of the University of Alaska system (Svrluga, 2019), they threatened the accreditation status of each the state's universities (Flaherty, 2019). Ultimately, "only" $70 million was slashed from the system (Lederman, 2019), but there was no substitution whereby monies could simply be transferred in to make up the difference. States tend to provide a consistent level of funding to systems even when costs rise. The deferred maintenance of New Delhi's campuses runs into the billions of dollars. India says it wants to attract foreign faculty—the best and the brightest are needed to make its universities more competitive in the global rankings—but, to do so, they would have to provide hundreds of millions of dollars, which are simply unavailable. When administrators are faced with budget shortfalls and they look to their peers, isn't it logical to think about how to compete in this environment? Nevertheless, they end up doing so in a manner that reinforces the challenges they face.

Temporal Acceleration

Globalization has accelerated neoliberalism in a manner that promotes a sense of confidence about how to survive in a competitive environment. The sense of confidence is intended to mask the inequities that will occur. Time becomes a commodity that is compressed and accelerated across geographies and peoples. In *Waiting for Godot*, Samuel Beckett (1955) has his two characters speak as if in step with the challenges we face today:

Vladimir:

That passed the time.

Estragon:

It would have passed in any case.

Vladimir:

Yes, but not so rapidly.

Time becomes compressed, and those who think of interactions as leisurely and unimportant will be left behind in the new economy (Castells, 2000; Hassan, 2003). The rapid integration of information and communication technology (ICT) into all facets of contemporary society has changed the way people make sense of time. How individuals and societies utilize, perceive, experience, and negotiate the passing of time has been a subject of academic discourse across disciplines, as the construct of time permeates all aspects of daily life (Duncheon & Tierney, 2013). The intensification of time in a globalized world only has brought a greater focus on how individuals' lives get become by the neoliberal assumptions about effectiveness, efficiency, and the underlying purpose of life.

Economists characterize time as a scarce resource, noting that each day is limited to 24 hours. Gary Becker (1965) observed that families and firms, alike, have a limited number of resources for the maximization of productivity. One of the most valuable resources is time; hence, individuals need to use their time in ways that maximize satisfaction. Since people cannot perform some important activities simultaneously, Gross (1984) further notes that people must constantly choose between activities such as working, sleeping, and playing.

How time is constituted therefore places pressure on the individual who must make essential daily decisions pertaining to the usage of time. The dominant temporal perspective in Western societies is "Clock-time, which neoliberal economists from Western societies have adopted as linear, continuous, and uniform (Usunier & Valette-Florence, 2007), along with the notion that individuals make time allocation choices based on a fixed number of hours in the day. Hallowell (1937) writes that "when one thinks of time, not as a sequence of experiences, but as a collection of hours, minutes and seconds, the habits of adding time and saving time come into existence . . . time, in short, became reified" (p. 649). Hence, time is money (Gross, 1984).

The neoliberal view of time in Western thought infuses the language around the concept, as time is "spent, saved, wasted, invested, divided, managed, budgeted, shared, and used up" (Tierney & Duncheon, 2013, p. 241; see also Birth, 2004; Gross, 1984; Lakoff & Johnson, 1980). Individuals use time wisely if they complete objectives within an allotted amount of time. "Clock-time" also has the potential to dictate work schedules and leisure activities; hence, it becomes a form of social control (Marx, 1877/1977; Segre, 2000). Marx was not the only sociologist to express misgivings about the potential for time to inscribe inequalities through class distinctions (between those who could take advantage of leisure and those who could not), Weber also was concerned about the ability of capitalist companies to regulate daily work by prescribing workers' time.

Globalization has compressed time even further. We all know that the internet, for example, makes it that much harder to make a distinction between home and work. The busy executive used to carry a briefcase and retreat to a home office to look over file folders and accounting sheets.

Today, executives check their iPhone on the way out the door to see if anything has happened in the time while the laptop has been in silent mode and the office door has been closed. Companies may make policies about not bothering staff on weekends and in the evening. Everyone knows, however, that, in a globalized world, one cannot afford the competition to get a jump on one's work. Workers around the world, and particularly in the United States, do not even take the vacation time allotted to them, in large part because they do not think they can afford to do so if they want to remain competitive (Maye, 2019). Likewise, the compression of time only has made academic life that much more harried.

Constrained Notions of the Public Good and Identity

In Chapter 1 I noted the social ramifications of neoliberal globalization. Inequality has increased, as has privatization. Regulation is seen as superfluous at best, and more likely harmful for curbing the enthusiasm of the market. An expansive notion of the public good runs counter to the belief that the market should determine growth, so support for government infrastructure shrinks. Academic staff—faculty, administrators, and personnel—are valued for how much they can produce and how cheaply they can be paid. The result is that tenure is superfluous, and part-time workers who are paid piecemeal are valued. One's identity becomes framed in economic terms, and other notions of who one is that might help frame how one approaches life are seen as either individual traits that reduce or increase utility or a group trait that helps one succeed or fail in the market. Once again, the world is framed in terms of winners and losers. The importance of critiquing this sort of world is unimportant and peripheral. One might be free to offer one's opinions at home, but not in the academic workplace. Academic freedom is either a luxury we can no longer afford or inimical to the goals of the organization.

Every organization confronts its environment in different ways. In an ecological framework, adaptation is key and different species adapt in different ways. There are also changes from one organization to another. Start-ups are different from mature industries, and we can track how organizations change over time where what once worked is no longer sufficient for a growing business. Informal interactions that determine how decisions get made may work in an environment of a dozen employees, but obviously they will fail in a large company.

The Aging of Academic Ideas

When neoliberalism and globalization took hold, higher education was already a mature industry. I pointed out in chapter two how academic life had been reorganized. An analogy is useful. Typewriters faded when computers came on the scene because the chief executive officers of typewriter companies did not understand the competition or the market. Universities, over time, saw their authority challenged. Observers of higher education have long held that universities are ivy-covered castles removed from society so academics could objectively study abstract notions such as truth, as well as applied ideas pertaining to society, such as crime and punishment. The laboratory became the model for how one investigates phenomena. Rather than messy and haphazard or moral and righteous, science—by way of the Enlightenment—enabled the faculty to come up with answers about truth and society.

Autonomy was essential. Outside interference was disdained because it had the potential to pollute objective findings. The result was a certain form of hegemony whereby questions of knowledge were largely deter-mined in the academy. The academic's voice gained credence, and, in larger society, the university was an admired organization that helped improve the well-being of society. Indeed, land grant institutions in the United States were part of a larger focus that suggested that what was learned in the academy could be passed on to society. We conducted tests, our colleagues verified them, and, once we had decided something, we would tell the pertinent constituency—agricultural audiences, for example—how what we had learned would improve what they were doing.

And then the walls collapsed on the structures we had created. Some of the cracks came from within the academy. Many of us critiqued how we thought about knowledge production, and we made valid points about the rigidity and historicism of the scientific paradigm. Knowledge could be circumscribed by one's biases, we asserted; the scientific paradigm was not sacrosanct. Enough of a critique existed that individuals began to acknowledge the flaws that existed with regard to women and people of color, and largely how we defined difference. Presumably, if the scientific method was to determine one's findings, then whoever did the study did not matter. And yet, enough evidence existed to point out the biases in the system that the academy could no longer simply reject out of hand any arguments being made about objectivity.

Globalization and neoliberalism added fuel to the intellectual fires. Lawmakers who bought into the ideas about the importance of the market thought higher education was getting a free ride; limiting the public good meant that individuals benefited more than society for a postsecondary education, so the burden of cost fell to the individual rather than on society. Further, even though the state was providing less funding, lawmakers argued that governmental oversight should not also be less. One oddity of the last 20 years is that, as public funding decreased, evaluation increased. One might think that if I now paid 50 percent of the funding for an organization whereas I used to pay 100 percent, my voice pertaining to the direction of the institution would recede. However, the opposite has taken place. Less funding and more supervision make intellectual sense, however, insofar as evaluation and oversight go hand in hand with reduced notions of the public good and the rejection of autonomy for any organization.

Social media and advances in technology also brought forward additional information, and, in some cases, different findings from that of the academy. Why turn to the academy for knowledge about a particular subject if we can find what we are looking for with the click of a mouse and the information will confirm what I know to be true? How we validate evidence changed as well. What used to be labeled "old wives' tales" became believable because they were passed with lightning speed from user to user. For example, although the vast majority of scientists believe the evidence is clear, consistent, and compelling that vaccines prevent illness, the internet has enabled others to hold contrary views (Ward et al., 2016).

If one can find alternative facts that confirm one's biases and we have an administration in Washington, DC, that supports the use of such facts, then we have an academy in crisis. The triad of academic privilege largely has eroded. First, the hegemony of knowledge production and definition is no longer in the sole province of the academy. If the arbiters of knowledge are not the professoriate who work within the academy, then any special status that the university once may have had is gone.

Second, the legitimacy of that organization as something special, apart from society because it has to be to do its work, is no longer a viable claim. A bookstore once had a niche where individuals knew they had no other place to go if they wanted to buy a book. A library was a public good paid for through taxes because it was the only building where one could go to read and take books home for free. The assumption behind the bookstore was that they would make a profit because they had a viable product that others did not sell. We did not go to a pizza parlor or a sporting goods store to buy a book. The assumption behind the public library was that we had a shared belief that reading was good, not just for the individual, but for the community. We all know what happened. Amazon made bookstores quaint and an artifact of the past. The internet made reading available in real-time, anywhere; all an individual needed to do was own a phone or tablet. The funding for libraries eroded as information became even more readily available and tax dollars decreased.

I know, of course, that the sort of reading one does when we surf the internet or read our friends' Instagram posting differs from that of the library. Some of us miss thumbing through a particular section of a bookstore with "real" books, rather than just clicking on the one we want to buy. But the raison d'être of bookstores and libraries certainly has come under attack from advances in software and technology, so why would we not think that the legitimacy of the university is also under attack?

Third, autonomy as a privilege works when the citizenry believes that, to do one's work, one needs to be autonomous. The steady drumbeat of intellectual bias, however, has eroded the idea that universities should be autonomous. They are arms of the state, and, to some, they should reflect what the state wants them to convey. Academic freedom has become irrelevant.

All these ideas are interrelated, of course, and the genesis for the attacks has come from similar forces that largely have to do with globalization and neoliberalism. If the university were still the arbiter of knowledge, then the legitimacy of the academy would not be under attack and a stronger case might be made for autonomy. If a country had a robust notion of the public good, then the traditional idea of university autonomy would be protected; furthermore, we would presumably have more say in how knowledge gets defined than we do today. If society agreed that crowdsourcing is not legitimate for the construction of knowledge, then the autonomy of the university would have remained important and its hegemonic status would be protected. We also know that organizations are always embedded in social and temporal contexts. The pandemic has framed certain issues, as has the murder of George Floyd in the United States. Racism, for example, always has undergirded academic institutions, but the knowledge of racism and the conundrum of action have accelerated.

We cannot, however, make wishes about what I am suggesting are now social facts. I do not see us returning to a day where what I have called the triad of university privilege was sacrosanct. What, then, becomes of the modern university? And, for my purposes here, how do we resituate universities, in however form they are defined, to fight fascism as a system? I can understand why the university voice has been muted in fighting fascism, but an underlying purpose of academic life must be to speak truth to power.

Disenabling the Academic Ability to Speak Truth to Power

A great deal could be written about how individuals choose their line of work today. At one point, choice was of little import. One's father was a carpenter, and the son became a carpenter; the daughter either married or became a schoolteacher. The wealthy made choices; the daughters still married, but the sons might choose professional careers in law, politics, religion, and the like. Until the late nineteenth century, we did not have a very rigorous career path for choosing to become a professor. Frequently, whether in India or Europe, class and religion played a role in who taught at a university. Eventually, however, students became graduate students and had to learn disciplinary knowledge in order to become a professor.

Even today, there are not many high school students in Hong Kong, Los Angeles, or New Delhi who aspire to the academic life. In today's neoliberal environment, students say they want employment largely based on what they perceive to be job availability and salary (even if their assumptions are mistaken). Traditional trajectories of students who aspire to an academic career occur because they enjoyed a particular subject in college and/or enjoy teaching. They enter graduate school, hopefully nail down an area of inquiry, and as they enter their final year of graduate study, they learn that the job market is very competitive. Depending on a variety of factors, including family obligations, students then look for employment and more likely than not do not find a tenure-track position.

If they are part-time faculty in an urban area, they may enter in a unique profession of becoming a "freeway flyer" whereby, to make ends meet, they teach on multiple campuses up and down the freeway. There is very little specific data about what happens to freeway flyers, but they do not have much luck turning part-time teaching into tenure-track positions. They generally fade out of academe and into more typical forms of employment for which they have not been formally trained.

Those who are lucky enough to get a position on the tenure track start teaching and trying to figure out what they need to do to get tenure.

The criteria for tenure and promotion are generally unclear, and contra-dictory advice will be given by one's colleagues. When a candidate comes up for tenure, they are likely to receive it. The averages mask, however, the number of individuals who voluntarily leave the academy prior to a vote for tenure. Nevertheless, it always has been the case (and is even more so in the current environment) that the individuals who receive tenure and promotion are a small percentage of those who initially thought they might like to become a professor. Ultimately, a microscopic number of individuals end up in academe as a profession, when compared to other jobs and careers. This small number has shrunk even more with the eco-nomic chaos that the pandemic caused, which essentially has frozen hiring.

One ought not to be surprised, then, that those who populate academe today have only a dim historical understanding of the academy and its role in modern society. They are experts in their field of study and they may have a better idea about today's students than their older colleagues, but they also are not aware of the "new normal." To them, what exists today is what they know. I raise this because, just as with other forms of identity, how one constructs who one is changes, not only because the individual changes, but also because the environment and context of one's life have changed. Today, being gay in Los Angeles means something entirely different from what it meant in 1975 when I was a college stu-dent. Although India only recently dropped the ban on homosexuality, it is a very different climate from when my gay Indian colleagues went to college. Homosexuality has been legal in Hong Kong since 1991, and its first gay pride parade was 2008. Although gay life may not be as open as it is in Los Angeles, there is certainly a difference now than what it was like for those who came of age in the 1970s. My simple point here is that we too often tend to create static definitions of identity when they are always in flux, always socially re-created. To be sure, groups such as African Americans faced historic discrimination a century ago and still face it today. But even racism shifts in frame and tone over time.

The same is true with an academic identity. The profession, such as it was in the nineteenth century, was a loose affiliation of individuals based around intellectual disciplines. One was more likely to say, "I am a teacher" than "I am a professor," and being a professor largely implied being a teacher. In the twentieth century, however, the formalization of the profession focused on three large ideas, or questions: First, how does one educate students? Second, how does one advance knowledge through research and teaching? And third, what are the limits of one's research and teaching? Obviously, the three questions have offshoots that have taken precedence at one time or one another. Who one teaches and their demographic makeup are of central import today, which was not the case a century ago. The advancement of knowledge was once done primarily through conferences that were smaller in size and pushed members to think about new ideas in a way that today's megaconferences are unable to do. At the turn of the twentieth century, academic freedom was not an enshrined idea of the academy in the same manner that it became a half-century later.

One's academic identity varies, just as we cannot essentialize what being African American or transgender or having a disability means. However, as I noted in Chapter 4, the idea of academic freedom was firmly implanted as a component of academic life shortly after the AAUP was created in the early twentieth century by John Dewey and his colleagues. One might have mistakenly thought that academic freedom is purely a concern of academics, but just as how one defines knowledge is of crucial import for all of us, so too is the concept of academic freedom. Curiously, in my discussion of how one chooses to study for academic life and how they are trained, I did not mention academic freedom.

Part of why an individual chooses to become a doctor or psychologist may be that they wish to save lives or cure individuals of an illness. Most people who choose disciplines to study do not have such lofty goals. However, people learn the ethos of their discipline through their study about what they can and cannot do, and what they might aspire to achieve, whether it is to write a great novel or cure an incurable disease. All graduate students also probably learn something about plagiarism, and they may learn technical aspects of how to make a presentation or curate one's CV. What they do not learn very much about is academic freedom, unless it occurs by osmosis. There may be informal and sporadic discussions about academic freedom, but most students learn very little about the roots of academic freedom or its purpose for the academy. Indeed, for those who are studying in the hard sciences or professions such as engineering or accounting, academic freedom may seem superfluous. Their teaching or research is not likely to be controversial. Such a feeling has only intensified as all disciplines have increased what needs to be known in the content area, so there is less time for activities that take them off-focus.

Academic freedom is at the core of one's identity as a professor. The idea gives us the ability to study at the frontiers of knowledge; the right to bring forward controversial ideas; the obligation to protect one's colleagues from nefarious interference; the ability to speak up when we see events that we believe threaten knowledge production and the greater common good. Because prospective academics, whether in Los Angeles, Hong Kong, or New Delhi, have vaguely understood the idea, one has "on the job" training once one becomes a faculty member.

Today, we are particularly at risk. In a neoliberal gig economy, there are more part-time professors than tenure line faculty than at any other time in the modern era. Salary compression makes academics more concerned about simply putting bread on the table for their family, especially after the pandemic. The ability to think through what the parameters of academic freedom might be is even less possible than when I entered academic life as an assistant professor in 1986. Because there are fewer tenure line faculty, they are stretched in a way that has not happened before. Professional obligations have increased, while the available professorate to meet those obligations has decreased. The need for largely free reviews of manuscripts and conference proceedings, for example, means there are more demands on us. There are more journals and more conferences and fewer reviewers. Similarly, committee work continues, even with fewer of us to do the work. I mentioned that the criteria for tenure and promotion also have increased; hence, junior professors need to work harder to get what senior colleagues once attained with less effort. Globalization also has led to the ubiquitous presence of technology in every waking hour. There is really not a time when one "turns off." Indeed, academe, perhaps more than other professions, has no sense of work as a nine-to-five job. Because many of us tend to write from home, we are always available via whatever social platform we use, and there is no down time. When we are awake, we are available.

Layer onto these pressures and obligations the larger cultural social context in which we currently live. Academics are largely not prepared for the rough-and-tumble interaction that one finds on Twitter, Instagram, or Facebook. Sure, a handful of academics are able to parry attacks and engage in the back-and-forth that occurs with lightning speed on social media, but most of us are not. We do not know how to participate, and, for those who chose academic life in large part because they want a more contemplative life, such conversations and attacks seem anathema to why they chose to become an academic.

Conversely, because many individuals feel comfortable with using alternative facts, or reaching a decision about an issue via crowdsourcing the idea, the academic is relied on less for advice and input. The result is that academic freedom is less used by today's academics, and the concept seems of less consequence to the larger public than in the past. Academic freedom was never really understood, but larger bodies, such as the Supreme Court, and legislatures continually affirmed its import, not for those who work in the university, but for the larger society. Now we see the opposite, and we are at a crossroads. The academic can further retreat into the monastery with fewer colleagues and assume that the esoteric work they do is of utility in some fashion—or we can figure out what academic freedom is in the twenty-first century and affirm the critical work we have to do in our way, on our own turf, as well as in newer forums such as Twitter, to ensure that democracy remains at the core of civic life. If academic identity is not, in some fashion, about the search for truth and the ability for us to investigate what truth is and how we go about enabling knowledge to inform the scaffolding of democracy, then are we not complicit in the rise of fascism and the recession in which democracy now finds itself?

In order to answer this question, I put forward four steps to action pertaining to the student and four steps for the academic that summarize the ideas I have presented in the previous chapters. In particular, the steps flesh out what I suggested in the previous chapter were axes to consider that might enable our institutions to be more vocal in the defense of democracy. I then turn to a larger discussion of how to promulgate change on an organizational and system level.

A Framework for Action

For the Student

Recognize that Jobs and Work in the Post-COVID-19 New Economy Matter

I want us to be mindful that, regardless of the points I am making, the vast majority of students and their families who attend a postsecondary institution anywhere look to their education as advancing their career prospects. Most students will not assume a one-to-one relationship between study and a job, but they expect that their time and money will be a good investment. Otherwise, why not spend that time and money in a better way? Those who wax eloquently about the need for educated citizens (e.g., Giroux, 1983, 2008, 2015) write with an abstract eloquence that, at times, seems divorced from present-day realities. When I was in college, my friends and I did not worry about getting a job on graduation because there were jobs. Indeed, throughout college, I worked at a homeless shelter in Boston, the Pine Street Inn, and, in my senior year, the head of the organization offered me a job and encouraged me to get a master's degree in social work that they would partially cover. I ended up going to the Peace Corps, but when I returned home to get my master's degree at Harvard, I did part-time work at a halfway house for troubled youth. Again, as I completed the degree, the psychologist who ran the home offered me a full-time job. This work history had less to do with any particular skills I may have had and more to do with an economy where jobs for college graduates were plentiful.

As I finished my PhD at Stanford, I started to apply for jobs. There was very little strategic direction at Stanford at the time about what grad students needed to do to make themselves marketable. Before I really even began the process, I got an offer from a research outfit in Boulder, Colorado, which recruited me based on my advisor's recommendation. Two years later, as I looked for tenure-track positions, I found myself in a bidding war for my services at two universities right off the bat. Again, I am not offering this vignette as evidence of a sterling career; the point is that those of us who wanted tenure-track positions found them, mostly in locations where we wanted them.

I also graduated with virtually no debt. Although my family was not flush with cash, my father was able to afford the tuition at a private university. I did work-study to earn extra cash and worked in the summers at a variety of jobs. A summer job was easy to find, whether I was in Boston or home in Westchester County, New York. I paid for my master's degree, and Stanford paid for the PhD. I had a research assistantship. The result is that, when I started to work first in Boulder, and subsequently at Penn State, I had payments of about $30 a month to pay back on my loans. With the jobs I took on the Fort Berthold Indian reservation after my master's degree, and then with the research position in Boulder, and after that at Penn State, I concentrated on the salary they offered me and the teaching load at Penn State. I didn't think about health care, much less retirement. Each job, however, had full health benefits and a generous retirement system. I didn't really know anything about retirement until I hit my 60s and started to think about how much I had saved.

I offer these memories to demonstrate how much the world has shifted; I think those of us who write from a particularly privileged position neglect the realities of what younger individuals face today. Indeed, to say that I am "privileged" is an odd word choice when I am referring to a full-time job that provides health and retirement benefits. Health care should not be a privilege; it is a right. Unfortunately, that is the very situation in which we find ourselves today, whether we are in Hong Kong, New Delhi, or Los Angeles. Although the protests in Hong Kong had a great deal to do with Hong Kongers' identification as Hong Kongers and what that meant for the city, rolled into the protest was the realization that locals could not find jobs that enabled them to buy a home and raise a family. New Delhi's higher education institutions have a mismatch between the courses students take and the jobs that exist, which has led to significant unemployment among college-educated students. Students in Los Angeles, more than in Hong Kong or Delhi, face a mountain of debt if they go to a four-year private university or a UC. If they go to the CSU four-year state school, they are likely to take six or more years to graduate, and if they go to the community college, the outcome is particularly questionable. Indeed, given the current economy, it should be no surprise to know that 41.6 percent of CSU students face food insecurity and 10.9 percent report being homeless during a 12-month period before and/or during attendance at a Cal State university (Crutchfield & Maguire, 2018).

We run the risk, then, of irrelevance when I write about the very real rise of fascism and offer a level-headed critique of globalization and neoliberalism, yet ignore the material conditions in which individuals live, whether they be in New Delhi, Hong Kong, or Los Angeles. I do not, however, believe that the solution to the problems I have outlined reside in simply making our postsecondary institutions job training centers, as if such a proposal would solve the financial circumstances that exist. Even if postsecondary institutions were able to transform themselves into cohesive units that trained students for specific positions and jobs, there are not enough jobs that exist for the students who graduate in New Delhi. In Hong Kong and Los Angeles, the graduates will need to move, which is possible, but the jobs in a neoliberal economy will not provide the sort of economic supports that I once had, and they will not be what students say they want when they go to university—a job that will enable them to raise a family, buy a home, have adequate health care, and save for old age.

Nevertheless, I do not think we can simply say that the economy is the culprit and that higher education has no role in enabling students to attain some sort of employment once they graduate. To be sure, I am not writing a training manual for universities about employment, but I am conscious of the conditions that exist for those whom we educate. When

I travel around to campuses in these three cities, I am repeatedly struck by how much of a disconnect exists between what we teach students and what they need to know when they start in their jobs. Such an observation is only that much clearer given the difficulty of finding employment because of the pandemic.

One Size Does Not Fit All: Honor Difference

Students need different learning activities to be employable and to be able to be engaged in the democratic sphere. Unfortunately, in today's environment, we have students who arrive at college—and frequently later graduate—without adequate literacy and numeracy skills. I appreciate that what we mean by literacy and numeracy is endlessly debated. This is not the place to enter into a soliloquy about my own definition of critical thinking. Suffice it to say, however, that we have students who cannot read simple forms, cannot write in a way that will enable them to get a job, and cannot do math at a level that enables them to understand how much money they are earning, how much taxes they will need to pay, and how much income they need to enjoy a comfortable existence.

We also know that different students arrive at college with different capabilities. I am not suggesting that there are inherent or innate differences among students, but rather that those who are poor have had fewer opportunities to learn in a manner that enables them to flourish in college. Again, I could discuss ad nauseum here the point that high schools need to do a better job of educating college-bound students—they do. The reality exists that our postsecondary institutions have to deal with the students who arrive on their doorstep. We solve nothing by spending time focused on the sorts of students we would like to have, rather than those we do have.

Students identities are also all too often submerged or marginalized. Black students on college campuses not only have different lives than their white counterparts on college campuses—they also have more difficult times. Recall the earlier points about microaggressions where I explained how individuals will think they are being complementary when they state, "Your writing is great. I never would have expected that of you." The consequences, however, are all too isolating and negative.

Similarly, gay students who are afraid to come out, a transgender student who has a binary option when using a bathroom, a student with a disability who can't make it into the third-floor classroom, and a first-generation student who cannot afford the lifestyle of their roommate all create unique challenges. An inclusive community based on difference builds support and understanding for everyone rather than assuming all students are more alike than different.

Training and Engagement Matter

Most students do not know very much about the world of work or how to be actively engaged in civic life. Indeed, in some respects, their lack of knowledge is growing, rather than shrinking. I mentioned that I had jobs throughout high school and college. I also was involved in a variety of civic actions—from protesting against the Vietnam War to working on behalf of farmworkers in high school and at Pine Street in college. Today's college graduates are more likely to be underemployed (Burning Glass Technologies and Strada Institute for the Future of Work, 2018), and they are less aware of the work and training needed for the job they say they want, much less where to look for employment (Abel & Deitz, 2013). They also frequently do not see civic involvement as something that pertains to them. Such points are even more true given the impact of the pandemic on the economy. In some respects, one ought not to be surprised. Children have long said in the United States, for example, that they want to be firefighters or nurses or president of the United States. They may associate the job with a particular feeling—"It's exciting!"; "I want to make a lot of money"—but they do not know what actually goes into firefighting, nursing, or holding office. They know even less about the panoply of jobs that exist.

A few institutions, such as Northeastern University in Boston, have internships embedded into their curriculum. Other institutions may have a community involvement program that some students take, and the more entrepreneurial universities may have a part of the institution that helps students pitch ideas for venture capital and learn what start-ups are all about in technology fields, and so forth. However, the vast majority of students graduate without understanding the sorts of jobs that exist in the field they say they want to do, and have even less of a sense about how to get engaged in democratic reforms of their communities.

Students also do not fully understand what may be required of them when they start work. Middle- and upper-class families may be more focused on their children's activities in the summer, but those who need advice the most, the lower-income students, often get the least amount of help. Frequently, internships happen at the eleventh hour before or during senior year. Something is better than nothing, but understanding the world of work should be a mixture of fun and work, trial and error. I regularly say to my graduate students that their first two years of a PhD program should involve studying different ideas to see if these ideas interest them. There's no harm, if framed correctly, to think that a particular idea is intellectually exciting, yet later find out that it's not what you thought it would be or that something else is more interesting. The problem occurs when the student has committed to the idea for their dissertation and finds out they don't like it. The same is true with employment. There's nothing wrong with someone thinking they want to be a nurse; but if they try it at the outset of their studies and discover they don't like dealing with blood or sick people, then the person can choose something else. It's harder when they don't really know, go down the road to become a nurse, and waste years to find out it's simply not their passion.

The result is that training and internships should be built into the start of everyone's academic career from day one and should comprise a mixture of vocationally engaged tasks and those that have to do with community involvement. It needs to be sustained, substantial, and meaningful. It should be something that all students get to experience, not simply the motivated few or those in a particular kind of program. The challenge is that what I am suggesting, as with my earlier point, calls for a significant reformation of the curriculum and outreach to multiple communities. It needs individuals to have a laser-like focus on what students say they want to do and what sorts of jobs actually exist, connecting students with people in the community able to involve them in democratic reform, and then monitoring and assessing how the engagement is going and what outcomes are likely. All of this is possible, but it calls for a different sort of academic environment than the one we have today.

Know What You Are Getting Into

My fourth point underscores my argument throughout this book. Students need a better awareness of the conditions that frame the world they are entering and in which they are participating, whether we are speaking of New Delhi, Hong Kong, or Los Angeles. On a practical level, students need to be much more sophisticated that I was with regard to a comfortable life in the twenty-first century. They need to be strategic about what sorts of loans they should tap into and what they should avoid. They need to be able to balance a budget, plan for the future, and understand the consequences of taking out a mortgage or buying a car on a loan from the car dealer rather than a bank. Students, especially those who are in their 20s and assume they will never get ill or grow old, need to have a better understanding of health care and saving for the future. These sorts of conversations need to happen regularly, and they should make up part of the curricular and cocurricular program of a school. I have dealt with too many students and assistant professors who cannot tell me the sort of health plan they have, what they are entitled to use for free, or what contributing part of one's paycheck means in terms of the institution's participation in one's retirement.

On a more significant level, students need to understand the world they are going to inhabit. The simple truism that a fish is the last to discover water simply points out that we all assume the pond in which we swim is the way it always has been and will be. Individuals who came of age in the Trump era think his actions are what all presidents say and do. Taking a job without health benefits is predicated, in part, on the assumption that people did not have health benefits in the past or that having to work three jobs to make ends meet is just the way it is. A university's task is to point out that we get to create our world, rather than simply inhabit it. Before one acts, one needs to understand the conditions that make the world, and academic organizations are those social units best able to help students comprehend the world that exists.

I have written at length about the various permutations of identity and intersectionality in this text. I do not now want to reduce one's identity to a singular component such as race or sexual orientation, but if we learned anything about the Black Lives Matter protests, it is that White people, however well intentioned, largely did not know how to respond. The point is less that one needs to read about "the Other"—although that it is certainly the case, especially in organizations dedicated to reading. More important, we have to create the intellectual spaces that enable people to reflect on their own lives and their position in the world. We cannot change the world if we do not understand it.

Each point that I have suggested here could be glibly accepted, or I could be told, "We're already doing that." The vast majority of institutions are not. We make political curricular compromises or we give up in frustration when we cannot come to agreement about a particular term or idea. Sustained and comprehensive engagement with the community to enable students to have meaningful interactions takes a great deal of time. Financial literacy is, more often than not, trial and error—and those errors can be quite painful. Based on what I am suggesting here, what we first need to do is to acknowledge that a problem exists to which universities need to respond, and, at the same, be more responsive to the felt needs of students.

For the Academic

We also need to think about the needs of the academic. It does no good to say that faculty should be more responsive if we are not clear about what responsiveness means. These sorts of recommendations involve the daily and long-term work of academics, which inevitably pertains to graduate education.

Understand the Four Cultures of the Faculty

The vast majority of faculty, whether in Delhi, Hong Kong, or Los Angeles, think of themselves in terms of their discipline. The statement, "I'm an engineer" or "I'm a professor of social work" simply reflects their disciplinary orientation and underscores what they learned in graduate school. They probably have a dim understanding of their nationality and its impact on faculty culture. They know, for example, that academic work is different in Delhi or LA. They also may realize that the culture of one institution differs from another—that not only is the University of Southern California different from the University of Hong Kong, but HKU also differs from its cross-town counterpart, the Hong Kong University of Science and Technology (HKUST), as much as USC differs from UCLA. Individuals will also know that they are in professions, that being a faculty member differs from someone who works in a business or is self-employed.

A professor's work involves all four cultures (Clark, 1963; Tierney, 1988; Tierney & Lanford, 2018), but they rarely understand the four cultures or how they relate to one another. The largest impact on an academic is the discipline in which they are trained. Their job generally lands them in a disciplinary department, and the reward structure is geared toward the discipline. Tenure, promotion, academic awards, and salaries are all focused on how well the academic has done in their discipline. One's nationality gets shrugged off as irrelevant, and there is never much discussion about what academic life means as a profession. Institutions matter in the sense that all these cultures get played out on an institutional level, but how we define institutional life frequently falls back on disciplinary norms and safeguards. Those who are most exalted are the ones who have shone in their discipline, and it is often a badge of honor to show the disdain and disregard one holds for academic service.

What we need to recognize is that academic life in the twenty-first century requires a more integrated understanding of what it means to be an academic. When we passively acknowledge that individuals differ based on their nationality, we also assume that what matters to Hong Kong should not concern us. I am suggesting the opposite. Academic life, writ large, pertains to a search for truth, and this search has no geographic or intellectual borders. A threat to an academic in New Delhi also threatens the academic in Los Angeles or Hong Kong. If we can understand the challenges we face across geographic and intellectual borders, we will be enabled to speak more confidently and forcefully about how universities can be linchpins of social reform, rather than isolated units unconcerned with what happens outside their intellectual frame. How an institution defines academic freedom should matter not simply to those in the institution but also to anyone who think of themselves as members of the professorate. Professional norms have to go beyond simply "how I define my work in a school or department" and force us to think of academic work in a broader framework.

The challenge, of course, is that both graduate work and work in one's discipline are geared in exactly the opposite direction. We tend to encourage narrow specialists because the accumulation of knowledge in an area of inquiry is so great. Only a very few might transcend their intellectual borders, and we tend to think of them as intellectual dilettantes. I am suggesting, however, that we can no longer survive isolated in intellectual silos. We have to encourage cross-border dialogues that help us understand the challenges that exist, and, in doing so, how we might participate in their resolution.

Teach to the Student

The norm for teachers is that they teach the way they learned or model those teachers they liked. Teacher training is frowned on, and very little has proven to be of much utility with regard to learning outcomes. The result is that students, like their professors, generally focus on what they need to know for the final exam. They also want knowledge that will further their potential for gainful employment. Even online learning has not changed the focus and outcomes of classrooms however pervasive it has become due to the pandemic. To be sure, some online classes are even more passive than a classroom, and students are more focused on very specific objectives and goals. Massive open online classes (MOOCs) also cannot provide the close interaction that we know frames good pedagogy. But it is also true that some online classes provide for learning experiences that may differ from the typical classroom but also have the potential for positive learning experiences.

What students are missing, however, is a synthetic experience about how they should see the world. I am not suggesting that students get indoctrinated with one viewpoint or that they largely learn social science facts in science classes. However, a university is a different sort of place when we focus on the education and the well-being of the student, rather than the learning outcomes of a classroom. Far too often we think of the sorts of experiences I am suggesting here as what takes place outside the classroom or under the aegis of student affairs. That's a mistake.

We need to encourage faculty to see their classes as filled with students with specific issues, problems and dilemmas unique to the twenty-first century. Not only Black students need to internalize why Black Lives Matter. An institution is not meeting its mandate unless all students grapple with issues of identity, equity, and democracy.

Further, to be sure, some students always have worried about loneliness, but the technological revolution that accompanied globalization has created isolation in entirely new ways. Couple that with a neoliberal work environment that I have discussed, and we have large numbers of students who are worried about their place in the world. They need connections, and faculty need to be observant, not simply for a challenge that a student may face, but more important, how they can help students think about their future.

We often talk about lifelong learning, but the norm for the faculty member is to focus on learning objectives of the classroom. What is happening around us, and on a daily basis, is not something that faculty feel trained to discuss or see as part of their job description. I want to be clear here, as well. Most faculty are not psychotherapists and do not have the training to deduce illnesses. Some students exhibit challenges that are beyond my capability to treat. I need to know whom the student should see and what the array of services are on a university campus. I also know that many students need thoughtful discussions on an ongoing basis, and we should fight the temptation to ignore problems. Rather than teach subject matter, we have to acknowledge that we teach students.

Acknowledge the Corrupting Influence of Nonengagement

I do not wish to put forward the idea that an ethos of engagement suggests that corruption will not occur. Democracy is not a utopia in which all individuals are sanctified and never err. However, the lack of a democratic voice and the politics of disengagement encourage corruption. Why should one care about a system if one is disinvested in it and assumes that their voice is irrelevant? India, for example, has become a poster child for corruption in higher education. The country received worldwide attention from a cheating scandal involving thousands of individuals who took medical examinations on behalf of students (Sharma, 2015). Answers for entrance tests to professional courses continue to be regularly leaked. Private and public colleges and universities systematically pay off individuals so that they will not have any problems with accreditation, and the individuals are able to augment their government salaries. Across the world, the "Varsity Blues" scandal exposed the lengths rich parents will go to enable their progeny to be admitted to an elite university. Los Angeles was the epicenter of the scandal (Jaschik, 2019; Medina et al., 2019).

Hong Kong is experiencing its own form of corruption of nonengagement with the new security law that has been implemented. As noted, two professors went to prison because they spoke out for democracy. One of them retired, and the other one returned to campus to discover that the governing body of Hong Kong University had fired him. For all intents and purposes, academic freedom in Hong Kong died with passage of this new law.

The problems speak to what I think of as a culture of corruption. They also are emblematic of larger issues I have been discussing throughout this work. To be sure, corruption is not anything new, but we need to continually ask ourselves why people are doing wrong today. Our answers may be different based on today's climate, rather than yesterday's. I mentioned earlier how the idea of a meritocracy once worked to eliminate prejudice. Jews were once excluded from some postsecondary institutions in the United States because administrators thought they were admitting too many Jews. In part to combat anti-Semitism, blind standardized tests were implemented. The assumption was that only students who merited admission, regardless of religious background, would be admitted. Over time, of course, the underpinnings of meritocracy showed biases toward those who could afford to school their children in how to study for an exam. A next step, although a bastardization of the idea of meritocracy, was to have someone take the tests in your absence, such as we have seen in India and the United States.

Times change, and the culture of corruption that I am speaking about today can be largely linked to the forces of globalization and neoliberalism that has resulted in the tenets of fascism at work. Competition, like a meritocracy, does not automatically lead to corruption. However, in the hypercompetitive environment that has come about because of globalization framed by neoliberalism, we have seen corruption rise at unprecedented levels. When we couple corruption on an academic level with the corruption of leaders in government, whether it be the Trump administration or the Chinese influence in Hong Kong, I am hard-pressed to think why there is not even more corruption. The problem, of course, is not simply that one or two individuals make mistakes and are caught for fraud or malfeasance, but the danger that the entire system can be viewed as a dysfunctional culture.

We are caught in a double-bind. On the one hand, if we believe in democracy, then we are less likely to enable corruption on a systemic level. When individuals make mistakes, we have remedies available that we continually tinker with in order to improve the system. Nevertheless, the underlying assumption of democratic engagement is that it is for all our benefit if we are involved in the system, rather than try to work around it or simply ignore it. We have looked to universities to help us understand the system and figure out ways to improve it. In part, academic freedom has enabled us to think through these issues that presumably bring us greater clarity and a better system.

On the other hand, if those of us involved in universities also have no faith in the system, then we either become disengaged, or we do not risk involvement for fear of sanction or wasted time—which is indeed a precious resource. Indeed, the temptation becomes to participate in corruption rather than to reject it, or to suggest ways to stamp it out. The disengagement of academics, then, leads to even greater levels of corruption on a systemic level because we have lost one pillar of a democracy. Precisely at a time when we need greater involvement by postsecondary institutions, we are witnessing their preference to stand back and let society continue on the path it is on.

The irony is also twofold in that we are ostensibly in an environment that obsesses about assessment, while at the same time we are not concerned about the underlying ideas of assessment that facilitate corruption. Schools are frequently judged by how well their students do on standardized assessments, irrespective of the socioeconomic or personal challenges that many students face outside the classroom. Therefore, the idea that education should be a liberatory process based on communal goals about citizenship has been replaced by a culture of assessment (Tierney & Rhoads, 1995) that underscores who is in control and who is relatively powerless. Outside evaluations, companies that create curricula, and other authorities have the control. Students, teachers, and administrators are relatively powerless and, in many cases, desperate to perform well on an assessment that may seem impossible to succeed in, given local challenges. Hence, the weight of responsibility for learning falls on them. If they do not succeed, then they must not have had the "grit" necessary for success.

As a result, a focus on what critical theorists (Tierney, 1991) have termed dispositional knowledge, such as the values and ethics that guide community life, becomes immaterial. One irony is that educational institutions have historically been viewed as cultural sites where knowledge gets defined. However, the prevailing assumption is that knowledge is static and preordained, rather than evolving. What it means to be a member of a democracy or to work for social justice is of little use because it cannot be evaluated and assessed for jobs in the marketplace. The notion that education could be a liberatory process based on communal goals about citizenship is not even entertained.

Thus, my concern is that counternarratives pointing out how educational institutions are cultural sites where knowledge not merely gets transmitted, but also defined, are being lost. As Crawford and McLaren (2003) noted, the culture of schooling is "fundamentally a struggle over meanings and about meanings. Furthermore, it is a struggle over events, representations, and interpretations" (p. 136). Relatedly, as Braverman (1974) commented, it is equally important to think about how academic labor is being reorganized, which in turn, changes the nature of social relations. The neoliberal agenda has reorganized education and its constituents in order to meet globalization's needs in the marketplace. The reproduction of already existing power relationships circumscribes action such that at times an alternative politics seems not simply difficult to achieve, but impossible to conceive.

However, rather than assume that the nature of social relations is preordained such that issues such as assessment are givens and corruption is the only viable alternative, I am suggesting that a transformation is possible. In such a transformation, the role of the academic moves away from that of a transmitter of knowledge and toward one that enables—foments—ideological dialogues and resistances. As Giroux (1988) has noted, "ideology becomes useful for understanding not only how schools sustain and produce meanings, but also how individuals and groups produce, negotiate, modify, or resist them" (p. 5). The transformative academic is someone who rejects overriding assumptions and struggles to isolate and interrogate beliefs and interpretations that globalization's proponents have made to appear as self-evident and necessary.

The responsibility of the academic, then, is to help focus dialogue on the reconstruction of the social imagination in order to advance a cultural politics of democracy that honors diverse voices rather than subscribes to notions of responsibilization. Such a stance stands in contradistinction to what I have described as neoliberalism, where the state's power becomes vast and invisible and the individual's voice mute and homogenous. I am concerned with how those of us in educational organizations might be more engaged in promoting democracy and empowering those who are most at risk of being responsibilized for failures that are not of their own making. A concentration on the cultures, ideologies. and discourses that enable them provides the potential, not to promote the submission or adherence to norms but instead to disrupts them, and in doing so, advances democratic organizations.

Trust develops through members' shared experiences in the culture. These shared experiences depend on how individuals learn about the culture. In turn, how members become socialized to the organization's mores is crucial for how they interpret and act in the organization. When we teach graduate students that the only meaningful knowledge is learning information from our discipline, then why should we be surprised that they assume faculty positions in which they focus only on their discipline? When we teach undergraduates that jobs are all important, then doesn't it stand to reason that they are more concerned about jobs? As opposed to assuming that an organization is a monolith whereby everyone interprets the organization in the same unchanging manner, I am suggesting that the organization is in flux and capable of significant reorientations, and that such changes are critical for the welfare, not simply of the organization, but for democracy overall.

One ought not to be surprised that responses to corruption are largely met in two ways. When allegations of corruption have been alleged, officials react as if the scenario were an anomaly rather than a cultural norm. When they are singular, then the aberration may be an individual lapse and the individual may be punished. However, I am suggesting that the culture itself has been corrupted.

When corruption occurs that is seen as a singular instance, the tendency is to provide a structural response. Structural responses relate to the culture's formal processes. Fix the "Varsity Blues" scandal by hiring another administrator, for example. Such a solution is entirely understandable. Rather than assume that the entire culture is corrupt, one looks to create rules and regulations that will not allow an individual to act in a manner that is abhorrent. In some respects, the reaction is in keeping with how democratic societies function in general. Stoplights, speed limits, car registrations, licenses, and the like regulate how drivers ought to drive and operate their automobile. When someone's car is not licensed or a driver blatantly goes through a stoplight, there are consequences. The system works reasonably well because the participants have a social network that enables trust to function.

Today, however, the system is broken. We are not simply in need of structural reform, but a rethinking of what we want of higher education in order to help sustain democracy in the twenty-first century. How might those of us in universities proceed?

Recognize the Responsibility of the Public Intellectual

We are not trained as public intellectuals. If anything, we are told to keep our heads down, to read, and to publish in specialized journals. Even those of us who aspire to be involved in issues beyond the academy have a very dim understanding of what it takes or how to do it. It's as if we are trained to be baseball players but also want to do ballet. Sure, some skills transfer, but most do not. If we want to educate students about the larger community, then we need to understand that community. Engagement for all but the most committed academics usually refers to a one-off event in the local community—or being involved with their child's potpourri of activities.

I am suggesting a different stance, given the rise of fascism. The university needs to explore ways that promote, support, and reward faculty engagement. The work of the engaged academic is, more often than not, something that is done in spite of, or on top of, everything else we do. At a time of national and international crisis, however, we need everyone to be involved. How can we call for a deeper engagement with students if the faculty and the administration are not similarly engaged? What message do we send to students in Los Angeles if we express ignorance about what's happening on other campuses in other countries? Just as I am suggesting that a math professor in Los Angeles cannot keep their head down when protests emerge to combat racism in Los Angeles, I am also calling for all of us to be more globally engaged. The circumvention of academic freedom in Hong Kong is a threat to everyone, not only those in Hong Kong.

To be an engaged intellectual, obviously, requires engagement. It's not something I can just say, and make the statement appear as if I am engaged. Former President Obama pointed out that simply tweeting this or that statement or disparaging someone with whom we disagree may make us feel good about ourselves (and self-righteous), but it doesn't change the world (Rueb & Taylor, 2020). If we want to change the world, then we need to find ways for sustained engagement. This is the work of the faculty at a time of rising fascism, whether we are in Delhi, LA, or Hong Kong.

The Democratic Imperative for Colleges and Universities

In 2019, the Brookings Institution put out a monograph entitled *The Democracy Playbook: Preventing and Reversing Democratic Backsliding* (Eisen et al., 2019). The text outlined the democratic recession that is at work in the world and put forward numerous suggestions about what important actors, such as legislatures and journalists, might do to ensure that democracy is safeguarded. In 2020, the American Academy of Arts and Sciences (AAAS) published *Our Common Purpose: Reinventing American Democracy for the 21st Century*. As with the Brookings monograph, AAAS also put forward useful suggestions for the reinvigoration of democracy.

Tellingly, there is no mention in either monograph of what postsecondary institutions or those of us who work in the academy should do to help advance democracy and retard fascism. As with many others (Albright, 2018; Diamond, 2019; Gessen, 2020; Levitsky & Ziblatt, 2018; Snyder, 2017, 2019), the authors believe that democracy is at risk and we must take aggressive steps to speak and act on behalf of the ideas behind democracy. I agree.

What troubles me is that higher education seems to be sitting on the sidelines as we watch democracy lose to fascists. The point is not simply that all of us who care about democracy should be involved in its protection, but that an organization that ostensibly is committed to the search for truth should be central to those efforts. I have pointed out why I believe colleges and universities should be critically engaged and why they are not. I also have suggested that however different Los Angeles, New Delhi, and Hong Kong are from one another, they have viable institutions, facing similar pressures, but also having distinct strengths in order to protect democracy.

I have written this book as a way to provoke discussion about how we might bring out more sustained engagement on our campuses. The norm for those on the left is to exhort their colleagues to reject neoliberalism and the more pernicious ramifications of globalization (e.g., Baru & Mohan, 2018; Giroux, 2005; McLaren, 2005; Thomas & Clarke, 2013). I appreciate exhortations, and I believe that setting an argument in a way that enables us to agree is critical. Nevertheless, more often than not, exhortations without agendas attached to them are like tweets without any links: I know where the authors stand, but what should we do?

An institution that faces declining enrollments because of a pandemic cannot be of much help if it goes out of business. Faculty who need three jobs to survive do not have much time to figure out for themselves what they should do to support democracy; they are having trouble supporting themselves and their families. Students who need jobs to stay out of poverty may agree with the ideals expressed by my more esoteric colleagues, but they do not have the time to do much else than take another internship to make them more marketable. I know full well the critique of these points and agree that each example highlights the pernicious aspects of globalization and neoliberalism. But acknowledging why I need to work three jobs does not suggest that I still do not have to work three jobs so my family will survive.

Accordingly, I put forward nine additional propositions for the university that serve as a framework for action for colleges and universities based on what I have written in this book. Given the broad diversity of institutions across type and nation, I am not proffering recipes that simply can be cooked irrespective of context. I do, however, wish to move ideas for action in a more concrete way than is typical so that critics of the current demise of democracy might rightfully think of what our postsecondary institutions might do to aid in the battle against fascism.

Define Civil Society

A large part of academic life pertains to what I discussed earlier with regard to Pasteur's Quadrant. The definition of civil society—and the relationships that groups and individuals have to one another and to the larger society—is a fundamental prerequisite to enabling democracy to flourish. As times change, we need to remind ourselves of what our obligations are to the nourishment of civil society. Sometimes, neutrality and even-handed analysis and voice can be useful, and academe is arguably the best suited organization to put forward what we mean by civil society in the twenty-first century. At other times, however, it cannot.

I raise this at a first step because unless we are clear about the contours of society itself, we will be unclear about how we might proceed to protect that society. Such a task is also not a manifesto that gets issued, but rather one that gets discussed as a living document. Students need to have a sense of what we mean about learning in a civil society so that their ambitions go beyond simply earning a job and making enough money to survive. Students need a critical consciousness, in addition to specific skills that translate into employment, so that they can to think about their relation to the world in more ways than simply that of jobs.

Some might suggest that setting the terms for a civil society is "old hat" or that it is what academe always has done. However, higher education as an industry, or as a collective, is not part of the conversation about how to define and protect democracy. We only need to look to Hong Kong to see the results of a society that is unclear what the parameters of civil society are, what the obligation of the citizenry is, and how universities might play a role. I want these definitions to be broad-based and inclusive of multiple interpretations of what such a society entails, and I want them to enable us to be proactive when democracy is at risk, as it is now in locations such as the United States and India.

Work on Ensuring Free and Fair Elections

A cornerstone of democracy is not only understanding its parameters but also working to ensure that the country has free and fair elections. As Eisen et al. (2019) stated, "Secure, free, and fair elections are the foundation of democracy, yet ensuring them is a complicated endeavor. Even in well-established democracies, measures must be taken to guard against partisan efforts to manipulate the vote. Conversely, governments should enact policies that promote broad access to the vote, such as automatic or same-day voter registration" (p. 15). To be sure, all citizens have a role to play in the establishment and maintenance of fair elections. However, colleges and universities have a unique role they could play but they largely do not on at least three levels.

First, what we mean by free elections needs to be clarified and communicated to the broad public. I am entirely comfortable with academics writing for other academics and presenting their work at juried conferences. However, if we are concerned about free and fair elections, then we also need to communicate what that means on a broad level to the multiple publics that exist in our communities.

Second, on an international level, we need to work with other universities to establish the contours of free elections, regardless of geography. Sometimes, especially in totalitarian societies, the imprimatur of international standards about a particular topic can be helpful and encouraging to those who wish to advance democracy. We too often work in isolated academic silos defined either by discipline or country, and instead we need to develop ways that put forward an academic understanding of what we mean by free elections and how to go about ensuring that such elections take place, irrespective of country. I appreciate that occasionally there are election monitors who come in to oversee elections; again, what troubles me is that our academic institutions are not more centrally involved in such oversight on a sustained and prolonged basis.

Third, free elections occur in some format, whether by mail or in person, over an extended time horizon or on a single day. Academic minds need to be more aggressive in putting forward what works best to enable participation and, in ensuring that whatever format is chosen, that get to vote. In the United States, we have election monitors and volunteers who participate on election day, which is all well and good. But if we take democracy seriously as a primary focus of academic life, then our universities need to be much more centrally involved in ensuring that citizens are enabled to participate. I am suggesting here that participation in a democracy is not simply a "nice" thing to do, but rather is a central obligation of everyone, especially those of us involved in academic institutions. If we are not active participants, then we can make no claim to saying that we speak truth to power or that we believe that academic institutions are actively involved in the search for truth. If democracy is imperiled, which I believe it is, then we need our academic institutions to step up and be more active in encouraging participation.

Enable Voter Participation and Dismantle Voter Suppression of Students

A commonplace observation is that students are disengaged and do not vote. We also know that numerous campuses in the United States encourage voter participation and occasionally will have "get out the vote" drives. If we are serious about voting, however, we need to be more aggressive in ensuring that all students vote. We should certainly be vocal in our work that points out how voter suppression works, but with our own constituencies, we also need to move more aggressively in ensuring that voting is not simply a "nice" activity, but almost mandatory.

We could, for example, require students to register to vote and then to vote as part of their registration as a student. Although some people may have a knee-jerk response about such a suggestion being in violation of the Constitution, there are a variety of remedies that could be put forward that ensure a more aggressive approach to voting. We could have a reverse checkoff or checkoff opt-out option whereby, in effect, a student has to say they do not want to vote. Voter forms could be part of registration packets at orientation; we could collect them and then do the necessary work to ensure that students are enrolled to vote. I am also aware that voter officials in some college towns can refuse to acknowledge the residency of students who are not from that town, but the university needs to work to clarify the rights of students to vote.

I want to emphasize that I am not saying that a college or university should be involved in supporting a particular candidate in any manner. However, in a book about democracy and higher education, we need to emphasize the importance of voting, not simply as a nice activity but rather as an obligation.

Make Equity a Central Value and Goal

Race, gender, caste, and class frame how people succeed on campus and in the larger society. The false narrative of merit and individualism is that if one works hard enough, then one will succeed. Those who do not succeed, the story goes, did not work hard enough. Every society has individuals from a group that has been historically marginalized who have succeeded. The personal narratives of grit and hard work are certainly compelling. We know of Dalits who have reached the pinnacle of society in India, and Black men and women who are captains of industry. Indeed, a Black man became president of the United States.

However, the structural constraints of society show how those who are able to succeed do so in spite of the society in which they live rather than because of it. A democratic society does not disable some and privilege others. Hong Kong's ability to ignore those who do the worst paying work, and various universities in the United States where racial and ethnic representation remains far below to state and national averages certainly highlight the outcome of neoliberalism and globalization. They also, however, point to an individual and collective inability to make equity a central value for a democracy. A democracy can make no claim to its inherent values when Black voters are disenfranchised from voting or Dalits remain underrepresented at universities. Democracy suggests individual initiative and hard work matter—but only when the playing field is fair.

Work Across the Globe for Democratic Engagement

Strength comes from working across groups rather than staying within one's own institution, or even one's department or school. I previously described the four cultures that the faculty inhabit, and we need to work harder to develop coalitions with colleagues across the globe. We need to be particularly aggressive with regard to institutions and faculty that come under attack. Scholars at Risk is a global network that highlights the dangers some faculty are under largely because of their willingness to speak out on issues that are critical to the state where they reside.[1]

New Delhi is a useful example of faculty who often have been outspoken on their campus, but they rarely get the forms of support that are crucial to their well-being from the broader academic world. The events that have led to the recent protests in Hong Kong have largely been done without foreign "interference"—and we need to reflect on what interference means. Ought faculty everywhere not be more centrally concerned with ensuring the safety of faculty who come under attack? Do we really have nothing to say when universities are closed, fire-bombed, or students come under attack? If Black faculty are targeted in the United States or faculty who are Dalits are targeted in India, do not we all have an obligation to speak out in support of them? I appreciate that we may not always know the nuances of what is happening "on the ground," but I am also aware that far too often we plead ignorance as a rationale for inaction. If we are concerned about advancing democracy, then we need to be more centrally engaged with democratic movements in specific areas, rather than assuming that it is not our business to know.

Encourage Civil Resistance—and Prepare for the Consequences

The question we need to ask in times of reform in our societies is what role academics should play. In Hong Kong, a few professors helped start the initial protests of the Umbrella Movement, and they were peripherally involved in the massive protests of 2019–20. Students were centrally involved at both moments, and, as might be expected, a variety of student voices were heard. Some called for peaceful protest, others worked the various legislative processes that were open to them, and still others called for violence and the closure of roads to the university's campuses.

What has concerned me is that the faculty and senior leadership of our universities are not more able to step forward as a moderating voice—moderating in terms of tamping down violence and putting forward workable solutions that might resolve, or at least ameliorate, the differences that now confront society. We know that nonviolent civil resistance works (Eisen et al., 2019). Nonviolent civil resistance can be an effective means of supporting and fomenting democracy. Engaged intellectuals embrace the role of leader and mediator, rather than shun it or look to others to formulate a response. In difficult times, we need leaders who can communicate and rise above the noise, rather than bureaucrats who worry about putting themselves out on a political limb. In Hong Kong senior administration has done the exact opposite: they have been mute in light of the government's crackdown on free speech and democracy, and at Hong Kong University they have fired a professor for speaking out for democracy.

If academe is an intellectual community that necessarily revolves around interactional meanings of what it means to be a citizen in a democracy, then such discussions are neither periodic nor informal. Conversations about the nature of democracy and our university's role in fomenting voice and enabling democratic engagement at times will mean that we need to think through how to resist those practices that subjugate democracy, and figure out how to ensure that violence does not occur or, when it does, how to end it.

A democrat is someone who works under the belief that all people's voices count, and when we resort to violence, then democracy has failed. There are those who might believe that violence at a particular moment in time is necessary to defend democracy, but even at that point, it is important that an academic voice investigate what has happened and try to examine the conditions that led to violence and how to ensure they do not happen again. Governance of the university involves faculty as equal partners; when we stay in our offices and focus on our academic work or a conference paper, we may well be doing one activity that necessitates time and energy, but we can no longer exclude those activities that enable all of us to do our work and teach our classes. When democracy dies, then those universities in democratic countries are inevitably harmed.

The result is that we need to develop structures that enable voice on the part of students, staff, and administration. If we do not have organizational structures that enable discussion, then either individuals will ignore the institution and/or they will act outside those norms of deliberation and discussion that are essential for democracy. How to speak up and support democracy does not just happen, or, if it does, it needs support structures to ensure that it does not simply fade away. Training and education are essential in helping people understand how to support democracy, and who better to do that than an educational institution?

Of necessity, what will happen is that we will reformulate the role of the academic, and our authority will be lessened. We will lead through example, but also moderate discussion, rather than be the "sage on the stage." When we lessen authority, we open the possibility for disagreement and conflict, but we also lessen the probability that violence will be seen as the only alternative. Rather than paper over differences. we have to learn to deal with them and find ways for those most in conflict to talk with one another. We move toward engaged communities of difference, rather than institutions interested in simply conveying data in a disinterested manner about our surroundings.

Act as We Want Citizens to Act: Model Behaviors and Provide Training

If we are putting forward strategies to ensure democracy occurs in the larger society, then we need our organizations to function democratically as well. Far too often, the opposite actually occurs. A president or vice chancellor ignores the faculty. Tenured faculty show little interest in the challenges that confront nontenured faculty. The custodians and other workers are ignored by everyone and are seen as disposable and unimportant.

We tend to model the behaviors of society, rather than set a model for behavior about how we would like society to act. The result is that what becomes paramount is job security and the perks that go with employment, rather than core issues such as academic freedom. The priority of an institution's goal also reflects back on academic life. As noted in Chapter 4, tenure came about to protect academic freedom. If it is just a sinecure for privileged elites, then there is really very little rationale to keep it. In a gig economy, we have gig academies (Kezar et al., 2019).

Higher Education for Democracy

I am not suggesting that presidents need to be elected or that a board of trustees should simply act like a senate with representatives from every group. Colleges and universities are corporations, and they have multiple models of good governance that can succeed. At the core of good academic governance, however, is a belief in shared voice and opinions. People will disagree, and because they have different perspectives, there will be creative conflict. All of that is to the good. People should disagree. Again, universities should be models for demonstrating how people can disagree with each other and not end up shouting one another down or extolling violence. If we want to have credibility on democracy, then we need to walk our talk. We need to be willing to take risks, to speak out, and to create broad coalitions across groups and campuses on behalf of the democratic imperative. We need to replace our timidity with speaking with courage.

In the campuses I have visited within Hong Kong, Los Angeles, and New Delhi, as well as other locations, those individuals who have acted most courageously in support of democracy are the students at the universities in Hong Kong. They have spoken up on behalf of democracy; they have protested, enacted various forms of civil disobedience, and risked a great deal to speak out on behalf of democratic reforms. I cannot support the violence that has engulfed the campuses, but what particularly troubles me is the muted responses of the faculty and senior administrators on behalf of the students. Creative nonviolent solutions also have not been tried. The vice chancellors, for example, could call for a committee to discuss the problems that exist and host the meeting on a campus. More dramatically, they could go on a hunger strike to protest any violence on their campuses and the harm that has come to students. That we do not even consider such actions as viable speaks to the paucity of ideas and actions that occur in higher education.

We also need a much more robust form of civic education and training. A democracy requires the participation of engaged citizens. All campuses should have some form of civic courses and training that encourages democratic dialogue and debate. We have to get beyond knee-jerk responses that are learned via Twitter. Academic institutions are the perfect organizations to enable learning of this kind in multiple venues and formats.

Build Trust

If we are going to call on society in ways that enable us to speak truth to power, then that society is going to need to trust us in ways that may not have happened for quite some time, and we are going to need to trust one another. What, then, are the conditions for trust that we need to create? Trust occurs over time. It depends on the competence of the trusted. It cannot occur if the trusted has no claim to do what he or she says will be done. Trust also can neither be coerced nor commanded. It depends upon overlapping and ongoing relationships that exist within social and cultural contexts. Such relationships generate a great deal of knowledge that individuals call upon to determine whether someone else is trustworthy. Further, personal characteristics like race, gender, sexual orientation, and the like not only impact how an individual views trust, but also how he or she comes to think about trustworthiness.

Colleges and universities in the twenty-first century are in highly unstable environments that necessitate risk-taking behavior, especially since the start of the pandemic. Academic organizations have tried to institute more managerial and hierarchical mechanisms in response to the turbulent external environment (Rhoades, 1998). Those strategies are precisely the wrong kind of actions; we need to enable people within academe and also outside the organization to participate in democratic forms of engagement that recognize higher education not as the sole voice on democratic, but as a conduit for helping us shape and build a new democratic environment. Students, for example, need to be heard and listened to rather than ignored. Those who argue for greater representation of faculty of color or increased representation in the curriculum of those who have been historically marginalized need to be brought to the table to make their arguments rather than simply having their ideas rejected out of hand.

Academic institutions continue to use decentralized decision-making processes in which power is diffuse and shared. The result is that the participants in colleges and universities will face change, not through a hierarchical chain of command, but by way of a system that necessitates collaboration and cooperation. A level of trust is critical if individuals are going to take risks and participate in shared decision making. A culture of obligation and cooperation is fundamental. Bureaucratic structures that try to outline and constrict individual behaviors are not useful, but trust also does not naturally develop in an organization simply because a leader sees its utility. Instead, trust needs to be nurtured over time. The manner in which trust manifests itself will be highly contingent on the culture of the organization

Trust does not come about without a framework and language for common understanding. As Russell Hardin (2002) notes, "When I trust you in the sense that your interests encapsulate mine in at least the matter with respect to which I trust you, we can, naturally, be said to share interests to some extent" (p. 144). One way to share interests is by common interpretation. Two parties view events similarly when they have a mutual interest in attaining the same goal, and they see the path to that goal in a similar manner. Trust occurs when both parties share interests such that what is good for one party is also good for the other. Such a view is context specific; one party trusts the other on a specific issue, but both parties may not have developed a generalized trust. Thus, trust develops through the ability of individuals to communicate, and we need to stand for what we believe in when we speak of democracy. On an organizational level, this form of trust also occurs through shared meaning of the culture.

Play the Long Game

I have written this book during troubled times. Violence and sectarianism are on the rise in India. Hong Kong is in flames. The murder of a Black man set off a national, indeed worldwide, surge of protests against police criminality. The president of the United States seems to lie on an hourly basis, and some say even if he loses the next election, he will not leave the White House. The pandemic not only killed millions of individuals but also created a global recession. Of course, the environment can change. A new government may tamp down passions in India. China may grant Hong Kong the autonomy the people desire. A Democratic majority and a resurgent, responsible Republican Party eventually may put to rest Trumpism. In Hong Kong, New Delhi, and Los Angeles, there will be a temptation for our universities to return to their ivy-covered walls and call the crisis over.

That would be a mistake. Democracy came into crisis not only because of the external environment where the conditions for fascism were on the rise, but also because those of us in academe were not vigilant. As Eisen et al. (2019) suggested, "Democracy's fate rests in the hands of people, and securing it begins at home" (p. 12). For those of who work in higher education, our home is academia. I am not suggesting a cause and effect in such a complex environment. I am, however, urging us to place the defense of democracy as central to the role of the engaged academic whether they are in Los Angeles, New Delhi, Hong Kong, or elsewhere. The academic's job is to engage in ongoing forms of critique pertaining to the abuses of power and authority. These discussions cannot only be with one's peers, but instead must be ongoing and systematic within the larger worlds in which academics live.

Those of us who work in higher education have the unique ability to envision a better world, and to figure out how to create the conditions to get there. We have the potential to be a critical conscience of and for society. When we struggle with such questions, we are representing the essence of the academic's search for truth, whether that truth be realist, positivist, postmodern, feminist, or critical. Ultimately, our job is to raise questions of society and point directions that support democracy and help defeat fascism. Each generation has the same struggle, the same potential, and the same hope for one another and for society.

Notes

Notes to Chapter 1

1. See https://about.coursera.org/press
2. For data relating to private higher education, see the Program for Research on Private Higher Education; https://prophe.org/en/global-data/

Notes to Chapter 2

1. See, for instance, http://www.calstatela.edu/univ/ppa/publicat/cal-state-la-ranked-among-best-universities-west-us-news-world-report
2. See http://newsroom.ucla.edu/ucla-fast-facts
3. See M. L. King (1963), "Letter from a Birmingham Jail"; https://www.africa.upenn.edu/Articles_Gen/Letter_Birmingham.html
4. Estimates from Government of the Hong Kong Special Administrative Region, Census and Statistics Department; https://www.censtatd.gov.hk/hkstat/sub/so20.jsp
5. See, for instance, the Center for World University Rankings; https://cwur.org/2018-19/china.php. See also the QS Top University Rankings; https://www.topuniversities.com/university-rankings/world-university-rankings/2019
6. Population estimates as of July 1, 2019, from the U.S. Census Bureau; https://www.census.gov/quickfacts/VT
7. See, for instance, https://www.bbc.com/news/world-asia-india-48090304. See also https://www.dw.com/en/why-narendra-modis-government-is-at-war-with-students/a-19051656
8. http://californiacommunitycolleges.cccco.edu/PolicyInAction/KeyFacts.aspx
9. https://www2.calstate.edu/csu-system/about-the-csu/facts-about-the-csu/Documents/facts2018.pdf
10. Statistics are for fall 2017 enrollment.

Notes to Chapter 4

1. See *Merriam-Webster* (n.d.)., No, "snowflake" as a slang term did not begin with *Fight Club*; https://www.merriam-webster.com/words-at-play/the-less-lovely-side-of-snowflake

Notes to Chapter 5

1. T. Morrison (1996, October 25), "The Place of the Idea: The Idea of the Place," speech at Princeon's 250th anniversary convocation; https://pr.princeton.edu/news/96/q4/1025spch.htm

2. The supplementary tutoring that is prevalent in Hong Kong (and other Asian countries) is often referred to as "shadow education" in the scholarly literature. For example, see Bray and Lykins (2012).

3. Also see https://www.newyorkfed.org/research/college-labor-market/college-labor-market_underemployment_rates.html

4. See, for example, the International Conference on World-Class Universities in Shanghai, China; http://www.shanghairanking.com/wcu/wcu6.html. Also see the World Summit Series sponsored by the *Times Higher Education* World University Rankings; https://www.timeshighereducation.com/events/summits

Notes to Chapter 6

1. See https://www2.calstate.edu/csu-system/about-the-csu/facts-about-the-csu/Documents/facts2018.pdf

Notes to Chapter 7

1. See https://www.scholarsatrisk.org/

References

Abel, J. R., & Deitz, R. (2013, May 20). Do big cities help college graduates find better jobs? *Liberty Street Economics.* https://libertystreeteconomics.new yorkfed.org/2013/05/do-big-cities-help-college-graduates-find-better-jobs. html

Aggarwal, M., Kapur, D., & Tognatta, N. (2012). *The skills they want: Aspirations of students in emerging India* (CASI Working Paper 12-03). University of Pennsylvania, Center for the Advanced Study of India.

Agrawal, R., & Salam, K. (2020, January 7). Why are India's students protesting? *Foreign Policy.* https://foreignpolicy.com/2020/01/07/india-student-protests-new-delhi-university-citizenship-law-narendra-modi/

Albright, M. (2018). *Fascism: A warning.* HarperCollins.

Almeida, D. J. (2016). Understanding grit in the context of higher education. In M. Paulsen (Ed.), *Higher education: Handbook of theory and research* (Vol. 31, pp. 559–609). Springer.

Altbach, P. G. (2005). Globalisation and the university: Myths and realities in an unequal world. *The NEA almanac of higher education.* National Education Association.

Altbach, P. G. (2007). Empires of knowledge and development. In P. G. Altbach & J. Balán (Eds.), *World class worldwide: Transforming research universities in Asia and Latin America* (pp. 1–28). Johns Hopkins University Press.

Altbach, P. G. (2009). One-third of the globe: The future of higher education in China and India. *Prospects, 39,* 11–31.

American Association of Arts and Sciences. (2020). *Our common purpose: Reinvigorating American democracy for the 21st century.* American Association of Arts and Sciences.

Amsler, S. S., & Bolsmann, C. (2012). University ranking as social exclusion. *British Journal of Sociology of Education, 33*(2), 283–301.

Angulo, A. J. (2016). *Diploma mills: How for-profit colleges stiffed students, taxpayers, and the American dream.* Johns Hopkins University Press.

Applebaum, Y. (2016, July 31). "I alone can fix it." *The Atlantic*. https://www.the-atlantic.com/politics/archive/2016/07/trump-rnc-speech-alone-fix-it/492557/

Arcidiacono, P., Kinsler, J., & Ransom, T. (2019). *Legacy and athlete preferences at Harvard* [Working paper]. Duke University, Durham, NC. http://public.econ.duke.edu/~psarcidi/legacyathlete.pdf

Arendt, H. (1973). *The origins of totalitarianism*. Harcourt. (Original work published 1951)

Aronowitz, S. (2012). The winter of our discontent. *Situations: Project of the Radical Imagination, 4*(2), 37–76.

Augoustinos, M. (1999). Ideology, false consciousness, and psychology. *Theory and Psychology, 9*(3), 295–312.

Auguste, B. G., Hancock, B., & Laboissiere, M. (2009). *The economic cost of the U.S. education gap*. McKinsey & Company. https://www.mckinsey.com/industries/social-sector/our-insights/the-economic-cost-of-the-us-education-gap

Augustin-Jean, L., & Cheung, A. H. Y. (2018). *The economic roots of the umbrella movement in Hong Kong: Globalization and the rise of China*. Routledge.

Autor, D. H. (2015). Why are there still so many jobs? The history and future of workplace automation. *Journal of Economic Perspectives, 29*(3), 3–30.

Axelrod, J. (2019, July 13). University of Alaska readies for budget slash: "We may likely never recover." *NPR*. https://www.npr.org/2019/07/03/738569508/university-of-alaska-readies-for-budget-slash-we-may-likely-never-recover

Baldwin, J. (2016). Quoted in R. Grellety, H. Peck, & R. Peck (Producer), & R. Peck (Director), *I am not your Negro* [Documentary]. Magnolia Pictures.

Bandurski, D. (2017). An umbrella closes in Hong Kong. *Dissent, 64*(2), 108–110.

Baru, R. V., & Mohan, M. (2018). Globalization and neoliberalism as structural drivers of health inequities. *Health Research Policy and Systems, 16*(Suppl. 1), 91.

Baum, S. (2015). The evolution of student debt in the United States. In B. Hershbein & K. M. Hollenbeck (Eds.), *Student loans and the dynamics of debt* (pp. 11–35). Upjohn Institute for Employment Research.

Beals, F., Kidman, J., & Funaki, H. (2019, April 22). Insider and outsider research: Negotiating self at the edge of the emic/etic divide. *Qualitative Inquiry, 26*(6), 593–601. https://doi.org/10.1177%2F1077800419843950

Becker, G. (1965, September). A theory of the allocation of time. *Economic Journal, 75*(299), 493–517.

Becket, S. (1955). *Waiting for Godot*. Grove Press.

Beerkens, E. (2003). Globalisation and higher education research. *Journal of Studies in International Education, 7*(2), 128–148.

Bellet, B. W., Jones, P. J., & McNally, R. J. (2018). Trigger warning: Empirical evidence ahead. *Journal of Behavior Therapy and Experimental Psychiatry, 61*, 134–141.

Bennett, W. J., & Wilezol, D. (2013). *Is college worth it?* Thomas Nelson.

Benson, L., Harkavy, I., & Hartley, M. (2005). Integrating a commitment to the public good into the institutional fabric. In A. J. Kezar, T. C. Chambers, J. C. Burkhardt, & Associates (Eds.), *Higher education for the public good: Emerging voices from a national movement* (pp. 185–216). Jossey Bass.

Berliner, D. C. (2013). Effects of inequality and poverty vs. teachers and schooling on America's youth. *Teachers College Record, 115*(12), 1–25.

Berman, S. (2019). *Democracy and dictatorship in Europe: From the Ancien regime to the present day.* Oxford University Press.

Bhardwaj, M. (2019, March 5). New Delhi is world's most polluted capital, Beijing eighth. *Reuters.* https://www.reuters.com/article/us-india-pollution/new-delhi-is-worlds-most-polluted-capital-beijing-eighth-idUSKCN1QM1FH

Birth, K. K. (2004). Finding time: Studying the concepts of time used in daily life. *Field Methods, 16,* 70–84.

Blight, D. W. (2018). *Frederick Douglass: Prophet of freedom.* Simon and Schuster.

Bourdieu, P. (1984). *Distinction: A social critique of the judgement of taste.* Harvard University Press.

Bourdieu, P. (1986). The forms of capital. In J. G. Richardson (Ed.), *Handbook of theory and research for the sociology of education* (pp. 241–258). Greenwood Press.

Bourdieu, P. (1994). Rethinking the state: Genesis and structure of the bureaucratic field. *Sociological Theory, 12*(1), 1–18.

Bourdieu, P. (2000). For a scholarship with commitment. *Profession,* 40–45.

Bradsher, K., Ramzy, A., & May, T. (2019). Hong Kong election results give democracy backers big win. *New York Times.* https://www.nytimes.com/2019/11/24/world/asia/hong-kong-election-results.html

Brandeis, L. D. (1913, December 20). What publicity can do. *Harper's Weekly.*

Braverman, H. (1974). *Labor and monopoly capital: The degradation of work in the twentieth century.* Monthly Review Press.

Bray, M., & Lykins, C. (2012). *Shadow education: Private supplementary tutoring and its implications for policy makers in Asia.* Asian Development Bank.

Bromberg, H. (1996). Revising history. *Stanford Lawyer, 30*(2), 116.

Brown, P., Lauder, H., & Ashton, D. N. (2010). *The global auction: The broken promises of education, jobs, and incomes.* Oxford University Press.

Burke, J. (2012). Sikh Golden Temple memorial reopens old wounds in India. *The Guardian.* https://www.theguardian.com/world/2012/oct/02/sikh-golden-temple-memorial-india

Burning Glass Technologies and Strada Institute for the Future of Work. (2018). *The permanent detour: Underemployment's long-term effects on the careers of college grads.* Burning Glass Technologies. https://www.burning-glass.com/wp-content/uploads/permanent_detour_underemployment_report.pdf

Bush, V. (1945). *Science: The endless frontier.* U.S. Government Printing Office.

Calhoun, C. (1998). The public good as a social and cultural project. In W. W. Powell & E. S. Clemens (Eds.), *Private action and the public good* (pp. 20–35). Yale University Press.

Campuzano, E. (2017, January 25). Chuck Palahniuk takes credit for coining "snowflake" as an insult. *The Oregonian*.

Cantwell, B., & Kauppinen, I. (2014). *Academic capitalism in the age of globalization*. Johns Hopkins University Press.

Cantwell, B., & Maldonado-Maldonado, A. (2009). Confronting contemporary ideas about globalization and internationalism in higher education. *Globalisation, Societies and Education, 7*(3), 289–306.

Caplan, B. (2018). *The case against education: Why the education system is a waste of time*. Princeton University Press.

Carlyle, T. (1841). *On heroes, hero-worship, and the heroic in history*. James Fraser.

Carnevale, A. P., Rose, S. J., & Cheah, B. (2011). *The college payoff: Education, occupations, lifetime earnings*. Georgetown University, Center on Education and the Workforce.

Carrico, K. (2018, January 22). *Academic freedom in Hong Kong since 2015: Between two systems*. Hong Kong Watch.

Cass, O. (2018). *The once and future worker: A vision for the renewal of work in America*. Encounter Books.

Castells, M. (2000). *The rise of the network society: The information: Economy, society, and culture* (2nd ed., Vol. 1). Blackwell.

Chaffee, E. E., & Tierney, W. G. (1988). *Collegiate culture and leadership strategies*. Macmillan.

Chan, H. (2019, April 9). Leading Hong Kong Umbrella Movement activists found guilty of public nuisance. *Hong Kong Free Press*.

Chan, J. M. M., & Kerr, D. R. (2016). Academic freedom, political interference, and political accountability: The Hong Kong experience. *AAUP Journal of Academic Freedom, 7*, 1–21.

Chan, M. (2020, February 28). Hong Kong pro-democracy figures arrested over banned rally. *Nikkei Asian Review*. https://asia.nikkei.com/Spotlight/Hong-Kong-protests/Hong-Kong-pro-democracy-figures-arrested-over-banned-rally

Chan, W. W., Tang, H. H., & Cheung, L. K. (in press). In Hao, Z. D., & Zabielskis, P. (Eds), *Academic freedom under siege: Higher education in East Asia, the US, and Australia*. Springer.

Cheng, K. (2019, November 13). CUHK announces premature end to semester as Hong Kong universities switch to online teaching. *Hong Kong Free Press*. https://www.hongkongfp.com/2019/11/13/cuhk-announces-prema-ture-end-semester-hong-kong-universities-switch-online-teaching/

Chiu, P. (2018, June 17). Why Hong Kong's private tertiary institutions may need to find their own niche to survive. *South China Morning Post*. https://www.scmp.com/news/hong-kong/education/article/2151175/why-hong-kongs-private-tertiary-institutions-may-need-find

Chopra, R. (2018, September 12). Fascist fest as Trump's America meets Modi's Hindus. *South China Morning Post.* https://www.scmp.com/week-asia/opinion/article/2163893/fascist-fest-trumps-america-meets-modis-hindus

Christensen, C. M. (1997). *The innovator's dilemma: When new technologies cause great firms to fail.* Harvard Business School Press.

Christensen, C. M., & Eyring, H. J. (2011). *The innovative university: Changing the DNA of higher education from the inside out.* Jossey-Bass.

Chung, K., Sum, L. K., & Lum, A. (2019, November 14). Chinese University: How a scenic seafront campus in northern Hong Kong became a fiery battlefield, scarred by petrol bombs and tear gas. *South China Morning Post.* https://www.scmp.com/news/hong-kong/politics/article/3037615/chinese-university-how-scenic-seafront-campus-northern-hong

Clark, B. R. (1963). Faculty cultures. In T. F. Lunsford (Ed.), *The study of campus cultures* (pp. 39–54). Western Interstate Commission for Higher Education.

Crawford, L. M., & McLaren, P. (2003). A critical perspective on culture in the second language classroom. In. D. L. Lange (Ed.), *Culture as the core: Perspective on culture in second language education* (pp. 127–160). Information Age Publishing.

Crutchfield, R., & Maguire, J. (2018). *Study of student basic needs.* California State University Basic Needs Initative.

Dean, T. (2017, June 1). The meeting that showed me the truth about VCs. *Tech Crunch.* https://techcrunch.com/2017/06/01/the-meeting-that-showed-me-the-truth-about-vcs/

Derrida, J. (2001). The future of the profession. *Filosoficky Casopis, 49*(6), 899–930.

Desai, A., & Vahed, G. (2016). *The South African Gandhi: Stretcher-bearer of empire.* Stanford University Press.

Deshpande, R., & Palshikar, S. (2008). Occupational mobility: How much does caste matter? *Economic and Political Weekly, 43*(34), 61–70.

de Sousa Santos, B. (2006). The university in the twenty-first century: Toward a democratic and emancipatory university reform. In R. A. Rhoads & C. A. Torres (Eds.), *The university, state, and market: The political economy of globalization in the Americas* (pp. 60–100). Stanford University Press.

de Sousa Santos, B. (2010. July 1). The university in the twenty-first century: Toward a democratic and emancipatory university reform. *Eurozine.* https://www.eurozine.com/the-university-in-the-twenty-first-century/

de Sousa Santos, B. (2016). The university at a crossroads. In R. Grosfoguel, R. Hernández, & E. R. Velázquez (Eds.), *Decolonizing the westernized university* (pp. 3–14). Rowman & Littlefield.

Diamond, L. (2015). Facing up to the democratic recession. *Journal of Democracy, 26*(1), 141–155.

Diamond, L. (2016). *In search of democracy.* Routledge.

Diamond, L. (2019). *Ill winds: Saving democracy from Russian rage, Chinese ambition, and American complacency.* Penguin.

Douglass, J. A. (2009). *Higher education's new global order: How and why governments are creating structured opportunity markets.* University of California at Berkeley, Center for Studies in Higher Education.

Duckworth, A. L., Peterson, C., Matthews, M. D., & Kelly, D. R. (2007). Grit: Perseverance and passion for long-term goals. *Journal of Personality and Social Psychology, 92*(6), 1087–1101.

Duderstadt, J., & Womack, F. (2003). *The future of the public university in America: Beyond the crossroads.* Johns Hopkins University Press.

Duncheon, J. C., & Tierney, W. G. (2013). Changing conceptions of time: Implications for educational research and practice. *Review of Educational Research, 83*(2), 236–272.

Dwyer, C. (2016, January 23). Donald Trump: "I could . . . shoot somebody, and I wouldn't lose any voters." NPR. https://www.npr.org/sections/thetwo-way/2016/01/23/464129029/donald-trump-i-could-shoot-somebody-and-i-wouldnt-lose-any-voters

Ebner, J. (2017). *The rage: The vicious circle of Islamist and far-right extremism.* I. B. Tauris.

Eggington, W. (2018). *The splintering of the American mind: Identity politics, inequality, and community on today's college campuses.* Bloomsbury.

Eisen, N., Kenealy, A., Corke, S., Taussig, T., & Polyakova, A. (2019). *The democracy playbook: Preventing and reversing democratic backsliding.* Brookings Institution.

Elliott, O. (1937). *Stanford University: The first twenty-five years.* Stanford University Press.

Erikson, E. (1968). *Identity: Youth and crisis.* Norton.

Evans, W. (2019, November). Ruthless quotas at Amazon are maiming employees. *The Atlantic.* https://www.theatlantic.com/technology/archive/2019/11/amazon-warehouse-reports-show-worker-injuries/602530/

Eyerman, R. (1981). False consciousness and ideology in Marxist theory. *Acta Sociologica, 24*(1–2), 43–56.

Faleiro, S. (2019, July 29). Absent opposition, Modi makes India his Hindu nation. *New York Review of Books.* https://www.nybooks.com/daily/2019/07/29/absent-opposition-modi-makes-india-his-hindu-nation/

Fearson, J. (1999). *What is identity (as we now use the word)?* Unpublished manuscript, Stanford University.

Ferber, A. L. (2017). Faculty under attack. *Humboldt Journal of Social Relations, 39,* 37–42.

Fernandes, L. (2006). *India's new middle class: Democratic politics in an era of economic reform.* University of Minnesota Press.

Filkins, D. (2019, December 9). Blood and soil in Narenda Modi's India. *The New Yorker.* https://www.newyorker.com/magazine/2019/12/09/blood-and-soil-in-narendra-modis-india

Findlay, C., & Tierney, W. G. (Eds.). (2010). *Globalization and tertiary education in the Asia Pacific: The changing nature of a dynamic market.* World Scientific.

Flaherty, C. (2019, July 10). Accreditation risk from Alaska cuts. *Inside Higher Ed.* https://www.insidehighered.com/news/2019/07/10/u-alaskas-accreditor-warns-funding-cuts-could-threaten-systems-status

Fong, B. C. H., Chan, E., Siu, K., & Chow, Y. T. (2020). *2019 Hong Kong academic freedom report.* Progressive Scholars Group.

Foucault, M. (1991). Politics and the study of discourse. In G. Burchell, C. Gordon, & P. Miller (Eds.), *The Foucault effect: Studies in governmental rationality* (pp. 53–72). University of Chicago Press.

Frey, C. B., & Osborne, M. A. (2017). The future of employment: How susceptible are jobs to computerization? *Technological Forecasting and Social Change, 114,* 254–280.

Fry, R. (2014, October 7). *The growth in student debt.* Pew Research Center. http://www.pewsocialtrends.org/2014/10/07/the-growth-in-student-debt/

Fuchs, D., & Klingemann, H-D. (2019). Globalization, populism, and legitimacy in contemporary democracy. In U. van Beek (Ed.), *Democracy Under Threat: Challenges to democracy in the 21st century* (pp. 3–21). Palgrave Macmillan.

Fukuyama, F. (1992). *The end of history and the last man.* Avon Books.

Fukuyama, F. (2008. February 9). The populist surge. *The American Interest.* https://www.the-american-interest.com/2018/02/09/the-populist-surge/

Fukuyama, F. (2018). *Identity: The demand for dignity and the politics of resentment.* Farrar, Straus, and Giroux.

Furedi, F. (2017). *Populism and the European culture wars: The conflict of values between Hungary and the EU.* Routledge.

Ganguly, S. (2019, January 7). The world should be watching Bangladesh's election debacle. *Foreign Policy.* https://foreignpolicy.com/2019/01/07/the-world-should-be-watching-bangladeshs-election-debacle-sheikh-hasina/

Gans, H. (2002). More of us should become public sociologists. *Footnotes, 30*(6).

Gee, J. P. (2000). Identity as an analytic lens for research in education. *Review of Research in Education, 25*(1), 99–125.

Gessen, M. (2020). *Surviving autocracy.* Riverhead Books.

Gettleman, J., Schultz, K., Raj, S., & Kumar, H. (2019. April 11). Under Modi, a Hindu nationalist surge has further divided India. *New York Times.* https://www.nytimes.com/2019/04/11/world/asia/modi-india-elections.html

Ghose, S. (2015, February 21). Academic freedom is under threat in India: Amartya Sen. *Times of India.* https://timesofindia.indiatimes.com/india/Academic-freedom-is-under-threat-in-India-Amartya-Sen/articleshow/46318446.cms

Giroux, H. A. (1983). *Theory and resistance in education: A pedagogy for the opposition.* Bergin and Garvey.

Giroux, H. A. (1988). *Teachers as intellectuals: Toward a critical pedagogy of learning.* Bergin and Garvey.

Giroux, H. A. (2003). *The abandoned generation: Democracy beyond the culture of fear*. Palgrave Macmillan.

Giroux, H. A. (2005). The terror of neoliberalism: Rethinking the significance of cultural politics. *College Literature, 32*(1), 1–19.

Giroux, H. A. (2008). Education and the crisis of youth: Schooling and the promise of democracy. *Educational Forum, 73*(1), 8–18.

Giroux, H. A. (2009). The attack on higher education and the necessity of critical pedagogy. In S. L. Macrine (Ed.), *Critical pedagogy in uncertain times* (pp. 11–26). Palgrave Macmillan.

Giroux, H. A. (2014). *Neoliberalism's war on higher education*. Haymarket Books.

Giroux, H. A. (2015). *Dangerous thinking in the age of the new authoritarianism*. Taylor and Francis.

Giroux, H. A. (2019). Neoliberal violence against youth in the age of Orwellian nightmares. In P. Kelly, P. Campbell, L. Harrison, & C. Hickey (Eds.), *Young people and the politics of outrage and hope* (pp. 27–43). Brill.

Goodstadt, L. F. (2014). *Poverty in the midst of affluence: How Hong Kong mismanaged its prosperity*. Hong Kong University Press.

Gordon, L. (2019, February 5). California State University graduation rates show uneven progress, some backsliding. *EdSource*. https://edsource.org/2019/california-state-university-graduation-rates-show-uneven-progress-some-backsliding/608158

Gross, D. R. (1984). Time allocation: A tool for the study of cultural behavior. *Annual Review of Anthropology, 13*, 519–558.

Grundy, T. (2017, September 16). Heads of top universities call Hong Kong independence unconstitutional, condemn free speech "abuses." *Hong Kong Free Press*. https://www.hongkongfp.com/2017/09/16/heads-top-universities-call-hong-kong-independence-unconstitutional-condemn-free-speech-abuses/

Grundy, T. (2019, September 28). Academic Dan Garrett banned from Hong Kong after testifying on city's rights situation in US. *Hong Kong Free Press*. https://www.hongkongfp.com/2019/09/28/academic-dan-garrett-banned-hong-kong-testifying-citys-rights-situation-us/

Gulson, K. N., & Fataar, A. (2011). Neoliberal governmentality, schooling, and the city: Conceptual and empirical notes on and from the global south. *Discourse: Studies in the Cultural Politics of Education, 32*(2), 269–283.

Gutek, G. (2006). *American education in a global society: International and comparative perspectives*. Waveland Press.

Hacker, A., & Dreifus, C. (2010). *Higher education? How colleges are wasting our money and failing our kids—and what we can do about it*. St. Martin's Griffin.

Hacking, I. (1990). *The taming of chance*. Cambridge University Press.

Haidt, J. (2016, October 21). Why universities must choose one telos: Truth or social justice. *Heterodox Academy*. https://heterodoxacademy.org/one-telos-truth-or-social-justice-2/

Hallowell, A. I. (1937). Temporal orientation in Western civilization and in a preliterate society. *American Anthropologist, 39*, 647–670.

Hamer, J. F., & Lang, C. (2015). Race, structural violence, and the neoliberal university: The challenges of inhabitation. *Critical Sociology, 41*(6), 897–912.

Hames-Garcia, M. R. (2000). "Who are our own people?": Challenges for a theory of social identity. In P. M. L. Moya & M. R. Hames-Garcia (Eds.), *Reclaiming identity: Realist theory and the predicament of postmodernism* (pp. 102–132). University of California Press.

Haney-Lopez, I. (2020). *Merge left: Fusing race and class, winning elections and saving America.* New Press.

Hardin, R. (2002). *Trust and trustworthiness.* Russell Sage Foundation.

Harper, V. (2014). Neoliberalism, democracy, and the university as a public sphere: An interview with Henry A. Giroux. *Policy Futures in Education, 12*(8), 1078–1083.

Hartmann, E. (2008). Bologna goes global: A new imperialism in the making? *Globalisation, Societies, and Education, 6*(3), 207–220.

Hart Research. (2015). Rising to the challenge: Views on high school graduates' preparedness for college and careers. *Achieve.* https://www.achieve.org/rising-challenge-survey-2-powerpoint

Hassan, R. (2003). Network time and the new knowledge epoch. *Time and Society, 12*, 225–241.

Hawkins, K., & Littvay, L. (2019) *Contemporary US populism in comparative perspective.* Cambridge University Press.

Hayes, J., & Hill, L. (2017). *Undocumented immigrants in California.* Public Policy Institute of California. https://www.ppic.org/publication/undocumented-immigrants-in-california/

Hentschke, G. C., Lechuga, V. M., & Tierney, W. G. (Eds.). (2010). *For-profit colleges and universities: Their markets, regulation, performance, and place in higher education.* Stylus.

Hershbein, B., & Kearney, M. S. (2014). *Major decisions: What graduates earn over their lifetimes.* Brookings Institute.

Hillman, N., & Corral, D. (2017). The equity implications of paying for performance in higher education. *American Behavioral Scientist, 61*(14), 1757–1772.

Hofstadter, R., & Metzger, W. (1955). *The development of academic freedom in the United States.* Columbia University Press.

Ives, M. (2019. June 10). What is Hong Kong's extradition bill? *New York Times.* https://www.nytimes.com/2019/06/10/world/asia/hong-kong-extradition-bill.html

Jaschik, S. (2019, March 18). The week that shook college admissions. *Inside Higher Ed.* https://www.insidehighered.com/admissions/article/2019/03/18/look-how-indictments-shook-college-admissions

Jayantha, W. M., & Oladinrin, O. T. (2019). An analysis of factors affecting home-ownership: A survey of Hong Kong households. *Journal of Housing and the Built Environment, 35*, 939–956.

Johnson, H., Bohn, S., & Mejia, M. C. (2017). *Addressing California's skills gap.* Public Policy Institute of California.

Johnson, H., & Mejia, M. C. (2016). *California's higher education system.* Public Policy Institute of California.

Kaeding, M. P. (2017). The rise of "localism" in Hong Kong. *Journal of Democracy, 28*(1), 157–171.

Kalleberg, A. L. (2011). *Good jobs, bad jobs: The rise of polarized and precarious employment systems in the United States, 1970s to 2000s.* Russell Sage Foundation.

Kapur, D. (2010). Indian higher education. In C. T. Clotfelter (Ed.), *American universities in a global market* (pp. 305–334). University of Chicago Press.

Kapur, D., & Perry, E. (2015). *Higher education reform in China and India: The role of the state.* Harvard-Yenching Institute Working Papers. https://harvard-yenching. org/features/hyi-working-paper-series-devesh-kapur-and-elizabeth-perry

Kaul, I., Grunberg, I., & Stern, M. (1999). Defining global public goods. In I. Kaul, I. Grunberg, & M. Stern (Eds.), *Global public goods* (pp. 2–19). Oxford University Press.

Kezar, A. (2004). Obtaining integrity? Reviewing and examining the charter between higher education and society. *Review of Higher Education, 27*(4), 429–459.

Kezar, A., DePaola, T., & Scott, D. T. (2019). *The rise of the gig academy: Mapping labor in the neoliberal university.* Johns Hopkins University Press.

Khan, N. (2019, April 24). Professor who inspired Hong Kong's mass protests is sent to jail. *Wall Street Journal.* https://www.wsj.com/articles/professor-who-inspired-hong-kongs-mass-protests-is-sent-to-jail-11556099967

Khwaja, T., Eddy, P. L., & Ward, K. (2017). Critical approaches to women and gender in higher education: Reaching the tipping point for change. In P. L. Eddy, K. Ward, & T. Khwaja (Eds.), *Critical approaches to women and gender in higher education* (pp. 325–336). Palgrave Macmillan.

Killion, J. (2011, March 23). Teachers agree that supporting diverse learners with high needs if a priority. *Learning Forward.* https://learningforward.org/press-release/metlife-survey-american-teacher-explores-needs-diverse-learners/

Kim, E. T. (2019, January 23). LA's school counselors strike back. *The Hechinger Report.*

Kirp, D. (2003). *Shakespeare, Einstein, and the bottom line.* Harvard University Press.

Knobel, M., & Verhine, R. (2017). Brazil's for-profit higher education dilemma. *International Higher Education, 89*, 23–24.

Kolko, J. (2019, May.). What the job market looks like for today's college graduates. *Harvard Business Review.* https://hbr.org/2019/05/what-the-job-market-looks-like-for-todays-college-graduates

Koseff, A. (2017, August 3). CSU eliminates remedial classes in push to improve graduation rates. *Sacramento Bee.* https://www.sacbee.com/news/politics-government/capitol-alert/article165342632.html

Kumar, V. (2016). Discrimination on campuses of higher learning: A perspective from below. *Economic and Political Weekly, 51*(6), 12–15.

Kwan, P., & Wong, Y.-L. (2016). Parental involvement in schools and class inequality in education: Some recent findings from Hong Kong. *International Journal of Pedagogies and Learning, 11*(2), 91–102.

Kwok, D. & Yiu, P. (2020, Februay 27). Hong Kong police arrest media tycoon Jimmy Lai on illegal assembly charges. *Reuters.* https://www.reuters.com/article/us-hongkong-protests-arrests/hong-kong-police-arrest-media-tycoon-jimmy-lai-on-illegal-assembly-charges-idUSKCN20M08V

Lakoff, G., & Johnson, M. (1980). *Metaphors we live by.* University of Chicago Press.

Lambert, M. T. (2014). *Privatization and the public good: Public universities in the balance.* Harvard Education Press.

Lanford, M. (2016). Perceptions of higher education reform in Hong Kong: A glocalization perspective. *International Journal of Comparative Education and Development, 18*(3), 184–204.

Lanford, M. (2019). Making sense of "outsiderness": How life history informs the college experiences of "nontraditional" students. *Qualitative Inquiry, 25*(5), 500–512.

Lazerson, M. (1998). The disappointments of success: Higher education after World War II. *Annals of the American Academy of Political and Social Science, 559*(1), 64–76.

Lederman, D. (2017, April 28). Clay Christensen, doubling down. *Inside Higher Ed.* https://www.insidehighered.com/digital-learning/article/2017/04/28/clay-christensen-sticks-predictions-massive-college-closures

Lederman, D. (2019, August 14). Budget compromise in Alaska. *Inside Higher Ed.* https://www.insidehighered.com/news/2019/08/14/alaskas-governor-and-university-reach-compromise-nearly-halve-budget-cut

Lee, F. (2020). Solidarity in the anti-extradition bill movement in Hong Kong. *Critical Asian Studies, 52*(1), 18–32.

Lee, F. L. F., & Lin, A. M. Y. (2006). Newspaper editorial discourse and the politics of self-censorship in Hong Kong. *Discourse and Society, 17*(3), 331–358.

Lee, S. Y. (2016). Massification without equalization: The politics of higher education, graduate employment, and social mobility in Hong Kong. *Journal of Education and Work, 29*(1), 13–31.

Legislative Analyst's Office (LAO). (2017). Overview of remedial education at the state's public higher education segments. State of California, LAO. https://lao.ca.gov/handouts/education/2017/Overview-Remedial-Education-State-Public-Higher-Education-Segments-030117.pdf

Leung, J., Talmazan, Y., & Bradley, M. (2019, November 18). Hundreds arrested, but 100 remain holed up at Hong Kong university. *NBC News.* https://www.nbcnews.com/news/world/china-says-hong-kong-can-t-overturn-ban-masks-protests-n1085376

Leung, J. H. C. (2019). Interpretive violence and the "nationalization" of Hong Kong law: Notes on the oath-taking controversy. *Law and Literature, 31*(2), 221–238.

Levitsky, S., & Ziblatt, D. (2018). *How democracies die.* Crown.

Lewis, S. (1935). *It can't happen here.* Doubleday, Doran and Company.

Li, A. Y., Gándara, D., & Assalone, A. (2018). Equity or disparity: Do performance funding policies disadvantage 2-year minority-serving institutions? *Community College Review, 46*(3), 288–315.

Li, A. Y., & Kennedy, A. I. (2018). Performance funding policy effects on community college outcomes: Are short-term certificates on the rise? *Community College Review, 46*(1), 3–39.

Lilienfeld, S. O. (2017). Microaggressions: Strong claims, inadequate evidence. *Perspectives on Psychological Science, 12*(1), 138–169.

Lilla, M. (2018). *The once and future liberal: After identity politics.* Hurst and Company.

Liu, J. (2017, June 29). Cantonese v. Mandarin: When Hong Kong languages get political. *BBC.* https://www.bbc.com/news/world-asia-china-40406429

Lolich, L. (2011). . . . and the market created the student to its image and likening: Neo-liberal governmentality and its effects on higher education in Ireland. *Irish Educational Studies, 30*(2), 271–284.

Long, H. (2018, October 5). Amazon's $15 minimum wage doesn't end debate over whether it's creating good jobs. *Washington Post.*

Lorde, A. (2009). I am your sister: Black women organizing across sexualities. In R. P. Byrd, J. B. Cole, & B. Guy-Sheftall (Eds.), *I am your sister: Collected and unpublished writings of Audre Lorde* (pp. 57–63). Oxford University Press.

Lorenz, C. (2012). If you're so smart, why are you under surveillance? Universities, neoliberalism, and new public management. *Critical Inquiry, 38*(3), 599–629.

Lukianoff, G., & Haidt, J. (2015, September). The coddling of the American mind. *The Atlantic.* https://www.theatlantic.com/magazine/archive/2015/09/the-coddling-of-the-american-mind/399356/

Lukianoff, G., & Haidt, J. (2018). *The coddling of the American mind: How good intentions and bad ideas are setting up a generation for failure.* Penguin Press.

Lum, A. (2020, January 4). American photographer who covered Hong Kong protests denied entry into city. *South China Morning Post.* https://www.scmp.com/news/hong-kong/politics/article/3044660/american-photographer-who-covered-hong-kong-protests-denied

Lum, A., Su, X., Sum, L. K., & Ng, N. (2018, November 9). British journalist Victor Mallet denied entry to Hong Kong as tourist. *South China Morning Post.* https://www.scmp.com/news/hong-kong/politics/article/2172383/british-journalist-victor-mallet-denied-entry-hong-kong

Lynch, K. (2015). Control by numbers: New managerialism and ranking in higher education. *Critical Studies in Education, 56*(2), 190–207.

Madani, S. (2019, May 31). The anatomy of unmaking the "Idea of the University." *The Companion, 1.*

Mahtani, S. (2020, January 12). Hong Kong denies entry to human rights watch head Kenneth Roth. *Washington Post.* https://www.washingtonpost.com/world/asia_pacific/hong-kong-denies-entry-to-human-rights-watch-head-kenneth-roth/2020/01/12/0ace9fdc-3548-11ea-a1ff-c48c1d59a4a1_story.html

Mangan, K. (2017, September 15). Cal state's retreat from remediation stokes debate on college readiness. *Chronicle of Higher Education.* https://www.chronicle.com/article/Cal-State-s-Retreat-From/241227

Marginson, S. (2007). The public/private divide in higher education: A global revision. *Higher Education, 53*(3), 307–333.

Marginson, S. (2011). Higher education and public good. *Higher Education Quarterly, 65*(4), 411–433.

Marginson, S. (2016). *The dream is over: The crisis of Clark Kerr's California idea of higher education.* University of California Press.

Marginson, S. (2018). And the sky is grey: The ambivalent outcomes of the California Master Plan for higher education. *Higher Education Quarterly, 72*(1), 51–64.

Marx, K. (1977). *Capital* (B. Fowkes, Trans.). Vintage. (Original work published 1877)

May, T. (2019, April 23). Hong Kong umbrella movement leaders are sentenced to prison. *New York Times.* https://www.nytimes.com/2019/04/23/world/asia/hong-kong-umbrella-movement.html

Maye, A. (2019, May). *No-vacation nation, revised.* Center for Economic and Policy Research. https://cepr.net/images/stories/reports/no-vacation-nation-2019-05.pdf

McLaren, P. (2005). Critical pedagogy in the age of neoliberal globalization. In P. P. Trifonas (Ed.), *Communities of difference* (pp. 69–103). Palgrave Macmillan.

McMurtry, J. (1991). Education and the market model. *Journal of Philosophy of Education, 25*(2), 209–217.

Medina, J., Benner, K., & Taylor, K. (2019, March 12). Actresses, business leaders, and other wealthy parents charged in U.S. college entry fraud. *New York Times.* https://www.nytimes.com/2019/03/12/us/college-admissions-cheating-scandal.html

Menand, L. (2001). *The metaphysical club.* Farrar, Straus, and Giroux.

Mérieau, E. (2019, March). How Thailand became the world's last military dictatorship. *The Atlantic.* https://www.theatlantic.com/international/archive/2019/03/thailand-military-junta-election-king/585274/

Ministry of Human Resource Development (MHRD). (2018). *All India survey on higher education (2017–18).* Government of India, Department of Higher Education. http://aishe.nic.in/aishe/viewDocument.action?documentId=245

Mishel, L., Gould, E., & Bivens, J. (2015). *Wage stagnation in nine charts.* Economic Policy Institute.

Mohanty, S. P. (1997). *Literary theory and the claims of history: Postmodernism, objectivity, multicultural politics.* Cornell University Press.

Mohr, J. C. (1970). Academic turmoil and public opinion: The Ross case at Stanford. *Pacific Historical Review, 39*(1), 39–61.

Mok, K. (2005). Globalization and educational restructuring: University merging and changing governance in China. *Higher Education, 50*(1), 57–88.

Mondon, A., & Winter, A. (2019). Whiteness, populism, and the racialisation of the working class in the United Kingdom and the United States. *Identities: Global Studies in Culture and Power, 26*(5), 510–528.

Moretti, E. (2012). *The new geography of jobs.* Houghton Mifflin.

Mounk, Y. (2018). *The people vs. democracy: Why our freedom is in danger and how to save it.* Harvard University Press.

Munn, N. D. (1992). The cultural anthropology of time: A critical essay. *Annual Review of Anthropology, 21*, 92–123.

Napolitano, D. (2019, November 19). Hong Kong arrests mount to 1,100 as campus siege continues. *Nikkei Asian Review.* https://asia.nikkei.com/Spotlight/Hong-Kong-protests/Hong-Kong-arrests-mount-to-1-100-as-campus-siege-continues

National Center for Education Statistics (NCES). (2018). *The condition of education 2018.* U. S. Department of Education, Institute of Education Statistics. https://nces.ed.gov/pubs2018/2018144.pdf

National Institution for Transformation of India (NITI). (2018). *Strategy for new India @ 75.* Government of India, NITI Aayog.

Neighborhood Data for Social Change (NDSC). (2018). *A snapshot of homelessness in Los Angeles county.* University of Southern Californiam, Price Center for Social Innovation. https://www.kcet.org/shows/city-rising/a-2018-snapshot-of-homelessness-in-los-angeles-county

Nelson, R. R., & Rosenberg, N. (1993). Technical innovation and national systems. In R. R. Nelson (Ed.), *National innovation systems: A comparative analysis* (pp. 3–21). Oxford University Press.

Neto, U. T. (2017). Democracy, social authoritarianism, and the human rights state theory: Towards effective citizenship in Brazil. *International Journal of Human Rights, 21*(3), 289–305.

Nevins, A. (1962). *The origins of the land grant colleges and state universities.* Civil War Centennial Commission.

Newman, J. H. (2015). *The idea of a university.* Aeterna Press. (First published 1852.)

Newton, D. (2018, June 25). Why college tuition is actually higher for online programs. *Forbes.* https://www.forbes.com/sites/dereknewton/2018/06/25/why-college-tuition-is-actually-higher-for-online-programs/#7474438ff11a

Oakes, J. (1986). Tracking, inequality, and the rhetoric of reform: Why schools don't change. *Journal of Education, 168*(1), 60–80.

Olssen, M. (2016). Neoliberal competition in higher education today: Research, accountability, and impact. *British Journal of Sociology of Education, 37*(1), 129–148.

Olssen, M., & Peters, M. A. (2005). Neoliberalism, higher education, and the knowledge economy: From the free market to knowledge capitalism. *Journal of Education Policy, 20*(3), 313–345.

Outka, P. H. (2002). Whitman and race. *Journal of American Studies, 36*(2), 293–318.

Page, E. (2012). Bureaucracy: Disregarding public administration. In J. Connelly & J. Hayward (Eds.), *The withering of the welfare state* (pp. 101–120). Palgrave Macmillan.

Palmer, A. W. (2018, April 3). The case of Hong Kong's missing booksellers. *New York Times.* https://www.nytimes.com/2018/04/03/magazine/the-case-of-hong-kongs-missing-booksellers.html

Pathania, G. J., & Tierney, W. G. (2018). An ethnography of caste and class at an Indian university: Creating capital. *Tertiary Education and Management, 24*(3), 221–231.

Paxton, R. (2004). *The anatomy of fascism.* Vintage Books.

Pérez Huber, L., & Solórzano, D. G. (2015). Racial microaggressions as a tool for critical race research. *Race, Ethnicity, and Education, 18*(3), 297–320.

Petersen, C. J., & Currie, J. (2008). Higher education restructuring and academic freedom in Hong Kong. *Policy Futures in Education, 6*(5), 589–600.

Pierson, P. (1994). *Dismantling the welfare state? Reagan, Thatcher, and the politics of retrenchment.* Cambridge University Press.

Piketty, T. (2014). *Capital in the twenty-first century* (A. Goldhammer, Trans.). Harvard University Press.

Pinchin, K. (2020). Hong Kong struggles with coronavirus, renewing residents' anger. *Frontline.* https://www.pbs.org/wgbh/frontline/article/hong-kong-coronavirus-renewed-protests-facemasks/

Post, R. (2018). The classic first amendment tradition under stress: Freedom of speech and the university. In L. Bollinger & G. Stone (Eds), *The free speech century* (pp. 14–34). Oxford University Press.

Postiglione, G. A. (2011). The rise of research universities: The Hong Kong University of Science and Technology. In P. G. Altbach & J. Salmi (Eds.), *The road to academic excellence: The making of world-class research universities* (pp. 63–100). World Bank.

Postiglione, G. A. (2017). *China's Hong Kong and the changing state of academic freedom.* Paper presented at the annual conference of the American Educational Research Association, San Antonio, TX.

Postiglione, G. A., & Xie, A. L. (2018). World-class universities and global common good: The role of China and the U.S. in addressing global inequality. In Y. Wu, Q. Wang, & N. C. Liu (Eds.), *World-class universities: Towards a global common good and seeking national and institutional contributions* (pp. 188–214). Brill.

Prasad, S. K. (2020, January 10). India is cracking down on university protestors. Here's what you need to know. *Washington Post.* https://www.washington post.com/politics/2020/01/10/india-is-cracking-down-university-protests-heres-what-you-need-know/

Raman, S. (2019). What budget 2019 needs to do to boost India's flailing higher education institutions. *IndiaSpend.* https://www.indiaspend.com/what-budget-2019-needs-to-do-to-boost-indias-flailing-higher-education-institutions/

Ramzy, A. (2019a, June 9). Hong Kong march: Vast protest of extradition bill shows fear of eroding freedoms. *New York Times.* https://www.nytimes.com/2019/06/09/world/asia/hong-kong-extradition-protest.html

Ramzy, A. (2019b, July 22). Mob attack at Hong Kong train station heightens seething tensions in city. *New York Times.* https://www.nytimes.com/2019/07/22/world/asia/hong-kong-protest-mob-attack-yuen-long.html

Rauhala, E. (2017, August 17). Hong Kong student leaders jailed for 2014 pro-democracy protest. *Washington Post.* https://www.washingtonpost.com/world/hong-kong-student-leaders-jailed-for-2014-pro-democracy-umbrella-protest/2017/08/17/ba7a92d4-8310-11e7-82a4-920da1aeb507_story.html

Reich, R. (2018). *The common good.* Penguin.

Rhoades, G. (1998). Managed professionals: Unionized faculty and restructuring academic labor. State University of New York Press.

Rhoades, G. (2011). A national campaign of academic labor: Reframing the politics of scarcity in higher education. *New Political Science, 33*(1), 101–118.

Riera, M. P. (2017). Venezuela: The decline of a democracy. *Development, 60*(3–4), 174–179.

Rizvi, F., & Lingard, B. (2009). *Globalizing education policy.* Routledge.

Rook-Koepsel, E. (2019). *Democracy and unity in India: Understanding the all India phenomenon, 1940–1960.* Routledge.

Ross, E. (1900, November 15). Indignation at the dismissal. *San Francisco Chronicle.*

Rudolph, F. (1962). *The American college and university: A history.* Vintage Books.

Rueb, E., & Taylor, D. (2020, August 10). Obama on call-out culture: That's not activism. *New York Times* https://www.nytimes.com/2019/10/31/us/politics/obama-woke-cancel-culture.html

Rustgi, A. K. (1999). Translational research: What is it? *Gastroenterology, 116*(6), 1285.

Rutledge, M. S., Wettstein, G., & King, S. E. (2019). *Will more workers have nontraditional jobs as globalization and automation spread?* (CRR Working Paper 2019–10). Center for Retirement Research at Boston College.

Saez, E. (2018). Striking it richer: The evolution of top incomes in the United States. In D. B. Grusky & J. Hill (Eds.), *Inequality in the 21st century: A reader* (pp. 39–42). Routledge.

Salmi, J. (2011). The road to academic excellence: Lessons of experience. In P. G. Altbach & J. Salmi (Eds.), *The road to academic excellence: The making of world-class research universities* (pp. 323–347). World Bank.

Schectman, N., Debarger, A. H., Dornsife, C., Rosier, S., & Yarnall, L. (2013). *Promoting grit, tenacity, and perseverance: Critical factors of success in the 21st century.* U.S. Department of Education, Office of Technology.

Schick, N. (2020). *Deepfakes: The coming infocalypse.* Twelve.

Scott, J. W. (2019). *Knowledge, power, and academic freedom.* Columbia University Press.

Scott, P. (2005). Universities and the knowledge economy. *Minerva, 43*(3), 297–309.

Sedmak, T. (2019, December 16). Fall enrollments decline for 8th consecutive year. National Student Clearinghouse. https://www.studentclearinghouse.org/blog/fall-enrollments-decline-for-8th-consecutive-year/

Segre, S. (2000). A Weberian theory of time. *Time and Society, 9*, 147–170.

Sen, A. (2015, August 13). India: The stormy revival of an international university. *The New York Review of Books.* https://www.nybooks.com/articles/2015/08/13/india-stormy-revival-nalanda-university/

Sharma, D. C. (2015). India's medical education system hit by scandals. *The Lancet, 386*, 517–518.

Sharma, K. (2018, July 30). IITs, IIMs, NITs have just 3% of total students but get 50% of government funds. *The Print.* https://theprint.in/india/governance/iits-iims-nits-have-just-3-of-total-students-but-get-50-of-government-funds/89976/

Shaw, J. S. (2010). Education—a bad public good? *The Independent Review, 15*(2), 241–256.

Shepardson, D. (2018, March 3). Trump praises Chinese president extending tenure "for life." *Reuters.* https://www.reuters.com/article/us-trump-china/trump-praises-chinese-president-extending-tenure-for-life-idUSKCN1GG015

Silver, A. (2019, November 19). Violent clashes at Hong Kong universities disrupt research. *Nature.* doi:10.1038/d41586-019-03515-2

Singh, P. (2007). The political economy of the cycles of violence and non-violence in the Sikh struggle for identity and political power: Implications for Indian federalism. *Third World Quarterly, 28*(3), 555–570.

Sklair, L. (2006). A transitional framework for theory and research in the study of globalization. In I. Rossi (Ed.), *Frontiers of globalization research: Theoretical and methodological approaches* (pp. 93–108). Springer.

Slaughter, S., & Rhoades, G. (2004). *Academic capitalism and the new economy: Markets, state, and higher education.* Johns Hopkins University Press.

Smith, J., & Lamb, K. (2019, November 14). Flaming arrows and petrol bombs: Inside Hong Kong protesters' "weapons factories." *Reuters.* https://www.reuters.com/article/us-hongkong-protests-weapons/flaming-arrows-and-petrol-bombs-inside-hong-kong-protesters-weapons-factories-idUSKBN1XO1A5

Smyth, J. (2017). *The toxic university: Zombie leadership, academic rock stars, and neoliberal ideology*. Palgrave Macmillan.

Snyder, T. (2017). *On tyranny: Twenty lessons from the twentieth century*. Tim Duggan Books.

Snyder, T. (2019). *The road to unfreedom: Russia, Europe, America*. Tim Duggan Books.

Solórzano, D., Ceja, M., & Yosso, T. (2000). Critical race theory, racial micro-aggressions, and campus racial climate: The experiences of African American college students. *Journal of Negro Education, 69*(1–2), 60–73.

Sotiris, P. (2014). University movements as laboratories of counter-hegemony. *Journal of Critical Education Policy Studies, 12*(1), 1–21.

Stacher, J. (2015). Fragmenting states, new regimes: Militarized state violence and transition in the Middle East. *Democratization, 22*(2), 259–275.

Stanley, J. (2018). *How fascism works: The politics of us and them*. Random House.

State Council, People's Republic of China. (2019, October 17). China's govt spending on education above 4% of GDP for 7 consecutive years. http://english.www.gov.cn/statecouncil/ministries/201910/17/content_WS5da82aa2c6d0bcf8c4c1549c.html

Stavrakakis, Y., & Katsambekis, G. (2019). The populism/anti-populism frontier and its mediation in crisis-ridden Greece: From discursive divide to emerging cleavage? *European Political Science, 18*(1), 37–52.

Stevenson, A., & Wu, J. (2019, July 22). Tiny apartments and punishing work hours: The economic roots of Hong Kong's protests. *New York Times.* Retrieved from https://www.nytimes.com/interactive/2019/07/22/world/asia/hong-kong-housing-inequality.html

Stokas, A. G. (2015). A genealogy of grit: Education in the new gilded age. *Educational Theory, 65*(5), 513–528.

Stokes, D. (1997). *Pasteur's quadrant: Basic science and technological innovation*. Brookings.

Sue, D. W., Capodilupo, C. M., Torino, G. C., Bucceri, J. M., Holder, A. M. B., Nadal, K. L., & Esquilin, M. (2007). Racial microaggressions in everyday life: Implications for clinical practice. *American Psychologist, 62*(4), 271–286.

Sullivan, A. (2018, February). We all live on campus now. *New York Magazine.* https://nymag.com/intelligencer/2018/02/we-all-live-on-campus-now.html

Svrluga, S. (2019, July 18). University of Alaska credit rating downgraded, reflecting financial turmoil. *Washington Post.* https://www.washingtonpost.com/education/2019/07/18/university-alaska-credit-rating-downgraded-reflecting-financial-turmoil/

Tannock, S. (2006). The trouble with getting ahead: Youth employment, labor organizing, and the higher education question. *Labor and Society, 9*(2), 185–198.

Thaler, K. M. (2017). Nicaragua: A return to Caudillismo. *Journal of Democracy, 28*(2), 157–169.

Thomas, D. A., & Clarke, M. K. (2013). Inequality, new sovereignties, and citizenship in a neoliberal era. *Annual Review of Anthropology, 42*, 305–325.

Thurow, L. C. (2000). Globalization: The product of a knowledge-based economy. *Annals of the American Academy of Political and Social Science, 570*, 19–31.

Tierney, W. G. (1988). Organizational culture in higher education: Defining the essentials. *Journal of Higher Education, 59*(1), 2–11.

Tierney, W. G. (1991). Critical theory and the study of higher education. In W. G. Tierney (Ed.), *Culture and ideology in higher education* (pp. 3–16). Praeger.

Tierney, W. G. (1993). *Building communities of difference: Higher education in the twenty-first century*. Bergin & Garvey.

Tierney, W. G. (1994). Cultural politics in a Latin American university. *La Educación, 118*, 265–284.

Tierney, W. G. (1995). La privatación y la educación superior publica en Costa Rica. *Universidad Futura, 6*(17), 49–58.

Tierney, W. G. (2020). *Get real: Twelve essays on the challenges confronting higher education*. State University of New York Press.

Tierney, W. G., & Almeida, D. J. (2017). Academic responsibility: Toward a cultural politics of integrity. *Discourse: Studies in the Cultural Politics of Education, 38*(1), 97–108.

Tierney, W. G., & Duncheon, J. (Eds.). (2015). *The problem of college readiness*. State University of New York Press.

Tierney, W. G., & Hentschke, G. C. (2007). *New players, different game: Understanding the rise of for-profit colleges and universities*. Johns Hopkins University Press.

Tierney, W. G., & Holley, K. A. (2008). Pasteur's quadrant: Knowledge production in a profession. *Educational Studies, 34*(4), 289–297.

Tierney, W. G., & Lanford, M. (2014). The question of academic freedom: Universal right or relative term? *Frontiers of Education in China, 9*(1), 4–23.

Tierney, W. G., & Lanford, M. (2017). Between massification and globalization: Is there a role for global university rankings? In E. Hazelkorn (Ed.), *Global rankings and the geopolitics of higher education* (pp. 295–308). Routledge.

Tierney, W. G., & Lanford, M. (2018). Research in higher education: Cultural perspectives. In J. C. Shin & P. N. Teixeira (Eds.), *Encyclopedia of international higher education systems and institutions*. Springer. https://doi.org/10.1007/978-94-017-9553-1_544-1

Tierney, W. G., & Lanford, M. (2020). Globalization in the United States: The case of California. In M. Priyam (Ed.), *Reclaiming public universities: Comparative reflections for reforms*. Routledge.

Tierney, W. G., & Rhoads, R. A. (1995). The culture of assessment. In J. Smyth (Ed.), *Academic work: The changing labour process in higher education* (pp. 99–111). Open University.

Tierney, W. G., & Sabharwal, N. S. (2016). Academic freedom in the world's largest democracy. *International Higher Education, 86*, 15–16.

Tierney, W. G., & Sabharwal, N. (2017). Academic corruption: Culture and trust in Indian higher education. *International Journal of Educational Development, 55*, 30–40.

Tierney, W. G., & Sabharwal, N. (2018). Reimagining Indian higher education: A social ecology of higher education institutions. *Teachers College Record, 120*(5), 1–32.

Tierney, W. G., Sabharwal, N., & Malish, C. M. (2019). Inequitable structures: Class and caste in Indian higher education. *Qualitative Inquiry, 25*(5), 471–481.

Tierney, W. G., & Sablan, J. (2014). Examining college readiness. *American Behavioral Scientist, 58*(8), 943–946.

Tilak, J. B. G. (2013). Higher education in Trishanku: Hanging between state and market. In J. B. G. Tilak (Ed.), *Higher education in India: In search of equality, quality and quantity*. Orient Black Swan.

Tomlinson, B., & Lipsitz, G. (2013). Insubordinate spaces for intemperate times: Countering the pedagogies of neoliberalism. *Review of Education, Pedagogy, and Cultural Studies, 35*(1), 3–26.

Twenge, J. M. (2017). *iGen: Why today's super-connected kids are growing up less rebellious, more tolerant, less happy—and completely unprepared for adulthood*. Atria Books.

Tyack, D. (1976). Ways of seeing: An essay on the history of compulsory schooling. *Harvard Educational Review, 46*(3), 355–389.

Usunier, J., & Valette-Florence, P. (2007). The time styles scale: A review of developments and replications over 15 years. *Time and Society, 16*, 333–366.

Vaknin, S. (2019). Education as a public good. *Journal of Educational and Psychological Research, 1*(1), 1–2.

van de Wetering, C. (2016). *Changing U.S. foreign policy toward India*. Palgrave Macmillan.

Venezia, A., & Jaeger, L. (2013). Transitions from high school to college. *The Future of Children, 23*(1), 117–136.

Verbeek, B., & Zaslove, A. (2016). Italy: A case of mutating populism? *Democratization, 23*(2), 304–323.

Vermont Higher Education Council. (2019). *Vermont higher education enrollment, fall 2019*. Vermont Higher Education Council.

Veysey, L. (1965). *The emergence of the American university*. University of Chicago Press.

Walby, S., Armstrong, J., & Strid, S. (2012). Intersectionality: Multiple inequalities in social theory. *Sociology, 46*(2), 224–240.

Walton, J. K. (2011). The idea of the university. In M. Bailey & D. Freedman (Eds.), *The assault on universities* (pp. 15–26). Pluto.

Ward, J. K., Peretti-Watel, P., & Verger, P. (2016). Vaccine criticism on the internet: Propositions for future research. *Human Vaccines and Immunotherapies, 12*(7), 1924–1929.

Waters, T., & Waters, D. (Eds.). (2015). *Weber's rationalism and modern society: New translations on politics, bureaucracy, and social stratification.* Palgrave Macmillan.

Weber, M. (1958). Science as a vocation. *Daedalus, 87*(1), 111–134. (Original work published 1917).

Weisbrod, B. A., Ballou, J. P., & Asch, E. D. (2008). *Mission and money: Understanding the university.* Cambridge University Press.

Wellmon, C. (2015). *Organizing enlightenment: Information overload and the invention of the modern research university.* Johns Hopkins University Press.

Wellmon, C. (2018, November 20). How professors ceded their authority. *Chronicle of Higher Education.* https://www.chronicle.com/article/How-Professors-Ceded-Their/245133

Wesley-Smith, P. (1998). *An introduction to the Hong Kong legal system.* Hong Kong University Press.

Wilkerson, I. (2020). *Caste: The lies that divide us.* Penguin.

Willis, D. J., & Allen, J. (2018, July 19). Searchable database: For-profit colleges in California. *EdSource.* https://edsource.org/2018/searchable-database-for-profit-colleges-in-ebnercalifornia-2010-16/600327

Wong, E., Ives, M., May, T., Li, K. (2019, November 17). Hong Kong violence escalates as police and protesters clash at university. *New York Times.* https://www.nytimes.com/2019/11/17/world/asia/hong-kong-protests-chinese-soldiers.html

Wong, S. H.-W., Lee, K.-C., Ho, K., & Clarke, H. D. (2019). Immigrant influx and generational politics: A comparative case study of Hong Kong and Taiwan. *Electoral Studies, 58,* 84–93.

Wong, Y.-L. (2019). Angels falling from grace? The rectification experiences of middle-class community-college students in Hong Kong. *Studies in Higher Education, 44*(8), 1303–1315.

Wong, Y.-L., & Koo, A. (2016). Is Hong Kong no longer a land of opportunities after the 1997 handover? A comparison of patterns of social mobility between 1989 and 2007. *Asian Journal of Social Science, 44*(4–5), 516–545.

Wood, G. (2019, May 15). Harvard's feast of grievance: The Ronald Sullivan affair is about everything—and nothing. *The Atlantic.*

Wu, J., Lai, K. K. R., & Yuhas, A. (2019, November 18). Six months of Hong Kong protests. How did we get here? *New York Times.* https://www.nytimes.com/interactive/2019/world/asia/hong-kong-protests-arc.html

Yeo, G. (2011). Nalanda and the Asian renaissance. *New Perspectives Quarterly, 28*(2), 73–76.

Yu, B., & Zhang, K. (2016). "It's more foreign than a foreign country": Adaptation and experience of mainland Chinese students in Hong Kong. *Tertiary Education and Management, 22*(4), 300–315.

Yu, E., Myers, S. L., & Goldman, R. (2019, November 18). Hong Kong protests: Over 1,000 detained at a university, and a warning from Beijing. *New York Times.* https://www.nytimes.com/2019/11/18/world/asia/hong-kong-protests.html

Index

Academic Freedom:
  overview of, 13–15
  autonomy and, 122–23, 234
  debate and, 137–45
  free speech and, 125–31, 136
  identity and, 143, 237
  limits of, 89–90, 123–24
  objectivity and, 100
  origins of, 102–5
  power and, 99, 141–42
  rankings and, 112
  safe spaces and, 135
  truth and, 101–2, 105–6, 124, 136–38, 141
  See also California; China; Hong Kong; India
adjunct faculty, 235
affirmative action:
  overview of, 9
  academia and, 72
  admissions and, 197
  caste and, 19, 83
  neoliberalism and, 167
African Americans, 73, 78, 82, 154, 205, 242
  See also black colleges; Black Lives Matter
Akhil Bharatiya Vidyarthi Parishad (ABVP), 113, 115
Amazon (company), 188

Ambedkar, B. R., 61
American Academy of Arts and Sciences, 254
American Association of University Professors (AAUP), 103, 237
anti-Semitism, 249
Arab Spring, 40
Arendt, Hannah, 209
Aronowitz, Stanley, 52
assessment, 34, 233, 251
assimilation, 11, 71–72
authoritarianism, 41–43
autonomy, 16, 31, 122–23, 221, 234

Babri Masjid, 115
Baldwin, James, 45
Banerjee, Abhijit, 63
Basic Law (Hong Kong), 112
Becker, Gary, 230
Beckett, Samuel, 229
Bharatiya Janata Party (BJP), 15, 43, 60–61, 204
black colleges, 158
Black Lives Matter, 66, 71, 84, 101, 154, 245
Bloom, Allan, 88
Bourdieu, Pierre, 48–49, 91, 180, 193
Brandeis, Louis D., 144
Brel, Jacques, 225
Brookings Institution, 8, 254

Buddhism, 11, 61
budget cuts, 35, 171
Bush, George W., 138–39
Bush, Vannevar, 172

Calhoun, Craig, 38, 44
California:
　academic freedom in, 118–19
　eugenics and, 104
　financial aid in, 10
　job market in, 186
　Master Plan, 18, 68, 158
　pandemic and, 69
　rankings and, 68
　Trump and, 65, 67
California State University (CSU),
　67–69, 185, 241
Cantonese, 12, 54, 221
capitalism, 30, 33, 34
Carlyle, Thomas, 211
Cass, O., 164, 187
caste, 12, 19, 83
　See also Dalits
censorship, 54–56, 110, 114–16, 121
Chan Kin-man, 106–8
Chan, Johannes, 111
charismatic authority, 39
charter schools, 66, 137, 154, 162
cheating, 62, 196, 249
child mortality, 4
Chin Wan-kan, 110
China:
　academic freedom and, 14, 57, 112
　democracy and, 7
　identity and, 12
　independence movement and, 55, 57
　rankings and, 59, 62, 112
　study abroad and, 165
　See also Hong Kong
Chinese University of Hong Kong
　(CUHK), 108–9
Christensen, Clayton, 6, 159

Chu Yiu-ming, 106
Chung, Robert, 109
civil society, 8, 255–56
climate change, 30, 45, 137, 207
colonialism, 4, 12, 153
community:
　difference and, 44–47, 94–95, 195–
　　96, 222
　engagement with, 178–81, 214–15,
　　244, 253–54
　identity and, 83–84, 87–88, 95, 180
　individualism and, 22
community colleges, 28–29, 67
competition, 224–29, 231, 250
compulsory education, 163
conspiracy theories, 14, 204
Carrico, Kevin, 111
corruption, 16, 62, 196–97, 249–53
cosmopolitanism, 210
cost efficiency, 32–33, 35
courage, 262
COVID-19. See pandemic
creativity, 46
critical race theory, 27, 91–92
critical theory, 91–92, 211
cultural capital, 30
cultural citizenship, 180

Dalits:
　affirmative action and, 19, 83
　Buddhism and, 11, 61
　student life of, 64
　violence against, 15, 61
de Sousa Santos, B., 27, 31, 50, 198, 212
Debs, Eugene V., 102–3
debt/loans, 10, 68, 240, 241
democracy:
　definition of, 7–8, 37
　comparative research and, 21
　recession of, 38, 40, 42, 199, 218
　See also specific topics
Deng Xiaoping, 19

deregulation, 16, 123
Derrida, Jacques, 194, 199
Dewey, John, 103, 237
Diamond, Larry, 40, 42, 200, 215
dignity culture, 87
disinformation, 26
Doniger, Wendy, 116
Drucker, Peter, 159
Duckworth, Angela, 192

Eggington, William, 84, 87, 95
elections, 18, 43, 220, 256–58
Eliot, Charles, 157
elitism, 51
English (language), 12, 54
equality, 43, 82, 85, 140
Erikson, Erik, 72
ethics of responsibility, 26, 79
eugenics, 103–5
evaluations, 34, 233, 251
examinations, 6
extradition bill, 57, 107

fake news, 18, 41, 220
fascism:
    free speech and, 208
    globalization and, 23, 223
    identity and, 90
    ideology of, 1, 210–11, 221
    myths of, 203, 205
    populism and, 38–39, 90, 218–20
    resistance against, 222
    truth and, 206–9, 212–14, 219, 235
    United States and, 199
Fearson, J., 76
Ferber, Abby, 120–21
financial aid, 10, 78
financial literacy, 246
Floyd, George, 75, 211, 234
for-profit colleges and universities,
    155
Foucault, Michel, 193

free speech:
    academic freedom and, 125–31, 136
    fascism and, 208
    Hong Kong and, 14
    objectivity and, 100
    power and, 99, 141–42
    Trump and, 118, 120
Fukuyama, Francis, 39, 44, 84

Galileo, 97–99
Gandhi, Mohandas K., 61, 64, 83, 204
Gans, Herbert, 94
gay marriage, 84, 138, 140
gender, 61–62, 73, 212–13
Germany, 101
GI Bill, 81
gig economy, 227, 238, 261
Gilman, Daniel Coit, 157
Giroux, Henry:
    ideology and, 32, 200, 251
    moral education and, 48
    power and, 201
    public sphere and, 26, 33–34, 36, 196
globalization:
    competition and, 224–29, 231, 250
    counter-hegemonic, 50
    diversity and, 166
    fascism and, 23, 223
    job market and, 161, 164, 177,
        224–25
    knowledge and, 31
    populism and, 3
    poverty and, 4
    psychological impacts of, 46, 248
    public good and, 163
    time and, 229–30
Goodstadt, Leo, 160
graduation, 185–86
Guru, Afzal, 113

Hacking, Ian, 173
Haidt, Jon, 77, 79–80, 89

Hamer, J. F., 47
Hames-Garcia, Michael, 75
Hardin, Russell, 263
Harper, William Rainey, 157
Harvard University, 197
hate speech, 100, 105, 120, 129–30
healthcare, 240–41, 245
high schools, 188–89, 242
Hinduism, 19, 64–65, 220
Hindutva, 61
Hitler, Adolf, 40
homosexuality, 78, 236
   See also gay marriage; LGBTQ
Hong Kong:
   overview of, 19–21
   academic freedom in, 53, 108–13,
      249
   censorship in, 54–56, 110
   citizenship in, 80–81
   free speech in, 14
   homosexuality in, 236
   housing market in, 54, 221
   identity of, 12, 220–21
   independence and, 109–110
   job market in, 188
   pollution in, 60
   poverty in, 160
   protests in, 9, 57–58, 108–10, 188
   public education in, 10–11, 16, 53,
      153, 154
   rankings and, 168
   See also Occupy Central; Umbrella
      Movement
Hong Kong Polytechnic University, 109

identity:
   overview of, 11–13, 71
   academic freedom and, 143, 237
   author and, 22, 76, 82
   community and, 83–84, 87–88, 95,
      180

   crises of, 25, 72
   culture and, 55
   difference and, 198
   epistemic closure of, 76–77
   fascism and, 90
   Modi and, 39, 42, 60–61, 204, 220
   mutability of, 236
   objectivity and, 27, 75
   politics of, 72–74, 82–86
   postmodernism and, 92–93
   Trump and, 12, 39, 121
   truth and, 77, 79, 239
   See also China; Hong Kong; India;
      United States
iGen teens, 175–77
immigration:
   assimilation and, 11
   diversity and, 66
   inequality and, 67
   populism and, 39
   undocumented, 78
income, 67, 157, 169, 186–87, 243
India:
   academic freedom in, 114–17
   caste system in, 9, 83
   censorship in, 114–16
   colonialism in, 153
   corruption in, 249
   gender in, 61–62
   homosexuality in, 84, 236
   identity in, 11–12, 64
   job market in, 188
   poverty in, 7
   public education in, 16, 63, 159,
      160
   rankings and, 168, 173, 229
   science education in, 80
   study abroad and, 165
   violence in, 15
Indian Institutes of Technology (IIT),
      18, 19, 62, 149, 190

individualism, 22, 38, 41, 79, 88, 225, 258
inequality, 4, 7–9, 63, 67
intellectual labor, 30
internships, 244
Islam/Muslims, 11, 15, 138, 204, 220
ivy metaphor, 30, 232

Japan, 10
Jawaharlal Nehru University (JNU), 113–14, 116
job market:
 curriculum and, 37, 184, 244
 globalization and, 161, 164, 177, 224–25
 income and, 186–87
 neoliberalism and, 46, 164, 188, 191, 235, 241
 pandemic and, 236
 underemployment and, 162, 243
 vocational education and, 29
 See also gig economy
Jordan, David Starr, 102–4

Kalburgi, M. M., 117
Kant, Immanuel, 202
Kashmir, 15, 43, 114, 115
Kearney, Denis, 104
King, Martin Luther, 43
Kirp, David, 5
knowledge society, 31
Kumar, Kanhaiya, 114

Lai Chee-ying, Jimmy, 221
Lam, Carrie, 107–8
Lambert, Matthew T., 160–61
land grants, 152, 157–58, 232
Lang, C., 47
Lazerson, M., 156
LGBTQ, 72, 78, 82, 135, 205, 236
 See also gay marriage

liberal arts, 9
libertarians, 38, 147
lifelong learning, 248
Lilla, Mark, 83, 87–88
Lincoln, Abraham, 158
Lipsitz, George, 41, 48, 165, 174
literacy, 242
loans/debt, 10, 68, 240, 241
Lopez, Ian Haney, 213
Lorde, Audre, 11
Lorenz, Chris, 5
Los Angeles:
 overview of, 18, 65
 demographics of, 175
 immigrants in, 66–67
 innovation and, 70
 pollution in, 60, 66
 poverty in, 68
 Trump and, 204
Lovejoy, Arthur, 103
Lukianoff, G., 87, 89

Malaysia, 167
Mandarin (language), 12, 54, 221
Mann, Horace, 163
Marginson, Simon, 5, 68, 150
massive open online classes, 248
Master Plan for Higher Education, 18, 68, 158
McCarthyism, 101
McMurtry, John, 156
Me Too (movement), 69, 84
mercantilization, 36
meritocracy, 34, 167, 258
microaggression:
 definitions of, 85, 132, 134
 curriculum and, 121, 133, 141
 dialogue and, 132, 134
 safe spaces and, 88, 135
 studies of, 69, 86
middle class, 9, 25, 54, 161–65

Modi, Narendra:
  discrimination and, 11, 89
  economic reform and, 61
  election of, 43
  national identity and, 39, 42, 60–61,
    204, 220
  opposition to, 113
  violence and, 220
Mohanty, Satya, 72
monasteries, 81
moral education, 48, 194
Moretti, E., 164, 178, 190
Morrill Land Grant Acts, 152, 157–58,
  232
Morrison, Toni, 149
Mounk, Yascha, 38, 43
Murray, Charles, 139
Muslims, 11, 15, 138, 204, 220

Nalanda University, 153
National Security Law:
  overview of, 15
  academic freedom and, 57, 249
  autonomy and, 16, 221
  democracy and, 53, 221
  pandemic and, 57–58
  rankings and, 168
Native Americans, 71–72, 158
Nehru, Jawaharlal, 26, 60, 64, 101
Nelson, Richard R., 46
neoliberalism:
  definition of, 5
  affirmative action and, 167
  authoritarianism and, 41
  competition and, 224–29, 231, 250
  diversity and, 166
  ideology of, 165, 171, 192, 200
  job market and, 46, 164, 188, 191,
    235, 241
  meritocracy and, 167
  populism and, 218
  privatization and, 34, 51, 161

public sphere and, 32, 160–64
  rankings and, 33–34, 168–70, 173
  time and, 229–30
New Delhi:
  overview of, 18–19, 59–65
  police in, 37
  pollution in, 60
  poverty in, 64
  violence in, 220
Newman, John Henry, 21, 29, 80, 81
nonviolent civil resistance, 260, 262
numeracy, 242

Obama, Barack, 16
objectivity, 27–28, 75, 79, 100, 214, 232
Occupy Central, 14–15, 43, 58
online education:
  inequality and, 63
  pandemic and, 2, 6, 176, 184, 247–
    48
  value of, 32, 35, 164, 227
organic intellectuals, 52

Palahniuk, Chuck, 133
pandemic:
  academic job market and, 236
  budget cuts and, 35, 171
  conspiracy theories and, 204
  democracy and, 38–39
  economic impact of, 50, 69, 159, 238,
    242
  online education and, 2, 6, 176, 184,
    247–48
  poverty and, 185
  protests and, 57–58, 107
  risk-taking and, 263
  school reopenings and, 20
Pasteur's Quadrant, 172–73, 198
Patwardhan, Anand, 115–16
Paxton, Robert, 219
Peace Corps, 1–2
peer review, 100, 124–25, 208

pluralism, 210
police, 37, 66, 75, 84, 151, 174
populism:
  definition of, 39
  fascism and, 38–39, 90, 218–20
  globalization and, 3
  inequality and, 7
  neoliberalism and, 218
  Trump and, 218, 220
post-positivist realism, 75
Post, Robert, 125, 126
Postiglione, Gerard, 6
postmodernism, 75, 91–94, 211
poverty, 4, 7, 8, 64, 68, 160, 185
privatization:
  overview of, 10–11, 156
  academic freedom and, 122–23
  neoliberalism and, 34, 51, 161
pronouns, 78
protests, 9, 12, 57–58, 107–10, 188
  See also Occupy Central; Umbrella
  Movement
public good:
  overview of, 15–17, 150–52
  debates over, 153–56, 161–165
  individualism and, 22
  land grants and, 152, 157–58
  neoliberalism and, 34, 160–64,
  233–34
  subsidies and, 159
  See also privatization
public intellectuals, 94, 253
public sphere, 22, 26, 32–36, 196

racism, 9, 47–48, 118, 198, 204, 211–13,
  234
rankings:
  academic freedom and, 112
  neoliberalism and, 33–34, 168–70,
  173
  responsibilization and, 193
  teaching and, 183

See also California; China; Hong
  Kong; India
Rashtriya Swayamsevak Sangh (RSS),
  113
Reagan, Ronald, 162
Reed College, 29
reflexivity, 49, 214
regulation, 34, 231
Reich, Robert, 43
religion, 76, 80, 143, 176
  See also specific religions
Republican Party, 18
research funding, 56, 124–25
responsibilization, 192–94, 201, 252
Rhoades, Gary, 5
riots, 60
Rosenberg, Nathan, 46
Ross, Edward, 102–5

safe spaces, 88, 132, 135, 139, 143
Schick, N., 204
Scholars at Risk, 117, 259
scholarship, 49
science:
  critical theory and, 92
  objectivity of, 27–28
  research and, 172–74
  truth and, 98, 232
Scott, Joan Wallach, 102–3, 125
Scott, Peter, 6
Sen, Amartya, 117
service, 179–80
sexual harassment, 133
shared governance, 14, 17, 30, 37, 123
Sklair, L., 192
Slaughter, Sheila, 5
Smyth, John, 33
snowflakes, 86, 133–35, 268n1
social media, 100, 120–21, 223, 238
Socrates, 206
Socratic seminars, 32
Sotiris, P., 49

South China Morning Post, 56
South Korea, 10
specialization, academic, 247
standpoint theory, 74, 76
Stanford University, 102–5, 190
Stanford, Jane, 102–4
Stanley, Jason, 203, 205, 210
Stokes, Donald, 172
student loans/debt, 10, 68, 240, 241
Sullivan, Andrew, 83, 195

Tai, Benny, 58, 106–8
Tannock, Stuart, 156
teacher unions, 137
teaching, 174–79, 183, 247–48
teenagers, 175–77
tenure, 6, 14, 35, 52, 105, 146, 236, 261
Thapar, Romila, 114, 116
Thatcher, Margaret, 162
Tiananmen Square, 54, 55
time compression, 229–30
Times Higher Education, 168
Tomlinson, Barbara, 41, 48, 165, 174
transformative academics, 200–201,
    252
transgender, 73, 84
translational learning, 197–98
translational research, 173
trigger warnings, 85–86, 119, 121,
    133–34, 139
Trump, Donald:
  academic freedom and, 132
  authoritarianism and, 42–43
  California and, 65, 67
  deregulation and, 16
  elections and, 43, 220
  free speech and, 118, 120
  identity and, 12, 39, 121
  Islam and, 138
  media and, 184
  populism and, 218, 220

racism and, 118, 204
  slogans and, 118, 205
trust, 262–64
truth:
  academic freedom and, 101–2, 105–
    6, 124, 136–38, 141
  authority and, 149
  fascism and, 206–9, 212–14, 219, 235
  identity and, 77, 79, 239
  public good and, 80
  science and, 98, 232
tuition, 53, 153, 158
Turkey, 10
tutoring, 268n2
Twenge, Jean, 175

Umbrella Movement, 106–7, 109, 214,
    260
underemployment, 162, 243
United Kingdom, 53, 55
United States:
  academic job market in, 240
  fascism and, 199
  identity and, 12
  inequality in, 7
  public institutions in, 15
  racism in, 9, 211–12, 234
University of Alaska, 228
University of California, 69
University of Delhi, 153
University of Hong Kong (HKU), 53,
    59, 108, 190
University of Southern California, 65,
    69
University Grants Commission, 63
use-inspired research, 172–74

vaccines, 137, 233
Vaknin, Sam, 150
Varsity Blues scandal, 196, 249
Vietnam War, 2

vocational education, 29–30, 80, 179,
     189, 191
voter registration, 258

Walton, J. K., 32
Weber, Max, 26, 48, 79, 171, 230
Wellmon, Chad, 80, 202
White nationalism, 78

Wilkerson, Isabel, 9, 213
Women's Marches, 43

xenophobia, 12
Xi Jinping, 42, 58, 107

Yiannopoulos, Milo, 89, 128, 208